*How to Survive
in Spite of Your Parents*

How to Survive
in Spite of
Your Parents

Coping with Hurtful Childhood Legacies

Dr MARGARET REINHOLD

HEINEMANN:LONDON

William Heinemann Ltd
Michelin House, 81 Fulham Road, London SW3 6RB
LONDON   MELBOURNE   AUCKLAND

First published 1990
Copyright © 1990 by Dr Margaret Reinhold

Reprinted 1991

A CIP catalogue record for this book
is available from the British Library
ISBN 0 434 11169 4

Phototypeset by Input Typesetting, London
Printed in England
by Clays Ltd, St. Ives plc

To William and Nora

Contents

My most sincere thanks to Clare McDonald
for her untiring help with the typescript

Preface

Little scenes of conflict between parents and children can be seen in public places all over the Western world – so common and usual we take them for granted and look on them as normal in our society.

For example, in our local supermarket tempers fray easily. It's a huge place, tiring and wearing for parents – mostly mothers – and for little children. Sometimes the air vibrates with noises of protest and distress. Babies scream for attention which they'll only receive when the family arrives home. Tight-lipped mothers drag shrieking offspring bodily along the heartless rows of washing powders and tinned food. Sharp blows – very humiliating – are suddenly dealt out to shocked and confused children for a trivial reason. Little faces, set in silent despair, break down; and when the toys on display, which are meant to tempt, are removed by tiny hungry hands, angry mothers snatch them back, loudly reprimanding.

Minor and normal as these scenes are, I find them distressing, as they return me, momentarily, to the dark depression of my own childhood. They're vivid reminders of the helplessness of small children and the ferocious power of adults. Painfully, I relive the life of a child at the mercy of hostile parents: fantasies of danger and death, anxieties so enormous they're hardly bearable, cringing fear and a slow burying of feelings which were once eager and intense.

No child knows its parents are at fault. It takes all the blame on itself for the rejection and cruelty it may receive – a cruelty often the more terrifying for being masked and mysterious. So the child suffers from guilt and a sense of acute inadequacy, storing experiences which will be re-enacted in adult life in the role of parent. All of us identify with children, since we all were children once. Consciously or unconsciously we all relive the past unendingly.

Knowingly or unknowingly, we make our children also relive our past, hurt for hurt.

This book is written for children damaged by parents and for parents who were damaged children: in the hope that it will help us to understand better how to avoid hurting our own children.

PART ONE

Introduction
to Psychiatry

ONE

Coming to Terms with Childhood Legacies

In my beginning is my end.

T. S. Eliot, 'East Coker', *Four Quartets*

In the course of the last century, we've slowly come to recognize that the experiences of childhood influence the ways in which we feel, think, act and respond throughout our lives. The events, circumstances and relationships of our early past have a profound and implacable impact on our adult years.

We've also begun to understand that the ill-treatment of children by their parents is more widespread than we once believed. Emotional and physical damage inflicted by parents on their children is probably responsible for much adult mental ill-health and unhappiness. Parents may harm their children in a great variety of ways – often unknowingly. The damage ranges from open and flagrant abuse to more subtle, concealed or even unconscious hostility. Most parents tend to re-enact their own childhood experiences when dealing with their own children. This re-enactment is usually unconsciously performed. In this way, contented and secure children become, in adult life, healthy, confident human beings and loving and reassuring parents. However, damaged children become damaged adults and, in turn, damaging parents to their own children. The cycle can repeat itself indefinitely, inexorably, generation after generation.

These patterns can't be changed by an individual's willpower, however strong. The reasons for their development are too deeply rooted in the unremembered past. Unconscious motivations are stronger than willpower. But for people whose lives are really unsatisfactory, or who suffer from mental or emotional ill-health, or who find themselves again and again involved in a fruitless repetition of disastrous relationships, or for a variety of other emotional problems, there is a solution. It is not an easy one, as I'll explain, but with courage and perseverance, a successful outcome is highly likely.

The solution begins, in the first place, with a visit to a psychiatrist. For many people this is an upsetting prospect. How would *you* feel if, when you went to visit your doctor he or she said, after listening carefully to your complaints – and after examining you, perhaps . . . 'I think, you know, we ought to send you to see a psychiatrist'. The doctor would probably say this tactfully and wait quietly for your reaction. Doctors know that in general, people are most nervous about and more reluctant to visit psychiatrists than any other kind of medical specialist. Would you be angry at your doctor's suggestion, or indignant, or frightened – or relieved? Would you say 'No! I'd rather not – I'd rather do anything than that. Isn't there some other solution?' Or would you say, 'Yes – I think that's a good idea'.

If you agreed to let your doctor make the appointment for you, would you tell your friends about it? Or would you go alone, secretly, praying not to bump into an aquaintance or colleague, perhaps pretending you were actually visiting the dentist who shared the consulting rooms?

Many people do fear psychiatry and psychiatrists and feel somehow it's a disgrace, a sign of weakness and failure if they need psychiatric help. Yet mental and emotional illness are more common than any other kind of illness in our Western societies. In spite of this, psychiatry has until recent years been the 'Cinderella' of the medical profession, and still is to some extent. Far more money is spent on building general hospitals and arranging treatment for the physically ill than on help for the mentally ill. Within the health service, physicians and surgeons tend to make diminishing and disrespectful jokes about their colleagues in psychiatry and some refuse to accept the importance of the mind in relation to the health of the body.

Yet in spite of the many reservations that doctors, health authorities and the general public have about psychiatry, thousands of people are referred to psychiatrists every year and many of them are very much helped by the treatment they receive. It's possible nowadays to alleviate, if not cure, almost every kind of mental and emotional disturbance, however severe. Psychiatrists deal with an enormous range of illness from the seemingly trivial to the very serious – and with people of all ages. I'll mention here a few well-known problems which need psychiatric help: depressive illness and simple depression, paranoia, schizophrenia and other mental illnesses, anxiety states, phobic symptoms, eating disorders (such as anorexia and bulimia), addiction to alcohol and other drugs, abuse of children, grief, psychosomatic illness, sexual problems (including frigidity and impotence), difficulty in forming and keeping relationships (including marriage), homosexuality and promiscuity.

I've mentioned only some of the innumerable reasons why people go to see a psychiatrist, but they all have one symptom in common: emotional suffering. This may be very severe even though the cause of it may seem small. In some forms of mental illness the suffering is so intense that the patient sees suicide as the only way out. Modern drugs – tranquillizers and antidepressants – have transformed the treatment of emotional suffering, but for certain forms of mental or emotional disturbance, psychotherapy is the treatment of choice, the 'best' treatment, the one most likely to have lasting benefits.

In this book I describe people with various reasons for emotional disturbance and how they can be helped though psychotherapy – what the treatment involves, how it works, which kinds of disturbance it's likely to help, and so on. The title of the book may seem flippant, but the fact is that, as I've already described, most of the suffering people endure in adult life has its roots in childhood. Children, vulnerable and very sensitive, respond vividly to the attitudes and feelings of those close to them – parents and brothers and sisters. Children are also quick to learn, and what is learned in childhood remains with a person for a lifetime. Children are like pieces of new blotting paper, mopping up whatever ink is applied to them, the stains then being fixed. Human beings, in common with all living creatures, have a tendency to form habits or patterns in the way they behave and feel and function. During childhood and adolescence, behaviour and feeling patterns are slowly assembled in response to – or in imitation of – the feelings and behaviour patterns of parents and siblings. Such patterns eventually become stable and are hard, if not impossible, to change.

Change may, very occasionally, come about as a result of chance encounters and adventures in life.

Here is an example, in a simplified form, of an emotional pattern and the circumstances which created the pattern. There was a father who seemed to be permanently bad-tempered and bullying to his little boy. The child learned to fear his father and, having tried in every way he could to please his father, without success, he did his best to keep out of his father's way. The pattern was fear of father, avoidance of father.

There is a powerful tendency in human beings to transfer from the particular to the general. Having learned one specific idea, we apply that idea to other situations which resemble the specific one. For example, we learn in infancy about our first chair; having taken in the concept of the seat, four legs, the back of the chair, and fixed the notion in our minds, we can apply the concept of 'chair' to all kinds of different chairs, armchairs, basket chairs, deck chairs and so on.

In the same way we transfer our complex notions of our own fathers, mothers, brothers and sisters to other people in the world. An older man in a position of authority becomes a 'father figure'. We tend to impose on that figure or 'project' on him, unconsciously, our feelings about our own original father. The pattern of feelings about father in the case of the little boy I've described was 'Fear, Avoid'. He was likely, in fact certain, to apply his feelings and ideas about his father to all older men in authority, his teachers, his bosses, his male superiors in every aspect of his life. He would fear them and try to avoid them throughout his life, long after his father had died. This pattern would, of course, be a great handicap.

Events, feelings and the reasons for one's behaviour tend to pass out of conscious awareness. We are able to 'blot out' experiences by means of what is called 'repression'. We may even refuse to attend – repressing or suppressing our attention – while events are taking place and so be hardly aware of what's happening. Or we may deny that something is happening, fooling ourselves. We may also forget what has happened. The outcome is that a great deal of our past is not available for our conscious inspection. The experiences of the past and also of the present are recorded by that aspect of our minds we call 'unconscious'.

The fearful little boy, once grown up, had probably no idea why he felt apprehension or dread when he had to have dealings with older men, why he shunned going to the office and found any excuse to stay away. He was always convinced that his boss disliked him. The angry father also succeeded in making his son feel a failure, since the child could find no way to please him and was always criticized. We present ourselves to the world according to the opinion we have of ourselves. The unhappy son presented himself as a failure in his dealings with men, made a muddle of his work, managed to be late at his desk most mornings, lost important papers, and so on. In the end, having been sacked from or resigned from a dozen or more jobs and feeling deeply depressed, he consulted a psychiatrist. The most suitable and helpful treatment for this man was psychotherapy. The job of the therapist was to try to relate what was going on in the present day to what went on in the past, during childhood. First, an investigation into the present circumstances helped lead to a clear understanding of the pattern. Having discovered the patient had problems with *all* older men, the therapist tried to steer him away from the general and back to the particular – the original and first experience of a relationship with an older man – his father.

In the beginning of his therapy, the patient said, 'My father? Oh yes, he was a good father, I believe he was a perfectionist and wanted us to be perfect.' In the course of the therapy, memories not normally available seemed to surface. 'My father used to hit me – hard – if I dropped things or was clumsy. I remember that once I was running to fetch a ball he'd thrown and I tripped over my shoelace and fell. He came storming up, I remember – and kicked me – as I was lying there – on the ground. I was only about five, I think. I suppose I was a very clumsy child . . .'

In the course of the therapy it became clear he was neither clumsy nor inept except in his relationship with father figures. The son in the process of discovering himself became more aware of his father's behaviour, began to feel angry with his father. The anger that sometimes develops in this way is something that makes some parents dread and hate therapists. 'It's not fair,' they cry, 'to blame it all on us! Surely he's got to take some responsibility also.' They are right. We are all responsible for our actions unless drugged, mentally defective or psychotic. But there are reasons why we are motivated – without being compelled – to act in a particular way. Psychotherapy uncovers these reasons. Having understood why he behaved in a particular way the patient, with the help of his therapist, must make efforts to change the pattern, rather than remain with his problems and continue to blame his parents.

Parents often try very hard, on a conscious level, to be 'good' parents. Much of the harm done by them is motivated and carried out unconsciously. Parents who are knowingly and deliberately cruel and dangerous are rare. Most parents who create problems in their children's lives are unconsciously repeating the lives they themselves led in their childhood, unconsciously re-enacting the behaviour of their parents. In this way, generation after generation will go through precisely the same hardships and endure and express the same hostilities.

Children do, of course, provoke hostility. The mothers in the supermarket, earlier mentioned, dragging their shrieking children along, are almost certainly exhausted, at the end of their tether. Part of the exhaustion will have arisen because the mother has been trying too hard to be a good, even 'perfect' mother. The idea that parents should be, or can be, 'wonderful' in their roles is quite unrealistic, a notion that is responsible for much anxiety and misery.

Human beings have a talent for conceptual thinking, for creating ideas, notions, formulae. Our lives are totally moulded and governed by 'man-made' concepts, in contrast to other animals who live and survive according to instincts and sensations. Some concepts are of course highly constructive as is that of democracy (perhaps), others destructive to the species, as is racism. Throughout human history there have been horrifying concepts, resulting in the Inquisition, the notion that animals other than man have no soul and so may be relentlessly tortured and destroyed, that 'witches' must be burnt at the stake, that black cats are the devil incarnate, that homosexuality is a crime – culminating in the most monstrous concept of all, Hitler's and other Nazis' idea of destroying millions of people in gas chambers, to 'purify' the race.

On a very different level, the mothers and fathers of Western societies have been subjected to concept after concept, one contradicting the other, on how to bring up children and how to be a good parent. Each succeeding generation has a different view. During this century bewildered parents have been told:

a: to feed their babies strictly every four hours and not more
often
b: to feed their babies on demand
c: never to pick up babies who cry
d: that breastfeeding is unnecessary
f: that breastfeeding is vitally important
g: to be strict with their children
h: to be permissive with their children

and so on.

Some concepts are simply out of date, but continue to have powerful influence. Victorian notions about sex still affect many people. Many concepts about family life are completely hypocritical. It would be far more useful and helpful to families to shed all notions except those which relate to the realities of human feelings and human relationships.

Psychotherapy searches for the reality of the feelings in the family. The man I described earlier, the son of a father who bullied him, tried to maintain an ideal about his father: 'He did try to be a good father. He worked terribly hard to send me to public school which we couldn't really afford. I was always being told how hard he worked so that I could have the things he'd never had . . .' But he also said, 'I was a very unhappy child. He made my life a misery . . .'

His father might have said, 'I did my best for the boy. I worked so hard I nearly killed myself, just to give him a good education and a nice home, and all the things I never had. . . .'

What was the truth? The answer is, there were, there are, many truths. One truth – but only one – lies in the unconscious mind. Was that father unconsciously jealous of his son for having the things in life he had never had himself? Was he unconsciously resentful about the cost to himself, in fatigue and boredom and anxiety, in trying to earn enough to give his child so much? Was he trying too hard, unconsciously, to placate 'society', following the conventional lines that society lays down for the 'good father' and the 'good life'?

Are the fathers and mothers of our societies, the law makers, the media men and women, the churchmen and women, those who create the climate of opinion, who are responsible for morality, customs, conventions, at fault? From the moment we're born, messages from the Establishment seep into our unconscious minds, transmitted by people whose unconscious motivation is often suspect.

To return to psychotherapy. Many different theories about the mind have produced more and more sets of concepts, but all schools of psychotherapy try to reach a non-conceptual truth: the truth of feelings.

Feelings, emotions, do, of course, change rapidly. Love gives way to hate, anger to laughter. Nevertheless, in day-to-day relationships, a thread of consistency runs through the feeling spectrum. If a feeling and its accompanying behaviour pattern is repeated often enough, it makes its mark. This is particularly true in childhood. Because a response to a stimulus is logical – for example, a large, angry father logically makes a small boy frightened – all behaviour and feeling patterns are logical responses to the events and attitudes of parents in a child's world. This logical sequence makes it possible for psychotherapy to relate the cause to the effect in dealing with disturbance of mind and emotions. There is logic (although it may be obscure) in the seemingly rambling ravings of very ill psychotics, and a limited and hideous logic in the worst of people's barbaric acts. Our evolution in the Darwinian sense has forced on us a cause–effect mode of being.

In this book I try to give an orderly, logical picture of the functions of the mind, a cause-and-effect picture of emotional disturbance and of normal emotional responses. I also try to encourage the acceptance of 'real' feelings, always remembering that reality as we know it is a hypothesis, an informed guess, perhaps a mirage seen through a glass, darkly.

TWO

Psychotherapy:
A Description and an Explanation

What is psychotherapy? How does it work? People are often afraid, as I've suggested earlier, of an investigation of their minds. The mind, more personal, more secret than the body, doesn't readily open itself to intrusion – especially if the intruder is a psychiatrist. Even if a person is willing to have therapy, resistance may occur, defences go into action, walls and barriers spring up to protect against invasion. The defences may come into action via the unconscious mind, not necessarily via the conscious mind. Silence is sometimes the outcome, the patient finding it difficult to speak – or else many irrelevant and deflecting thoughts are discussed, the real issue being avoided.

But if people knew more about the process of psychotherapy, they'd be less afraid, less protective and more willing to co-operate with the therapist, even on an unconscious level. The exploration of the mind can only take place if the person with the problems, the patient, works together with the doctor or therapist.

Psychiatrists don't have X-ray eyes. They can't tell what's going on in a person's mind any more than a lay person can read another's thoughts. What's revealed in the course of therapy is exactly what the patient wants, consciously and unconsciously, to reveal about him or herself. Sometimes people try to resist therapy as if they were resisting rape. But psychiatrists aren't opponents. They want to help their patients. They don't make moral judgements and they're less critical of human feelings and behaviour than most other people. The psychiatrist or therapist is often a kind of friend. And psychiatrists or analysts approach their patients quietly, hesitantly and passively as a rule, waiting until the patient is ready to begin – and waiting again, each time a patient stops in his tracks, fearful of what might be revealed.

We are afraid of ourselves, our inner thoughts, observations, longings, because of conventional morality. Our main inhibitions are to do with aggression or sex, two great driving forces. But as far as an experienced psychiatrist is concerned, human beings are only subtly different from one another. Psychiatrists are seldom surprised and seldom shocked. As far as they're concerned, 'There's nothing new under the sun' – a sad fact perhaps, but also a reassuring one. Human minds resemble one another closely.

Psychotherapy literally means treatment of the mind or soul. In the practice of medicine, there are many ways of treating a disturbed or ill mind, for example, with drugs or electro-convulsive therapy (ECT). The term psychotherapy, however, is reserved for a specific treatment which involves communication between a patient and a therapist. The therapist may be a medically qualified psychiatrist or he or she may be a 'lay' therapist, not medically qualified but, nevertheless, an orthodox therapist who has had a rigorous training. There is also a good deal of unorthodox therapy to be found, but, in general, this does not help the patient as successfully or as enduringly as orthodox therapy may do.

In orthodox psychotherapy, the communication between the patient and the therapist is partly verbal – perhaps largely verbal – but there is also an exchange of feelings and a more mysterious element, perhaps a kind of telepathy.

There are many schools of psychotherapy and many, many theories about how the mind works. The theories are notions, or concepts, or ideas. Many theories may be applied to the workings of the mind and most of them may be valid, since there are infinite possibilities for symbolizing human thinking. In general, the theories of psychoanalysts are abstractions and not related to what is known of brain/mind relationships.

The techniques used in psychotherapy vary. Some psychoanalysts, notably Freudians and Kleinians, prefer their patients to be on a couch, out of sight of the therapist. Some therapists like to face their patients, who may sit opposite them. Talking then begins.

It's best if the patient initiates the talking. Some patients find this very difficult. In 'strict' psychoanalytical therapy, analysts may wait for days, weeks, or even months for a patient to begin or continue to talk without intervening. The theory behind this technique is that there is a valid (for the patient) reason for the silence. In eclectic psychotherapy (that selecting ideas from various schools of thought), the therapist is likely to encourage conversation by asking questions, or chatting about the weather, or other harmless subjects, simply to begin the flow of talk. A patient's silence may indicate hostility or depression or other states of mind and emotions.

The talking usually goes on for an hour at a time (or the analyst's rigid 'fifty minutes'). Analysts believe it important to see their patients at least three times a week, preferably more often. Eclectic therapists or psychiatrists may limit the sessions to once or twice a week. Sometimes just a few hours of eclectic or supportive psychotherapy may be extremely helpful to a patient. The treatment may go on for years, depending on the problems and the personality, capabilities, and so on, of the patient, and also depending on the patient's physical and emotional circumstances. If a patient is in insuperably difficult circumstances, which cannot be changed, the patient may need the support of a therapist indefinitely.

Psychoanalysts try to keep their own personalities out of the therapeutic situation, hoping to exist only as grey, neutral figures. The idea behind this is that patients may then regard their therapists in any light, without the real personality of the therapists intervening. In spite of these attempts at camouflage, patients often – perhaps almost always – become intensely inquisitive about the private lives of their therapists. They want to know about the real person, where he or she may live, whether they are married, if they have children and so on.

But the reason for the analyst's camouflage is to give a better chance to the patient to endow the therapist with characteristics of a figure from the patient's past. Part of the benefit derived from psychotherapy results from the fact that the therapist is unconsciously used by the patient to represent some childhood ghost, usually a parent.

The patient will tend to 'project' on to the therapist feelings originally experienced in early life – and later – in relation to a mother or father or sister, brother, aunt, uncle, 'nanny', grandparent – depending on circumstances. The process of 'projecting' feelings on the analyst happens easily and unconsciously, often without conscious recognition that the phenomenon is taking place. The therapist is a symbol, in a sense, of the real parent.

The feelings of a patient for his therapist may be very intense, very profound. A patient may fall deeply in love with his or her therapist. Sometimes the sex of the therapist is irrelevant, a male therapist being endowed by the patient with, say, characteristics of a female from childhood – mother or sister – and vice versa.

The patient's feelings in relation to the therapist are one of the most important talking points in the course of psychotherapy. These feelings help to reveal the feelings of childhood towards the real parent or sibling. We may transfer wholesale the feelings we had for a mother or father in childhood, thus exactly re-enacting the past. On the other hand, a therapist may represent an idealized version of a parent or other figure, a version which the patient longed for and never received: a loving and caring mother, instead of a rejecting one, an affectionate and kind elder sister, instead of a jealous and angry one. If a patient had a very unpleasant parent and received rough treatment from him or her, the patient may have been an angry and troublesome child and this anger and hostile behaviour may, perhaps, be felt towards the therapist.

The transfer of such feelings from patient to therapist is called 'transference'. The transference may be 'positive', meaning the feelings are harmonious and pleasant, or 'negative', meaning the feelings are angry and stressful. The therapist's feelings for the patient are likely to be compassionate, affectionate and often respectful. There is often a great deal to be admired in a patient. Feelings intensify, of course, if the therapy has taken place over a long period. It's important for the therapist to keep a firm control over both his or her feelings and the patient's. The therapy's value to the patient is much diminished if feelings are 'acted out' to excess. For this reason, therapists abstain from social contact with their patients. Another interesting fact is that it seems more embarrassing for a patient to meet a doctor or therapist in a social context if he or she has been baring his or her mind rather than body. Patients don't seem to mind social intercourse with their dentists, physicians or even gynaecologists, but they tend to be anxious about meeting their psychiatrists in public places.

There do, of course, exist therapists who are bored by and hostile to their patients – but these are few. Patients 'pick up' the therapist's feelings very quickly and are quick to respond to them.

Most people in distress are over-sensitive to the attitudes of those around them. Therapy may take place on a one-to-one basis of patient to therapist. Or therapy may take place in groups. In group therapy, there's an opportunity for using the other members of the group to represent a variety of people from childhood, brothers, and sisters, schoolmates and so on. The doctor or therapist who conducts the group is likely to represent a parent.

All therapy, no matter what the theory, is directed towards an understanding of events and feelings in the past, those of childhood. All therapy is aimed at revealing, at making conscious, that which has been recorded in childhood by the unconscious aspect of our minds. If we could be clear about how our parents really felt about us when we were children and how we felt about them, there'd be less mental and emotional illness – and less need for psychotherapists – and the process of psychotherapy would be quicker and easier. But most people are very unclear as to what precisely went on when they were little children. We have a curiously obscure and shadowy view of our early years, because events and feelings are partly forgotten, partly 'repressed'. Some events and feelings were never consciously perceived although recorded unconsciously.

There was also confusion. Our parents generally tried to present themselves according to some formal notion – some idealized version of parental behaviour, conforming to what they felt society expected of them. This presentation may have been very different from their true feelings. There are, of course, concepts of morality which dictate how parents should act and feel towards their children. These moral notions vary from society to society. In sophisticated present-day Western societies, for example, all except the mildest aggressive and sexual feelings and behaviour are supposed to be suppressed both by parents and by children. There are also social concepts which silently dictate to *children* how they ought to feel and behave towards their parents. Many parents and many children try to obey these rules. Children are supposed to love and revere their parents. It's hard to say precisely how the rules are known, but social morals creating guilt are in the air, 'between the lines', implicit in advertisements, plays, films, television, in books and newspapers and in the very walls of the houses in which we live.

The conventional pictures of parent–child, child–parent

relationships are unreal, like cardboard images, from which the ferocious passions, normal in human life, are missing. All living creatures struggle to survive, spilling blood, sweat, and tears in the process. Human beings are no exception. But because the conventions insist on pretence, pretend we do, suppressing and repressing the realities, or genuinely refusing to recognize the truth. 'Human kind,' said T. S. Eliot, 'cannot bear very much reality'. But psychotherapy attempts to establish the reality – for the reality, although sometimes depressing, sometimes cruel and hurtful, is nevertheless therapeutic.

Why is it necessary to bring the past out of its shadowy resting place, why essential to make conscious the seemingly disposed-of, dealt-with, events and feelings of childhood? The reason is that recorded happenings and experiences, although unconscious, continue to motivate us – continue to make us behave or think or feel in certain specific ways. The unconscious mind is much more powerful than the conscious aspect of our minds. The events of childhood and our reactions to them stay with us forever. The experiences of our youth are the most intense and formative of our lives, as is well known. The first sixteen to seventeen years are the most important. After this, we are formed, stamped and almost sealed. The patterns are set and fixed in our unconscious minds. They'll continue to make us follow lines of behaviour, lines of feeling and even of thinking. However hard we try to rule our lives by conscious intentions, by willpower, or 'pull yourself together' methods, we'll fail if our conscious wishes are in conflict with powerful unconscious motivations.

Our unconscious drives trick us time and time again into fulfilling the old patterns. Here's an example of how this happens. Miss M. J., now aged thirty-eight years has, since the age of seventeen, longed (as far as she consciously knows) to be married, to have an agreeable home and children. She's constantly on the lookout for Mr Right. But he never seems to come along. She's an intelligent and very attractive woman, has a good job in a public relations firm and is valued by her friends and colleagues. 'Poor Marie-Claire', her friends say after the breakdown of her twenty-fifth relationship. 'She doesn't deserve to have this happen to her. Why does such a nice person always seem to get involved with such hopeless men?' Marie-Claire has had endless affairs with men. All end in disaster. Her friends are accustomed to having to come round with gin and sympathy, accustomed to the sight of a tear-stained, pale, sleepless Marie-Claire, slowly recovering from yet another débâcle. The truth is that there exist in Marie-Claire's unconscious mind strong reasons, or motives, for *not* getting married. She has completely forgotten that, between the ages of three and six, she had a glorious love affair with her father, as a result of which he unconsciously decided he must keep her for himself for the rest of his days. She in turn 'betrothed' herself to him and made a resolve to marry him when she grew up. The whole business might have come to a natural end during Marie-Claire's adolescent years had not circumstances forced them together again. Marie-Claire's mother became disabled by a serious illness which was to cause her death a few years later. Marie-Claire, the only girl among the children, adopted the role of mother to the family. She and her father drew, once more, very close to one another and he became very dependent on her.

By the time she was thirty, however, he too had died, so at the present moment she's under the impression that her old relationship with her father couldn't possibly affect her feelings and behaviour. But that early 'betrothal' is still operating, the pattern being that she must remain free for her father, 'Daddy's girl', until that mythical, impossible moment when past will become present and he will claim her as his bride.

The relationships she has had with men have failed because they were unconsciously planned to fail and so doomed before they started. She chose to be involved with men (the choosing was unconscious) who were unsuitable for marriage. The sensitive antennae of her unconscious mind picked out from the many possible partners those who would be impossible to marry, those who were neurotically unwilling to marry, those who were already married and could not leave their wives, those who were homosexual, those who were impotent, and those who were wildly and openly promiscuous. There were men who lived in Antarctica, Jesuit priests, Mormons and transvestites. She brushed aside all those sensible and reasonable suitors who were the right age, in the right income bracket, compatible, sensitive, intelligent and suitable. She called them 'boring' or dull or ugly and managed to find a reason to disentangle from them.

Thus the conflict between conscious wish to marry and unconscious need to remain faithful to her father was resolved, in endless repetition, by her entering enthusiastically and optimistically into a relationship only to find, surprise, surprise, that she was once again involved with a man unsuitable for marriage.

A psychotherapist faced with Marie-Claire and her problems (which are not uncommon in our Western societies) would hope first to help her to see exactly what she is doing, and why she behaves as she does; then to help her change that pattern of faithfulness to a dead father. But to begin with, the pattern must be defined. The buried, unconscious feelings and events of childhood may be brought into consciousness in a variety of ways.

The therapist might begin by discussions regarding present-day behaviour and feelings, fairly certain that a reenactment of the past is taking place from time to time. The present mirrors the past with uncanny exactitude. And, when talking about the past – and the present – astonishing fragments of memories, whole stretches of forgotten life, or sudden, telling episodes, tend to swim into consciousness. We have the classic and magical example of Proust's *À la Recherche du Temps Perdu*. So analytical psychotherapy depends on memories which link themselves to some experience of the present and become available for conscious inspection; on the events and feelings of today which reflect the past; and also on dreams, which may describe unconscious feelings in symbolic terms (and also events of the past). Dreams are an important item in some schools of analysis, notably the Jungian school.

The process of psychotherapy is very like a detective story – patient and therapist joined in efforts to sleuth out the past. The rule is 'softly, softly', as the unconscious mind is easily alarmed and may quickly resist investigation. Our patterns of thinking, feelings and behaving have been set up for a reason. We defend ourselves from change, which may seem to bring insecurity or danger. We take it for granted, mistakenly, that the childhood reasons for the patterns, the childhood circumstances, are still operating – although, of course, they're never relevant to adult life. It takes a long time to be rid of old fears.

Here's an example of psychotherapy in action. The patient is a young woman called Serena. She's happily married. She's come to the psychiatrist because, recently, her husband has begun to talk about the importance of her having a child. He longs for children – and so does she, in theory, but when he first mentioned the subject, Serena found herself suddenly and inexplicably overwhelmed by unbearable panic. Without any reason, she thinks. Why should she feel so terrified? The answer is that she simply can't face the idea of giving birth.

To start with, the talk between Serena and the psychiatrist is about the present day – simple chat about her husband, other people's children, the weather, where to buy good bread, what life was like in Toronto where she was born. One day the patient suddenly mentions that her husband would like her to have shorter hair. This would mean she'd have to go to the hairdresser more often than she does now, and she hates the hairdresser's.

'Oh? Why is that?'

As a child – a very small child – and also later, until she was old enough to wash her own hair, her mother used to send her by taxi once a week to a hairdresser to have her hair shampooed.

'That's rather unusual. Why was that, I wonder? Couldn't she have washed your hair for you?'

'My mother didn't like to do it. She . . . I don't know why . . . I have a feeling she didn't like to touch my hair.'

'Ah. . . . . . . !'

Here is clue number one, a definite suggestion of something strange about Serena's mother and her relationship with Serena as a young child.

'Does your mother like to touch you now?'

'She does in a way, that's to say she kisses us hello and goodbye, my sister and me – but I don't like her to touch *me* somehow . . .'

On another occasion, apropos of discussing diets, Serena mentions that she can't stand milk.

'Oh? Why is that?'

'I don't know. I hate it. I've always hated it – even as a small child. At the nursery school, when all the others were having their milk, I had to have something else, orange juice or something . . .'

Clue number two. Could something have gone wrong in the very early days of the relationship between Serena and her mother?

And later the patient reports that one of her worries about having a child is that she won't be able to feed it.

'Why not?'

'My mother couldn't. She had terrible problems with me, breastfeeding. I believe I screamed a lot – so she told me. She didn't even try, with my younger sister . . .'

Another piece of evidence. A woman who can't bear to touch

her child's hair is likely to have problems about a child sucking the nipples of her breasts.

And again, on yet another day, Serena suddenly asks: 'Is there something wrong with me do you think – about my breasts? Johnny [her husband] likes very much to touch them and hold them. I can't bear it – everything else is OK – any other part of my body – but not my breasts . . .'

And later we learn that Serena is very intolerant of even the slightest frustration. Recently her husband had to postpone a week-end trip that she had been looking forward to very much and she became hysterical, with a night-long scene. And the same thing has happened when he firmly said he would not allow her to go on smoking if she became pregnant (Serena smokes only rarely).

After a while we begin to suppose that Serena's mother had the greatest difficulty having any physical contact with her child. We picture the scene with her mother perhaps trying desperately to breastfeed her infant daughter – giving her her breast and at the same time holding herself away from her child – so that the baby screamed and screamed in terrible frustration, within inches of the milk yet not able to get at it – and developing an aversion to breast and milk and to having children of her own, when this experience would be re-enacted.

All this, of course, can't be consciously recalled by Serena – but the experiences are recorded in unconscious mind – and promote the panic which she feels at the thought of having a child.

Without the help of psychotherapy, even if she forced herself to have a child because of her husband's insistence, the chances are she would precisely re-enact the dramas that went on between her and her mother.

Here's another example of the exploring technique of psycho-therapy. A famous painter arrives in the psychiatrist's consulting room saying he simply cannot get down to his work. However hard he tries to make himself get to his studio, he simply can't manage it. He says he feels frustrated to the point of violence – either to himself or to others.

Questioning tells us: first, that he's only been so frustrated and so 'blocked' since he became really successful. Second, that the reason (apparently) he can't get to the studio is that he is too busy doing other things, which he feels he can't put aside for the sake of his own work.

'Such as?'

'Such as teaching young painters at the various colleges and art schools, entertaining younger colleagues from abroad, listening to their problems, visiting them in their studios, at their request, giving them advice and guidance.'

'Always *younger* artists?'

'Yes, almost always, or those less successful than myself; usually poor and not very talented, struggling . . . That's why I feel I owe it to them . . .'

'Do you enjoy your own success?'

The artist quickly denies that he *is* very successful, although he is famous in Europe and the US.

We have two clues. The first is that the 'patient' spends a lot of his time looking after painters younger than himself. Could these represent the younger siblings of his childhood? The second clue is that the patient is uncomfortable about his success, finds it hard to accept and enjoy.

On another occasion, the patient arrived in a depressed and penitent mood. His wife was ill with her duodenal ulcer, as she often was. He'd felt unreasonably angry and aggressive towards her, shouted at her that it was all her own fault – and, quite irrationally, that it was she who prevented him getting on with his work. He hates illness, he says, especially in someone close to him – and while his wife is ill, she seems to take up all his energy – although he doesn't have to do anything physically, as the au pair looks after her from that point of view.

The present reflects the past. Could his wife be a kind of mother figure to him (unconsciously, of course)?

The clues so far suggest that the patient feels a guilty need to care for possibly sibling figures, that his own success makes him feel bad, and that he hates illness in someone close to him; also that – is it possible? – he felt his 'mother' somehow obstructed him from doing the work which brought him success. The psychotherapeutic investigation, proceeding slowly, gradually lets us understand that the patient was the only truly thriving child in a family of two parents and four children. The other three, two boys and a girl, were frail and often ill. In addition, they were less intelligent than the patient and did less well at school. One boy died at an early age – perhaps suffering from leukaemia. The other limped along, to end up in a not very successful job in a country town. The only girl suffered from epilepsy due to an injury at birth. The parents were constantly urging our patient to 'play things down'. His father would say, 'Keep it quiet, old chap. You don't have to shout about it.' His mother: 'You don't need to make such a performance, dear. It's very good – but if you make such a noise about it poor Rosie's [or poor Ronald] going to get upset.'

He'd been sent away to boarding school, the only child in the family to be away from home. He was told by his mother this was a great privilege – but we can suppose he might have felt it was because he was too powerful, too dangerous, perhaps wicked. He must be removed from his siblings for their safety.

In the end, we understand he may have felt unconsciously responsible for the frail condition of his siblings, perhaps even responsible for the death of his brother. The more successful he was, the more damaging he felt himself to be – at the same time blaming his parents (now wife) for this state of affairs. And perhaps it was also true that he was carrying his parents' guilt about *their* aggression in causing fragility, ill-health, death, and epilepsy in their children. His unconscious guilt and fears force him to find reasons not to work, arrange for him to spend a great deal of time caring for the symbolic siblings, the younger, less talented, poor and suffering artists. And we see that he has a conflict of driving forces, one motivating him to work and success, the other to diminish himself and efface himself, in favour of the less privileged.

These two brief sketches illustrate the exploratory nature of the journey on which one embarks when entering psychotherapy. The journey may be rough and difficult, but in the end it's infinitely rewarding. Serena was able to bear her child in peace and emotional comfort and to breastfeed her. The artist gave up some of his teaching commitments and most of his social counselling sessions and returned to his studio. And his wife was cured of her ulcer.

Yet even without a clearcut outcome such as I've just described, psychotherapy is usually enriching and often enjoyable in the end after, perhaps, some stormy times. Understanding unconscious motivation adds another dimension to life. The inner world is marvellously interesting. We may find links with our distant past; with our evolution, in Darwin's sense; and a closeness to the other animals on earth. And we also find ourselves subject to certain laws – the tendencies towards integration and dissolution – re-integration, separation, rhythms, patterns, alternatives . . .

But first, before our inner world is formed, we must have a relationship with the outer world.

PART TWO

The Inner World
of the Mind:

**How We Relate to
and Cope with the
Outer World of
the Environment**

THREE

Conceptual Thinking and Feelings

Conceptual thinking

First of all, we must recognize one very important fact about human beings. The way in which we deal with our world and with one another is based largely on conceptual thinking. Concepts are ideas – notions which are arrived at as a result of assessing information we receive, by means of our senses, from the environment. Both the unconscious and the conscious aspects of our minds function in terms of concepts.

Our whole way of life is governed by conceptual thinking. In this way we differ hugely from all other animals on earth, whose way of life is governed by instincts. I use the term 'instincts' here in a special sense, meaning impulses which spring from within an animal which motivate that animal to behave in a fairly precise, ritualized way – a way which doesn't in any way depend on learning or experience or reasoning, but which is inherited, carried by the genes from generation to generation. For example, birds migrate instinctually at certain times of the year. Cats, when afraid, climb trees. Mice rush for cover.

Much aggressive and sexual behaviour in animals other than man is performed at the 'instruction' of instincts. Instincts mould and modify animal behaviour, restraining and restricting and making animals conform, very often, to a kind of symbolic ritual, so avoiding excesses.

Instincts evolved – in the Darwinian sense of the term – and so are of value to the survival of a species. They probably have very great survival value, in fact, perhaps more than human beings have so far achieved with conceptual thinking.

It's interesting and mysterious that we humans have little instinct-motivated behaviour. Somewhere along the road of man's evolution, we lost touch with instincts, perhaps as the ability for conceptual thinking became more advanced.

Certainly our cousins the apes are still in possession of instinct-motivated behaviour. But the hominid line must slowly have either discarded instinctive behaviour or become unable to attend to or respond to instinctual impulses. We might say that the behaviour of other animals is imprisoned by instincts, since instincts force rigid behaviour responses.

Equally humanity is imprisoned by conceptual thinking since we have no other way of operating or being. But it hasn't yet fully dawned on us that our survival depends wholly on concepts. We have escaped – by means of conceptual thinking, by being free of instinct-motivated behaviour – from one of the fundamental rules of evolution: the survival of the fittest. As a result, our future as a species is threatened. And what is more, our concepts themselves are dangerous to the survival of man.

Feelings

Our saving grace is that in addition to our ability for conceptual thinking, we have the capacity for experiencing feelings and emotions.

The ability to experience feelings is shared by many other animals and, via our feelings, we are more closely in touch with a world that existed before the advent of humanity. Feelings and emotions accompany conceptual thinking and often promote further conceptual thinking. They are experienced as a response to stimulation – a response to events, to other people's feelings and behaviour, to happenings in the world outside us, or within us.

Sometimes the true cause or reason for a feeling or emotion may be unconscious, in which case we tend to find a spurious conscious reason for our response. We have only a limited range of feelings and emotions – just as we have only limited sensory organs, which allow us to have limited sensations. Other animals may have more possibilities for feeling experiences – which we shall never know, since we can only encompass and understand the world in our own image.

Because we are limited as to how we respond, one kind of feeling or emotion occurs in relation to a great variety of circumstances. For example, happiness is the response to:

a) A sunny day in Spring.
b) Being in love.
c) The children doing well at school.
d) Winning a prize

and so on

Anger is the response to:

a) Being hurt physically or mentally.
b) Seeing a man run over a dog in the street and drive on without stopping, leaving the wounded animal in the road.
c) Losing one's wallet.
d) Having one's adolescent child stay out till 4 a.m. without telephoning, i.e. acute anxiety.
e) Seeing one's neighbour cut down a tree without a permit and get away with it, i.e. another person breaking the law without being punished

and so on.

We're at a loss for words to describe and define feelings and emotions and moods. Our language can describe quantity but not quality. We couldn't, for example, explain to a man from Mars what pain feels like, what the colour red looks like, what an orange tastes like, or what it is to feel sad or happy. Look in the dictionary for the definition of 'compassion' and you may see 'pity' mentioned. Turn the pages to 'pity' and you'll see it defined as 'compassion'.

Nevertheless, for almost all of us, the only true reality is the reality of experiencing sensations and emotions. I say almost all, because there are some people who are so out of touch with their feelings they live largely on the level of conceptual thinking.

But for the majority, feelings are the stuff of life. A world without 'feelings' is arid and dreary. The more intensely we're able to feel, the richer our lives.

We must suppose that our feelings evolved, one by one, in the Darwinian sense and that each feeling has some survival value. The ability to experience fear, for example, might cause an animal to run away, escape in good time from a predator, or freeze, or hide.

We share our ability to experience feelings and emotions with other animals – and certainly, millions of years before our ancestors made their gradual appearance on earth, there were animals who could see and hear and taste, who could perhaps experience excitement or fear or anger or love. It has been one of our peculiarly arrogant assumptions that animals other than ourselves have no 'feelings' or minds or emotions. This has been partly the fault of the Christian Church which denied that other animals had a soul. For all we know, there are creatures on earth far more loving and caring of one another than we have ever been of our fellow men and women. Darwin himself wrote that 'animals could clearly feel pleasure, pain, in terror their muscles trembled and their hearts palpitated, like man's. Such faculties as maternal love, self-sacrifice, jealousy and love of praise and such complex attributes as imitation, attention, memory and rudimentary reason were not the exclusive property of man . . .'

It is, in fact, through our feelings that we're more closely in contact with that other world, the world beyond the realm of conceptual thinking, the world of our animal past. This is a world accessible to other animals, from which we're excluded (as from the Garden of Eden) where creatures live in accordance with their feelings, their behaviour always guided by instincts. They move with a sense of sureness through jungles, climb trees with unthinking agility, swim calmly in the great rivers and huge oceans of the earth. Their consciousness is in no way diminished, but conceptual thinking is perhaps minimal.

It may be that animals bypass conceptual thinking but achieve the same results. For example, a herd of buffalo, sniffing the air, will know from the scent alone that a lion is near. Their acute and well-organized ability to hear also gives many animals information which doesn't need to be processed and put together by means of conceptual thinking. But we, homo sapiens, have comparatively poor hearing and a poor sense of smell – or, at least, our senses are not well enough organized in the nervous system to give us, by means of sensation alone, a wide range of accurate information.

Be that as it may, what is more sure is that we humans enjoy feelings, crave feelings and emotions, except when they're painful. When the pain of feeling is severe, we ignore and avoid feelings, as happens often in a disturbed childhood. Having developed the habit of avoiding feelings, we live barren lives.

In adult life some people tend to seek out situations where feelings and emotions are enhanced and intensified. Sometimes alcohol and other drugs are taken for this purpose. Sometimes people out of touch with their own feelings link themselves to others who feel very intensely, and so enter a feeling world vicariously. Or they may link themselves to those who behave outrageously and 'sensationally', so opening themselves to the reception of violent stimulation of the senses and emotions. The 'numbed' person wants, unconsciously, the partner to perform and feel exaggeratedly – and often the partner unconsciously 'obliges', not always to his or her advantage.

So, it seems, we all unconsciously strive to reach that more mysterious, perhaps more wonderful world where animals live, where feelings are paramount and conceptual thinking takes second place.

FOUR

Consciousness and the Unconscious

Rationalisation and repression

At the end of the nineteenth century and the beginning of the twentieth, Western societies were rocked and shocked by the writings of two men, Darwin and Freud. Previous views about the human species had to be changed, amid loud uproar. Was man created by God on the sixth day, woman born out of Adam's rib? Or were we cousins of the apes, evolved with the fittest, our strange, hairless bodies a chance trick of the genes? Then, an announcement from Freud . . . We were at the mercy of an unconscious mind, motivating us to act, think and feel without understanding why! The 'unconscious' was more powerful than conscious mind and housed our sins and weaknesses.

Evolution and unconscious mind . . . Putting together the ideas of Darwin with those of Freud, surely we must say that our minds evolved in the same way that our bodies did, slow change after change, unconscious mind preceding conscious? We must suppose that attributes of the mind, gathering together over millions of years, made either a contribution to survival – or, on the contrary, assisted in the downfall of a species – and we should consider the ability to achieve consciousness as a remarkable feat of the evolutionary process.

Looked at in this way we might say that unconscious mind is the rule, and consciousness a special function, an act of being aware, of focusing and attending.

The ability to be conscious isn't a voluntary performance. We, in common with many other animals, are conscious the moment we're born and the moment we open our eyes after sleeping, provided our brain and nervous system are intact. But we can, by an act of will, heighten consciousness and pay particular attention.

And we can lower consciousness by not attending to what we are doing, seeing, hearing and so on.

Experienced car drivers will know that, occasionally, on a long road free of traffic and obstacles they may suddenly 'come to' and find that an unconscious pilot had taken over the management of the car – that is, their attention to driving has diminished, but nevertheless, they have successfully driven along the road, followed the curves and so on without being fully aware of what they are doing. In the same way, if we're reading, absorbed in a book, we're a great deal less aware of our surroundings – although far from being generally unconscious. The same might be said of someone listening intently to music, while his or her eyes might be fixed, say, on a bookcase or a vase of flowers. Neither the books nor the flowers will be attended to or noticed. In a sense, we'll be unaware or unconscious of them. Yet switch off the music or put down the book and, instantly, the objects and people around jump into focus.

So we can see there is an ongoing interchange between the conscious aspect of the mind and the unconscious aspect of the mind.

This to-ing and fro-ing between consciousness and the unconscious mind allows a variety of mental performances to take place. One such activity is called 'rationalization'. Rationalization in this special sense means that, on a conscious level, we believe we are acting or thinking or feeling for a particular reason, a reason that seems rational. But the true reason for our actions or thoughts or feelings lies in unconscious mind and is different to the apparently rational reason. The true reason is something we would rather not face because, perhaps, it puts us in a bad light, or shows us something about ourselves we'd rather not know or is painful to us.

For example:

1: *Conscious rationalization*: I think I'd better just clean the kitchen floor with my new vacuum cleaner because the cleaning lady is not good with machines and could break it.

   Unconscious true reason: I ought to be upstairs writing my book but I'd do anything rather than that. Besides my mother hated me to be successful.

2:   *Conscious rationalization:*I never give my children sweets because it's so bad for their teeth.

Unconscious true reason: My mother never gave me sweets when I was a child. Why should they have what I didn't get?

3:   *Conscious rationalization:* I simply can't decide which of these two pairs of shoes to buy so I'm going to take both of them. They're a bargain, anyway.

Unconscious true reason: I'm feeling deeply deprived. My husband doesn't seem interested in me any longer and I'd really like to have a love affair. My husband reminds me of my father who couldn't be bothered with me.

4:   *Conscious rationalization*: I think I ought to eat this biscuit because I feel so bad when my blood sugar is low. Besides I'm not really fat – I've got big bones.

Unconscious true reason: I'm lonely and sad and I've had a miserable childhood. Eating is my only consolation.

Rationalization is often very complex, masking deep and long-standing problems. Clearly, rationalization depends on the interchange of information, the connections between unconscious and conscious aspects of the mind.

Another ability which depends on these interchanges is called repression – or suppression. This is a phenomenon which allows experiences which begin in conscious mind to be dismissed from conscious awareness or recognition. These experiences are absorbed, but unconsciously, and make their effect via unconscious mind, provoking behaviour and feelings which must be 'rationalized'. Painful experiences, frightening experiences, information which a child or adult would rather not have – these and many other unwelcome experiences may be allowed to drift out of conscious awareness. But whether the mind can actively repress or suppress selected information is in question. Perhaps we simply withdraw our attention. But whether we repress actively, or fail to notice, the outcome is that we can allow ourselves to be unaware.

These two phenomena, rationalization and so-called repression, play a great part in daily life and a great part in our ability to be hostile, cruel, neglectful and aggressive to our children and to one another without accepting responsibility for our behaviour and feelings. We simply rationalize – or repress.

Repressed feelings don't disappear. They continue to operate in unconscious mind, just as past experiences which have been forgotten remain recorded in unconscious mind and make themselves known in conscious mind in a variety of ways.

Transferral from unconscious mind to conscious awareness takes place in everyday life all the time. A smell, a taste or any other sensation or event may suddenly recall a whole complex of experiences, as Proust described in *A la Recherche du Temps Perdu*, the taste of a madeleine suddenly reminding him of a whole period of his childhood. There is also traffic in the opposite direction. We relegate the experiences of today into unconscious mind to become buried and forgotten, perhaps never to be remembered, or perhaps until some incident, some trivial happening, some sight or sound brings them back to us. Psychotherapy relies on this to and fro of information, the association of present with past, to bring into consciousness the true circumstances of a person's childhood.

FIVE

Our Sense of Our Own Image, Our Identity

Our relation to the world depends on an image we have of ourselves, which is partly conscious and partly unconscious. This image, or sense of self, depends very much on the views our parents had of us. If they loved and respected us we developed a sense of being valuable. If they rejected us we regard ourselves as worthless. Whether we value ourselves highly or put a very low value on our worth is of great importance when it comes to the way we deal with others, our careers, our successes and failures, our confidence in ourselves.

We all know that we are individuals, each of us different from everybody else, each of us separate and distinct, and with a personality and identity of our own. We all have a picture of ourselves – our appearance, our tastes, likes and dislikes, abilities and qualities. We have a conscious image of ourselves as if we could see ourselves reflected in a mirror. In this way, we're different from other animals who aren't, perhaps, capable of recognizing, consciously, an external image of themselves. But we're in line with other animals regarding an *unconscious* image of ourselves which we all also possess.

During our childhood, beginning perhaps at birth, we slowly develop, unconsciously, a 'feeling' about ourselves, an emotional self image to which we apply (also unconsciously) a kind of moral assessment, or critical judgement. The outcome is that we have a fundamental sense of ourselves as being either worthy, or valuable – a 'good' feeling – or, on the contrary, unworthy, unvaluable, undeserving. This *unconscious* self image strongly influences our *conscious* image of ourselves.

If a person grows up unconsciously feeling unworthy and not

36

valuable then, no matter how good-looking or clever, the person will be consciously convinced he or she is ugly and stupid. The unconscious sense of self distorts the conscious one, so our view of ourselves is as if we were looking in one of those fairground mirrors which make us seem fatter or longer or weirder than we actually are.

On the contrary, people who grow up feeling valuable and worthy on an unconscious level are calmly confident about themselves, no matter what they look like. These people find survival in our aggressive and hostile world much easier than those with a 'bad' or 'poor' self image. A 'good' self image allows a person to be free of anxiety about his or her self and so to be tranquil and realistic – well balanced, in fact.

Those who believe themselves unworthy tend to be less balanced, suffering from anxieties which can deform all our attitudes and behaviour. Lack of belief in self worth may make people go through life with bowed shoulders, keeping sadly in the shadows – or, in a kind of over-compensation, such people might try to be noticeable, try to do better than others, be richer, more powerful, more remarkable than others. But the world sees us, accepts us, treats us intuitively according to the way we see and accept ourselves – that is, according to our unconscious image of ourselves.

We too, in fact, are inclined to treat ourselves according to that image. If we like and respect ourselves we'll be cherishing and caring of ourselves. If the opposite is the case, we're liable to treat ourselves badly, without realizing consciously what we're doing or why we're doing it.

Those people with a poor self image are likely to be taken advantage of by friends and enemies alike, pushed around, trampled on and ridiculed, however brave a face they put on and however much noise they may make. Of course, if the trappings of fame and wealth have been acquired, those trappings will call for respect, but no one will be deceived about how the person really feels about him or her self.

From what I've just said, it follows that a poor self image doesn't necessarily prevent success and achievement. Sometimes people succeed in spite of themselves – or because the sense of inferiority is the spur to prove the opposite. Success and achievement depend on ability and courage, both of which may be attributes of a person with a sense of inadequacy and worthlessness.

The way a person feels about him or her self, the unconscious self image, bears, in fact, very little relationship to the true character and talents and quality of the person. The self image is no mirror of the person. The self image is the mirror of the feelings and attitudes of parents and siblings during the childhood of the person.

There are two aspects to the image of self. The first aspect is related to the body and the second to the mind. The body image depends on a vast network of nerves and nerve impulses bringing information from every part of the body – skin, muscles, tongue, intestines, joints and so on. As a result of this information, we're able to carry, unconsciously, a plan or map of our body in our minds. We're able to manoeuvre in space, reach out and touch within our range, jump over obstacles – or avoid them in our path, to catch and to hold. We're able to say just where, in our bodies, the pain is, if we're in pain. We can detect a single hair on the tip of our tongue. We can also drive cars, ride bicycles, plough fields because we extend the notion of our body into the machine. We are born with the abilities needed to create the body image. Even before birth, the network of nerves, the brain, the muscles and joints are in readiness to receive the wealth of sensory stimuli which, the moment we're born, will begin to bombard the body.

The body image, like the psychic image, remains largely unconscious throughout life, unless attention is consciously paid to any aspect of the body or its activities. The other image of ourselves involves our mental and emotional ability to receive 'messages', to hold up mirrors to the feelings of others, mainly our parents. This image is a psychic one. A child searches for clues, watches the faces of its parents and of other people around it. The child listens. Its contact with the hands of those who change its nappies, wash it, dress it, perhaps cuddle it, gives vital information. The child is not deceived. Is it loved and therefore lovable?

Unlike the body image, the psychic image takes years to consolidate. The messages it receives must be consistent if they're to make any lasting impression and be received over a long time. A child's response to these messages depends partly on the personality or character with which that child is born. Why human and other animal characters differ so much from one another is mysterious. Some children are rebellious and tend to fight back, others are meek, others try to manipulate by means of charming or amusing parents and others just express distress by crying. But whatever the child's response, the unconscious image of self will be 'bad' if the messages from parents imply rejection or hostility, or 'good' if parents genuinely respect and care for their child.

Over the long period of infancy, early and late childhood and adolescence, the conscious image of the self is fluid, fluctuating and uncertain. By late adolescence, the image becomes solid and fixed. The sad thing is that children are so susceptible and helpless that their sense of their identity has very little to do with their own qualities, and is almost entirely dependent on how they believe others, mainly parents, feel about them. As children we would hardly know we existed without the reassuring or disturbing reflections from those around us. We are, in fact, hardly ourselves; we are as we believe 'they' see us.

The child questions itself continually – but always unconsciously. 'Am I lovable?' asks the child, but has to respond with another question, 'Am I loved?' In this search for identity we see human beings at their most sensitive and most touchingly vulnerable.

Extraordinary as it is, the concept of self has, perhaps, had a greater effect on the mental health of humanity than any other concept. Loved and respected children who value themselves as a result of their parents' feelings towards them are the truly confident, healthy people of this world. They are perhaps rare. Out of unloving, rejecting homes come drug addicts, criminals, racists and fascists, suicides, anorectics, kleptomaniacs, mentally ill and unhappy men and women who can never love themselves nor anyone else. But even though unloved children may find it hard to love, some are certainly capable of caring and sometimes they care more intensely and effectively than loved children do.

The sense of identity, carefully and painfully built up by direct experience, is complicated by another human tendency: re-integration. Having separated – as the child separates from its mother – there's a tendency to merge again. We're strongly inclined to join, to imitate, to take on the characteristics, habits, tone of voice, facial expressions, manners, of a person, usually a parent, who's close to us during our developing years. This process is known as 'identifying' with another person. Without realizing it – because the process is unconscious – we almost become the other person.

While identifying with a well-balanced, successful and cheerful parent is a great advantage, the opposite is the case if the parent is, for example, mentally or physically ill, an alcoholic, or extremely disagreeable, and so on.

For example, the child of a very anxious mother might find herself in excellent circumstances where there isn't the slightest need for anxiety. But if she's 'identified' with her mother she'll feel as anxious as her mother did and need to search out or even create reasons to justify her anxiety.

Sometimes people who've identified with a parent are convinced they'll have the same illnesses, or even die on the same date and in the same way as the parent. Identification may take another form. We tend to identify – again unconsciously – with people or creatures who seem to resemble ourselves, or who seem to be experiencing something similar to our own experiences.

A child who has had a wretched childhood will tend to identify with all other (apparently or really so) unhappy children. He or she will also tend to identify with all other helpless defeated creatures – cats and dogs in distress, trapped birds, hunted foxes, maimed and beaten horses and so on. The re-experience of our own unhappiness and fear may be searing.

People who are able to identify with the more wretched people of this world and the more ill-treated animals are often those who make great efforts to alleviate distress. I said earlier that while rejected children found loving difficult, they were certainly able to care.

The anxious, less loved children of this world are, in addition to being sometimes great carers, very prone to respond to the anxiety-creating messages from the media and society in general. Do we have the right car, toothpaste, shoes, coffee? Do we have the 'right' kind of friends, orgasm, education, accent, income? Should we do better? Can we do better? If unemployed, is it our fault? – and so on. But underneath this the most haunting questions of all recur again and again. 'Am I lovable?' 'Am I loved?'

Here are some descriptions of how people with a poor self image might behave and feel.

Delia was an orphan and an only child. Her mother died when she was three years old. Shortly afterwards, her father went off with another woman to another country. It was left to the state to take care of Delia. She became one of many unwanted children and was put in an orphanage. Delia was a meek child, gentle and sad and physically a little frail. She tried to be very 'good', that is, docile and obedient in order to please members of the orphanage staff. The latter were fond of her and wanted to help her. But Delia grew up with the characteristics of a deeply rejected and abandoned child. Without recognizing this fact, she felt herself to have no value whatever. Sometimes she mutilated her body, hating herself so much she cut marks in her skin with a sharp pair of scissors or a kitchen knife. She went though periods of near starvation, alternating with passionate greed. She would become emaciated, then grossly overweight, only to starve again for a while.

When she was fifteen she was apprenticed to a dressmaking establishment in the centre of London. She was very pretty, although shy and tongue-tied. People tried to help her. In the course of time she was encouraged to model some of the clothes which she helped to make and this led to her becoming a professional model during one of her thin phases. In this way she began to meet a number of men, most of whom made sexual advances to her. Unable to say no, she became very promiscuous. Confused and alone, with no parent figure to advise her, she failed to take any contraceptive measures. She became pregnant three times and had three abortions, two of which were performed in wretched circumstances.

The first termination of pregnancy was performed late at night in a doctor's back-room surgery in a seedy district, without any form of anaesthesia. The doctor had tried to have sexual intercourse with her as one of the conditions of the operation being performed, but a profound sense of disgust and horror came to her rescue and she was able to resist him. The men who had made her pregnant were never told by her that she might have a child by them and so these abortions were lived through alone.

The second termination took place in a nursing home in north London that specialized in this operation. She was admitted for only twelve hours together with a large number of other unfortunate women. Almost as soon as she came round from the anaesthetic her clothes were brought to her and she was asked to leave. Anyone might think after two such experiences that Delia might be more careful in her sexual life or at least make sure she had contraceptive protection. But withdrawn and incapacitated as she was, Delia couldn't bear to discuss her situation with anyone. By a lucky chance she developed a very sore throat and cough while at work and was sent to the firm's doctor who came to her rescue. She managed to tell him of her predicament. As a result, the last pregnancy was terminated in a general hospital under proper anaesthesia and precautions against infection.

There were no more pregnancies because by now Delia had become sterile, following a chronic infection of her Fallopian tubes, which became obstructed.

Delia's next involvement was with a man who was addicted to hard drugs. He did his best to turn Delia into an addict also. She escaped, assisted by an elderly man who became her lover. He persuaded Delia to live with him and was kind and supportive. With his help Delia found her way to a number of study courses in various subjects. She finally passed some exams and was able to get a small job earning a regular income. She began to study at night and she wanted, if possible, to become a children's nurse. (She particularly wanted to look after small children.)

Her first steps in the direction of self-respect had been taken. The elderly man continued to befriend her and also educate her. She was fond of him and he of her, but the sexual side of the relationship appalled her, although she was able to 'switch off' a great deal of the time and feel only weary numbness. She believed also that she could never leave him and was terrified that he might grow tired of her. He had a friend, a woman of his own age who liked Delia and was kind to her. This woman was responsible for persuading Delia to have some psychotherapy. It was arranged that she would join a group at a psychotherapy clinic. The group helped Delia a good deal.

A year later, she had recognized that she no longer truly depended on anyone, that she was grown up, strong and fit and beautiful.

She decided she would try to find her father of whom, for years, she'd had a fanciful vision. In this dream about him she saw him as a handsome kindly man, who, once he recognized her, would take her to his heart, welcome her into a beautiful family of charming, loving people and dote on her ever after.

She managed, with great difficulty, to locate her father. He was living in Canada with his wife and several children. She wrote to him. To her surprise, it took a long time before she received a reply. He seemed less than enthusiastic and didn't say he wanted to see her. She wrote again, saying she was proposing to visit him.

This time she had a quick reply. He didn't think this was a good idea. Wouldn't it be better to get on with her life in the UK and forget all about him?

But Delia, supported by certain members of her group, determinedly went ahead with plans to visit her father. The doctor who ran the group warned her that she might not be welcome. But she insisted on going.

The encounter was a disaster. Rows and quarrels broke out almost at once, not only between her and her father, but with her stepmother and stepbrothers and sisters. Delia's father turned out not to be a handsome, smiling man but a weak, sulky child at the mercy of his strong wife, who was absolutely determined not to allow the intruder, Delia, into the family.

Poor Delia suffered torment, reliving all the desolation of her early childhood. She returned, defeated, to London. She never saw or heard from her father again.

It was hard for Delia to recover from such a bitter rejection. But she did in the end recover, with the help of her group, by understanding the truth of her circumstances. The truth was that her father had always been a weak, irresponsible, unlikeable man; if he had not, he would never have abandoned Delia in the first place; that Delia's self-hate was the outcome of her belief that her father was a powerful and admirable man who'd abandoned her because she lacked the qualities which are essential if one is to be loved. Her belief in her father's excellence was wrong. Her belief in her own inadequacy was wrong.

She had also believed unconsciously that her mother, in abandoning her by dying, might also not have disappeared had Delia been more remarkable. This idea also she recognized as false. Delia realized she had spent a large part of her life mutilating and damaging herself in the mistaken belief that she was worthless. She had now to allow herself to feel sorrow at her mother's death, compassion for herself and anger towards her uncaring father. Delia recognized also that she had offered herself to men and submitted to their needs rather than her own in order to gain acceptance and in the hope that she would not be rejected. She became aware that a deeply unconscious sense of her own tragic circumstances of childhood had motivated her to become a children's nurse, caring particularly for young children. This awareness strengthened her resolve to reach her goal.

Old habits are hard to break. Delia made many mistakes before she finally fulfilled herself. She became a nurse, she married, she adopted children for whom she passionately cared and struggled to love. Her life, heading for disaster, was saved. But the earlier miseries illustrate what I earlier described. We receive in this world what we expect to receive. Our expectations are high if in childhood we've been privileged emotionally – cared for, cherished, made to feel valuable. Our expectations, if rejected, are of blows and hardships, mental and perhaps physical, and these we arrange to receive.

Here's an example of a woman who did believe in herself. I once had a patient, Derek, who was a handsome bachelor. Dashing, exciting, glamorous, he lived a hectic city life, amusing himself by an endless series of affairs. His relationships were always with beautiful women, often as glamorous as himself, but insecure, anxious to please, clinging and dependent. Because of his own unconscious problems in his relationship with his mother, Derek received some satisfaction in leading these women on, getting them to fall seriously in love with him and then abandoning them. He was quite unaware, that is unconscious, of what he was doing and why, and would always find some good, apparently rational, reason for his behaviour. Before he finally abandoned his 'loves' he would play a kind of game with them, like a cat playing with a mouse. Once he had them completely enthralled, then – and only then – he began to 'let them down'. He'd make an appointment and not turn up. He'd say he would telephone, then never did – or rather he waited until they had decided to give him up and then he *would* telephone and persuade them to be involved with him all over again. He might try this performance not only once but many times with the same girl or woman. Usually he succeeded in charming her back – and he could be very charming indeed if he made the effort.

But once he made the mistake of becoming entangled with a well-known and very successful actress. She fell for him and the routine began. He was at first very attentive, seeming to be quite bowled over by her. Then, slowly, he began to behave in his usual way, distancing himself, slowly at first, then more vigorously but all the time continuing to swear total and utterly faithful love. This state of affairs is of course confusing for any woman, and the actress was confused.

Then she finally decided she'd had enough. He let the situation rest for a little while. One night, very late, he telephoned. His speech took its usual course. How troubled he'd been because he'd never felt such strong emotions for anyone before. How afraid he was of being hurt, how he'd tried hard to keep away because he was so vulnerable, but he found he couldn't bear not to see her – wouldn't she give him one more chance. Wouldn't she agree to see him just once more?

Yes, she said, she would. The day and the time were arranged. He turned up with one red rose and a bottle of her favourite scent. She threw the rose on the ground and trod on it. She threw the scent in the fireplace where a fire burned. She slapped his face and told him that *she* was not a child and she couldn't be bothered with men who were children. If ever he tried to contact her again she would call the police and say he was molesting her. 'Get out,' she said, and out he crept.

While he was telling me this story in a woebegone way soon afterwards, I couldn't help being a little amused – but I didn't allow him to know this. 'She had a better sense of her value than most of the others,' I told him. 'She wasn't going to let herself get involved in a situation that caused her suffering.'

This is the truth. Those who value themselves consciously and unconsciously are not prepared to lend themselves to catastrophic relationships. They are able to use their aggression to save themselves or defend themselves in a thousand little ways in daily life. Our ability to deal with children, teachers, professional advisers, tradesmen, waiters, plumbers, electricians and mechanics, and domestic helpers, depends upon an inner sense of self value which allows us to be firm and even tough. The valued child is able, as an adult, to cope with all the difficulties, sorrows and setbacks that life may bring. Survival is greatly enhanced by the possession of the most precious of all attributes which parents can give their child, a sense of worth. But it's possible to achieve a sense of worth later in life, even if this was not the case in childhood, if insight produces the understanding, 'There was something lacking in "*them*" not in me.'

SIX

Our Differences in Personality and Character

I've described how we acquire a sense of ourselves. There is an additional facet to this achievement. Each of us is unique. Each of us is born with characteristics and personality traits which determine to some extent how we're going to react to adverse or propitious circumstances. Each child in the same family might react very differently to exactly the same environment, the same attitudes of those around, the same events. Each of us has an inherited personality – a character – a compound of attitudes and traits. It's hard to analyse exactly what gives a person a particular flavour – but we do each have our particular and individual flavours. The way we deal with our feelings, the way we respond and react, depend on these inherited characteristics. We tend to react in a consistent way, according to our nature. Ill-treatment during childhood tends to intensify and harden the mode of reaction, 'fixing' it, whereas children who are well looked after and cherished tend to be less extreme in their reactions. The ill-treated child, must, in a sense, grow up alone, unable to rely on or trust the adults around it. The child's survival depends on itself. It gathers together its inherited characteristics and ruggedly tries to defend itself – an unconscious performance which produces echoes in the conscious mind.

Some children are better at self-defence than others. Some cope better with adversity.

'All are equal but some are more equal than others.' Orwell's statement applies very much to the mental and physical attributes which we've inherited.

All *are* equal in the sense that we can't and shouldn't make value judgements about 'better' or 'worse' characters. But some are tougher and more robust, some more sensitive and fragile.

Carl Jung divided the human race into two camps. Half of us are, he said, 'introverts', half 'extroverts'. Introverts are people who turn inwards rather than outwards, who withdraw feelings, who 'absorb' pain and so in whom pain is retained. Introverted people are thus more vulnerable to pain. They have a tendency to try to avoid situations where they may be 'attacked' and so they avoid contact with other human beings if possible. Introverted people feel safest and more comfortable when alone. They love animals, who are not hurtful as human beings may be, and they enjoy scenery, nature, solitude. Sometimes the term 'schizoid' is applied to introverted people. This means they have some of the characteristics of a certain category of schizophrenics – although in no way do they suffer from this illness. But, like those who suffer from one kind of schizophrenia, they are, as I've said, 'loners', asocial, hypersensitive, brooding, liable to dreams and fantasies, unable to share emotionally, often not very articulate about themselves and their own needs. Ill-treated introverted children become more withdrawn, more silent, more numb, more rigid than their well-treated counterparts. As adults they may learn to present to the world a brittle, superficial normality of feelings which in no way co-ordinates with their inner life. It's 'as if' they have normal feelings – but the 'as if' is a trick learned by imitating others. People who have shut themselves off from their feelings as children may be helped to learn to get in touch with their feelings as adults, but they'll always retain the characteristics of the introvert. Physically, they're more still and rigid than the extrovert.

Extroverts are outward-going, jolly, talkative, aggressive people who 'make the party go', hale, hearty and vigorous. They may be demanding and articulate. Often very sociable, many extroverts hate to be alone. They tend to fight off pain, rather than absorb it. They scream instead of withdrawing, fight and shout and resist noisily. Whereas an unhappy, introverted child might sulk silently for hours without being able to cry, an extroverted child has tantrums, complains, shows off, weeps easily, and draws attention to itself and to its troubles. The introvert hides; the extrovert rushes shrieking into the street. The introvert finds contact with other people a strain, has to make efforts to converse. The extrovert 'flows', chatting easily, making friends easily, finding it easy to protest and throw limbs and body about. From the point of view of mental health, we believe it's better to be extrovert and to express our feelings rather than to suppress them. This doesn't mean that extrovert children don't suffer just as much as introvert children. They do, but the way they cope with their distress is different.

Both introverts and extroverts can be valuable members of our societies, achieving a great deal, leading fulfilled and contented lives if all has gone well for them.

There are other qualities and characteristics with which we are born. Some of us are determined and resistant, while others are easily defeated. Some are very susceptible to pain (physical and emotional), while some others tolerate suffering more easily. Some are more intelligent, some less so.

The way in which we'll try and cope with life will depend on our inherited characteristics. Some are conscientious and dogged, others more dashing and flighty. Some are more susceptible to guilt, others less so. It's well known that different personality types do better or worse at certain jobs. Nowadays psychologists have worked out complex tests, as a result of which it's possible to predict whether a person will make a good or bad fighter pilot, diplomat, marine, officer (that is, leader), scientist, architect, student and so on. 'Career guidance' is a great industry of our times.

Another way of classifying people's characters is to divide them into the 'active' or 'passive' categories. All children who are ill-treated are victims since they're at the mercy of their parents. Some accept the victim role without a struggle, others protest, fight back and draw attention to their plight. A passive child isn't necessarily always a child who's inherited a 'passive' character. Children who've had a severe or long physical illness early in life may remain passive victims throughout their lives, as may those with a chronic physical illness – a malformed heart, kidney disease, leukaemia. Some children who have to be in hospital for months at a time may become inert, withdrawn, silent little creatures who've given up hope and accept suffering as the natural way of life.

Occasionally a child with a chronically ill parent who is bedridden or a severe invalid will identify with that parent and take on the inevitably passive behaviour of that parent.

Yet another classification of character is to divide people into those who are 'obsessional' and those who aren't.

Non-obsessionals have few very special characteristics. They are more carefree than obsessionals, travelling through life 'without luggage' – and able, in fact, to travel literally without luggage – arriving late at the airport, having forgotten to bring a passport, without suffering the overcaring anxieties of an obsessional. Non-obsessionals may be careless in their dress and general appearance, untidy, unpunctual and unconcerned. While non-obsessionals may cause irritation, anxiety or misery to other people, they suffer less from the symptoms which affect obsessionals.

By 'obsessional' we mean very particular, perfection-seeking, fussy, caring people, who are interested in detail. They are usually clean and tidy in appearance, conscience-stricken, easily made to feel guilty and often suffer from anxiety. Obsessionals tend to be early rather than late for appointments, are generally reliable, find it difficult to delegate and feel the need to have everything under control. They also might feel the need to control others. The striving for perfection doesn't necessarily apply to every aspect of an obsessional's life, but to the more important ones. Obsessional people may make very good parents – or very bad ones. If their attempts to control their children and their wish to have their children perfect are not exaggerated, then the caring and responsible aspects of their personalities are, of course, of great value to their children.

But there are some obsessional parents who nag their children from morning to night and who demand excessive cleanliness, tidiness, orderliness and good behaviour. They may cause anxiety in their children, rebellion – and depression, in a child who fails to live up to its parents' wishes for it. Obsessional anxieties increase under stress as does obsessional behaviour. By obsessional behaviour I mean ritual acts which people with an obsessional personality tend to perform: locking the doors of the house at night and verifying, not once or twice but many times, that the doors are truly locked. Always folding a newspaper in a particular way. Obsessional behaviour is linked to superstition and it is obsessionals who are most likely to touch wood, avoid walking under ladders and murmur spells to avoid bad luck. Children, too, may be obsessional, touching every rail in a row of railings, trying not to walk on the lines of paving stones and so on. Many obsessional children have routines which they hate to be disturbed. The toys must be placed around the bed in a particular way, the curtains drawn to leave a specific gap, the bedtime story, known by heart, repeated yet again. Such rituals take on even more painful importance if a child feels anxious for other reasons.

Breaking the pattern of a ritualized piece of behaviour causes anxiety and distress in both adults and children. Obsessional behaviour is shared by many other animals – cats, dogs, even geese. It maybe an inherited trait which in other animals enhances chances of the species' survival. In human beings, obsessionalism causes people to be good citizens but perhaps makes life more difficult for them. Some people suffer from pathological obsessionalism – the trait being carried to an extreme point, causing very distressing illness.

While obsessional parents may overdo concern and control, they do tend to be more practically efficient than some non-obsessional parents. They don't, as a rule, forget to provide food, milk, clean clothes and other essentials of life and will drive themselves to fulfil their roles as parents even if they're suffering from a minor illness.

Non-obsessional parents on the other hand may make careless, unreliable parents, especially if casualness is exaggerated. It's emotionally damaging for, say, a child to be kept waiting, habitually, at school long after all the other children have been fetched home, because a parent thinks time is of little consequence. A child feels neglected and unloved if its material needs aren't properly catered for. Something between a marked laissez-faire attitude – and an excess of detachment – and an over-attentive, hovering attitude is the ideal for a parent, but it is difficult to achieve.

SEVEN

Morality, Guilt and Conscience

As a result of our ability for conceptual thinking, we humans have formulated notions of what we believe to be 'good' and what 'bad', what we think of as 'right' and what as 'wrong'. Such ideas vary from culture to culture and generation to generation. But no matter what the current ideas for 'good', 'bad', 'right' and 'wrong', humans are able to respond to 'bad' and 'wrong' thoughts and behaviour with a sense of guilt and possess what is called 'conscience'.

These concepts are of great importance in the interaction between parents and children. Psychotherapy tends to release people from inappropriate or unjustified feelings of guilt, with beneficial effects.

Most of us carry in our minds a kind of inbuilt notion of what we believe to be right and what we know to be wrong, of what is 'good' and what is 'bad' in terms of behaviour, feelings and thoughts. But unless we stop to analyse our beliefs, these ideas are more or less unconscious and automatic, they are 'conditioned' by teachings in our early years. There are laws and rules, customs, taboos, 'good form', 'bad form', 'etiquette', things that are 'done' and things 'not done' All these teachings are part of our culture. Most people take them for granted and never stop to question them. Most of us behave in fact like a very well-trained troupe of laboratory rats conforming obediently to the rules of an experiment: rewards if you go this way, frustration and punishment if you go the other.

Every now and then a society gets restive and there are rumblings of rebellion against the indoctrination, like a volcano about to erupt. Some exceptional thinkers crystallize the discontent and a cataclysmic upheaval – like the French and Russian revolutions – takes place; a king is beheaded or a dictator murdered. Things change, but they have a habit of returning to a slightly modified status quo.

Most of the basic laws and rules can't change because they're essential for the running of any community. But there are an infinite number of moral attitudes which hem us in a vast network of invisible and subliminal rules, threats and encouragements. Most human societies keep their members in place by a tyrannical system of punishments and rewards – together with the human ability to have a 'conscience'.

Our moral values, in early years absorbed more or less unconsciously, have been handed down from generation to generation for many centuries. We're still carrying a load of Victorian morality – useless today, and even harmful – a century later.

At birth, we have delivered to us a package of moral messages – transmitted largely unconsciously, and unconsciously received. The moment an infant arrives in this world he or she is immediately swaddled and swathed in all the trappings of our Western way of life. Together with throw-away nappies, handknitted socks, baby soap, powder and cream, soft toys, pram, name, and health visitor, the child receives the entire culture, religion, and materialism of its family and its community. He or she also has to take on the job of fulfilling the parents' expectations and ambitions and learns very quickly that conforming means 'good', rebellion 'bad'.

The child will easily sense that some aspects of his or her behaviour cause approval or even delight in the parents, other aspects giving rise to disapproval, anxiety or consternation and anger. Before long, the child must obediently drink milk at breast or bottle, must sleep, if possible through the night, smile, sit, crawl, walk and talk at the 'right' time. Later he or she must empty the bowels to order at a suitable place and time and keep 'dry' – that is, control the muscles of its bladder.

If a child complies in all these matters, the satisfied parents will think of the child as 'good' and 'easy'. A good and easy child is easy for its parents to love. A 'difficult' child arouses disturbed and disturbing feelings in parents – feelings which may be conscious and also unconscious.

The emphasis on the virtues and rewards of conforming will be transmitted to the child throughout life – in every human society on earth. The instructions are given by the establishment, beginning with the parents.

'Do this! Do that! Don't do that!'

'Why?'

'Because Mummy says so.'

The child will have to decide what line to take – and will have a limited choice on whether to go along with what's required, or whether to rebel. Toeing the line means being accepted by the parents, family and community. There are other later rewards: employment, prizes, admission to learned societies, medals, ribbons, birthday honours and so on.

But these rewards are reserved for the few. The great majority have to be satisfied with a sense of virtue, material benefits and the absence of guilt.

Guilt is a mysterious, unpleasant emotion, closely linked to depression. Feelings of guilt are alleviated by forgiveness and by atonement and punishment. The notions of 'good' and 'bad', 'right' and 'wrong' are understood early in a child's life because of the reactions of parents to various kinds of behaviour. The child does what the parent asks, the parent smiles. The child feels happy. The child refuses to obey the parent – the parent is angry. The child feels unhappy, so the child understands that obeying is 'good', disobeying 'bad' – entirely in response to the parents' approval or disapproval. The unhappy feeling at the parents' disapproval (or hostility or rejection) we call 'guilt'.

So the parents are in a powerful position to control the child by their ability to produce guilt in the child – simply by showing disapproving attitudes. They might produce these attitudes even though the child hasn't done anything wrong – but the child will think it *has* done something wrong, and will feel guilty, searching itself for sin. Later in life, the establishment will take on the role of the parents, accepting or rejecting citizens according to whether they conform or rebel.

Parents may make a child feel guilty for matters that are not the child's fault. If parents wanted a boy and a girl was born instead, the girl could be made by the parents to feel guilty at not being a boy. One patient I used to see, the fifth girl in a family, where the parents desperately wanted a boy, was told by her mother at an early age that when she was born in the local hospital she, the mother, had instantly tried to get her adopted as the parents simply didn't want another girl. Sometimes a child might feel guilty because it doesn't come up to the parents' expectations in other ways – intellectually, or as a sports person. I can remember one father who was bitterly disappointed that his son wasn't a good golfer – as he himself was; and the son felt deeply guilty over this failure, although he tried hard to play golf as well as he could manage.

Parents may make a child feel guilty for excelling as well as for failing if, for instance, they'd rather the child didn't do better than they themselves had done. In the same way, the establishment of the society is able to make some people feel guilty over matters which aren't their fault: homosexuality, for example, and the illness AIDS. A senior police officer was once reported as saying that the spread of AIDS in so-called civilized Western society could be blamed on the increasingly degenerate conduct of the human race and a cesspool of immorality, infested by homosexuals, prostitutes and unfaithful husbands. Here is a member of the establishment assuming that people choose, as it were, to be homosexual. If they pulled themselves together, the police officer implied, they could be heterosexual. The Archbishop of York rightly responded: 'The result of [the] message has been to spread guilt and fear among AIDS victims, who now hide as hapless victims in a ghetto, instead of seeking medical help . . .'

In earlier days, people suffering from tuberculosis or smallpox could easily infect husbands, wives and children but they would not have been labelled 'morally degenerate' or 'infesting a cesspool'. Nor today would people with influenza or meningitis, dangerous potential killers which are equally infectious, be labelled in this way. The moral indignation stems from the fact that AIDS is a sexually transmitted rather than an airborne disease. The police-man's tirade indicates that sex is still linked to sin in the minds of many – a Victorian legacy.

The *fear* of sinning, the fear that one might sin, is as powerfully disturbing as guilt itself – that is, as our reaction might be after having actually committed a sin. Man alone among the animals has the conceptual ability to make moral judgements and so to decide in advance which actions are bad and which are good. This knowledge of 'good and bad' and therefore 'right and wrong' is 'conscience'. The great majority of citizens in the Western world would rather not do wrong – not so much because they fear punishment if they're 'bad', but because they prefer to be good rather than bad. To do wrong is to go against the indoctrination by parents, teachers and others in childhood and to become unacceptable, unlovable. So 'conscience' holds people in check, helps them refrain from committing a 'bad' act: 'So conscience doth make cowards of us all'. Ours is a society prey to guilt – easily made to feel guilty whether for not using a suitable deodorant, being unable to buy one's wife a diamond, or failing to love a child. We're all so indoctrinated about the right and the wrong way to feel or think and behave that guilt is an experience we all share, and doing or saying or feeling the wrong thing – either trivial or major – is inevitable. When we're guilty, we are depressed – and may even sink into a depressive illness, when guilt may be a prominent symptom.

Guilt can be relieved by punishment and forgiveness, as I've said earlier. Here's the story of a man who committed a crime and found his guilt unbearable. The story is a true one. It was told to me by the prison psychiatrist who tried to help him. John X was driving his van down a narrow country lane. Ahead of him was a girl on a bicycle. She had long fair hair and she looked young and attractive. Just for a lark he decided to touch the wheel of her bicycle with the wheel of his van. Accelerating slightly he did this – but to his horror the girl wavered wildly and fell to the ground under the wheels of his van. She was dead.

John X could have told any story he chose – there weren't any witnesses – but he insisted on telling the truth to the police and later to the judge. He was sent to prison for a number of years. He was a model prisoner. But every so often, about once a year it seemed, he behaved as if he'd gone mad. He broke up the furniture in his cell, he attacked a prison officer. In this way he lost all the remission of sentence he might have earned.

The prison governor, unable to understand the man, asked the psychiatrist to see him and it was discovered that the days on which he behaved so badly that he lost the remission were the anniversaries of his crime. His feelings of guilt returned to him so forcefully he craved the punishment his bad behaviour brought him.

It's a fact that unconscious guilt makes people crash their cars, cut their fingers, deprive themselves, abase themselves and ruin their lives. Hostile parents may enjoy making their children feel guilty. One mother I know never tired of telling the story to friends in front of her seven-year-old child of how the little girl, when asked to pull up some weeds in a garden bed, mistakenly pulled up all the newly planted seedlings instead. Another mother left her unloved three-year-old, suffering from a cold, in a cot next to a newly papered wall. The child was left alone for hours. Becoming bored, he dipped his fingers in a pot of face cream which was standing on a little table beside the cot and began to smear the wall. He had managed to grease all the area around him before his mother returned. Her rage and hate and his ensuing guilt haunted him the rest of his life.

Some parents are able to make their child or children feel permanently guilty by organizing a provocation and then blaming the child for responding to the provocation. Mr and Mrs Z had two daughters. The younger daughter, Lettice, was the apple of her mother's eye, but the mother never cared for her elder daughter, Marjorie. Mrs Z managed to make Marjorie endlessly jealous of her sister, but at the same time she criticized Marjorie for feeling jealous and made it clear that jealousy was a wicked sin. Marjorie, confused and bewildered, watched her mother giving Lettice special attention, special treats, special food, special toys and all kinds of privileges – of all of which Marjorie was deprived. Mrs Z's excuse was that Lettice was more frail and sensitive than Marjorie. Each time Marjorie saw her mother doting on Lettice, the poor child felt pangs of terrible jealousy. She struggled to suppress these feelings – but failed – and her jealousy was provoked again and again by her mother's actions. And again and again Marjorie felt both jealous and also wicked and guilty for being jealous. She was 'conditioned' or trained to believe that her natural inevitable responses were sinful. She grew up with great insecurity about herself and a feeling that she was to blame if anything went wrong. Other people could always make out that Marjorie was the one at fault – not they themselves. For example, if a workman, say the plumber, made an appointment to come on Wednesday and failed to turn up, Marjorie immediately concluded that *she* was the one who'd made a mistake about the day. The plumber had only to say, blusteringly, that he'd said he'd come on Friday, not Wednesday, for Marjorie to believe him and apologize. She spent her life apologizing. She was always ready to take the blame for other people's mistakes. The kind of childhood she'd experienced sets the scene for a depressive illness later in life and also for paranoia. Marjorie felt so blameworthy she was liable to believe that other people were criticizing her, whispering about her, laughing at her, talking about her behind her back – even plotting against her. These paranoid feelings weren't based on reality but were the exteriorization of her own feelings about her 'badness'.

Parents are in such a very powerful position with small children that once a child has been 'conditioned', that is, trained to feel 'bad' or guilty, only very small gestures are needed to make the child feel he or she has done something wrong. Grim facial expressions, ominous silences, a frown, a mutter, averting the head, one threatening word and the child immediately feels it's done something wrong.

There was once a cartoon in the *New Yorker* – a drawing of a woman with face adamantly turned away while a supplicating man knelt at her feet. The legend read:

'Is it something I've done?'
Is it something I haven't done?
Is it something I've said?'
Is it something I haven't said?'

That sums up the position of the child in relation to the parent. But the child is not, as a rule, sufficiently articulate to voice those questions. Its reaction to a disapproval which it may not understand may be a grey blur of misery, a helpless apprehension.

I said earlier that guilt is a human emotion. Other animals in the wild don't suffer from guilt, following instinct determined behaviour which has no 'good or bad' qualification. Domestic animals can, it seems, be taught that some behaviour is 'good' i.e. acceptable, other behaviour 'bad' – that is, meets with disapproval and perhaps punishment. But any dog, cat, horse or other animal trained by its master or mistress to know 'right' from 'wrong' is only reflecting human morality. Only human beings among the animals are able to make moral judgements, as mentioned earlier. But what is extraordinary is that man, with all his morality, has done more damage to the earth, been more cruel and more destructive to other animals and to his fellows than any other animal.

EIGHT

Inherited Abilities, or Drives

We have all been born with inner motivating forces, sometimes called 'drives'. We are all at the mercy of these 'drives' which are shared by many other animals, which give rise to 'feelings', thoughts and behaviour. The two major motivating forces are aggression and sex. The outcome or expression of stimulation by a drive may be unconscious or conscious.

We are stimulated to feel or think or act aggressively or sexually by means of very complex inherited attributes – partly emotional or mental, partly physical. These attributes are united to form the 'drive'. Our responses to 'drives' have been moulded – or distorted and deformed – by the conceptual thinking of our particular culture. Thus human beings differ from other animals whose responses to drives are wholly guided by instincts as I've earlier described.

'Drives' in human beings give rise to feelings, thoughts, fantasies – and behaviour. Human beings are rightly forced, by laws and attitudes derived from conceptual thinking, to modify the behaviour stimulated by the drives, since uninhibited and uncontrolled aggressive and sexual behaviour is, of course, highly destructive to a society and to other individuals. But we're also instructed, or we instruct ourselves, to modify the thoughts and feelings in a way less useful to us – and, in fact, sometimes harmful – as I've earlier described.

As a result of our moral attitudes towards aggression and sex and other drives, we often defend ourselves from the acceptance of these drives within ourselves. The effects of the drives then become unconscious. The harm which parents do to children is, on the whole, related to aggression and sex – but also may occur as a result of cruelty, distorted love and over-possessiveness and jealousy. The next chapters discuss these phenomena.

Destructive aggression

As in the famous advertisement for a certain brand of gasoline, in each of us there sleeps a tiger. Each of us is capable of violence when sufficiently aroused. Not all of us could kill, but we might certainly have thoughts of murder or at least veiled wishes for the death or disappearance of others. All of us feel at times the need to hurt or punish other people, who have hurt us, or of whom we're jealous or afraid.

All of us do commit acts of aggression towards one another – from the overt to the disguised. All of us have feelings of aggression and thoughts about aggression which are inescapable because they're part of our nature. We're born with our potential for aggression. It is part of our inheritance, a mysterious, complex driving force which is shared by many other animals. The ability for aggression evolved – in the Darwinian sense – and for all animals apart from men it clearly improves chances of survival.

In human beings, the ability to be aggressive seems to be anti-survival of the species, the whole population of the world being threatened by the atom bomb, chemical warfare and war-oriented disasters which we all know well. In other animals, aggression is limited by instinctive ritualized behaviour and is acted out only in relation to self-defence, hunting, mating, rearing young and preservation of territory.

We human beings have no restraints imposed by instincts. We have to depend on curbs arising from laws and customs, brought about by conceptual thinking. Nevertheless, we've inherited, like other animals, the aggressive response to threats of various kinds.

In daily life, in normal times and circumstances, our actual physical survival isn't often threatened. But we are at the receiving end of emotional aggression, verbal aggression and social aggression (racism and unemployment for example), and our own aggressive response is aroused probably dozens of times every day. We look upon any threat to our wellbeing – let alone our survival – as an aggression against us. Quite often 'things' threaten us, like cars breaking down when we're in a hurry or washing machines flooding the kitchen floor or the weather being rainy when we've planned a meal out of doors. Children provide innumerable threats to our wellbeing, just as adults provide threats to children.

The ability to be aggressive was, of course, of great value to man in the early days of his evolution, and also in the days before men began to live in groups and communities. In the jungle it was just as important for early men and women to be able to kill in self-defence, or for food, as for other animals. It was important to compete with other men for shelter and territory. But once people began to live together, the instant overt aggressive response was anti-social and became prohibited by the community. Aggressive behaviour became unacceptable, it was and is regarded as 'bad' behaviour, except in warfare. Today, overt and unrestrained aggression is the last remaining major 'sin'.

Nevertheless, our Western societies have a confused and ambivalent attitude to aggression in certain forms.

Here is Chamber's dictionary's definition of aggression and aggressive:

> **Aggression:** the first act of hostility or injury; the use of armed force; self-assertive, either as a good characteristic or showing emotional instability.

> **Aggressive:** discourteously hostile or self-assertive; showing energy and initiative.

We tend to admire aggressive business tactics, the aggressive salesman. Young people admire huge motorbikes, 'aggressive' leather clothes, violent rock and pop music. Heroes in 'Westerns' shoot their way out of trouble. Sportsmen whip up their aggression in competitive games. People hunt foxes or shoot birds. But other forms of aggressive behaviour are quite rightly condemned. Yet in a 'double-think' attitude, while finding war absolutely abhorrent, we often admire the men in uniforms, the soldier and the sailor, the brave men in their flying machines.

The ambivalence towards aggression varies, so that at one end of the scale we feel guilty about tiny inconveniences caused to other people – keeping someone waiting, for example, having arranged a time to meet – or breaking a friend's teacup. At the other end of the scale, the news of an annihilation of the enemy in wartime – thousands of men, women and children having met a ghastly death – is received with exhilaration, dancing in the streets, fireworks, ticker-tape processions and so on.

In general, however, in 'normal life', aggressive behaviour is morally condemned. From our earliest days, we're taught that aggression is 'bad':

'*Don't* push that spoon off the table!'
'Be careful of that cup!'
'*Don't* shout!'
'*Don't* be rude to your father!'
'*Don't* hit your little brother!'
'*Don't* splash the bath water.'
'That's a wicked thing to say!'
'That's Mary's toy! Give it back!'

and so on.

The indoctrination extends to feelings. We're taught that it's wicked to feel angry, to feel jealous, to be greedy, to hate. The outcome is, we must repress our aggressive feelings, although they are a logical, inescapable sequence that correspond to events and to other people's behaviour, words and feelings which affect us.

The aggressive response, an inherited characteristic, doesn't disappear. Instead it becomes relegated to unconscious mind, there motivating indirect aggressive behaviour, or distortions of aggressive feelings, in a dangerous disturbing mystifying way.

Moral condemnation of conscious, overt aggressive *feelings* and *thoughts* is a fairly recent event in human history. In earlier days, aggressive *actions* were prohibited. It was taken for granted the feelings and thoughts would be there. The children of Israel, about six thousand years ago, while waiting in the Sinai Desert to enter the promised land, were handed a brisk tabloid of what not to *do* rather than what not to feel – in a series of exhilarating tableaux (which Saatchi and Saatchi might have envied – and which were surely the work of the top PR consultants of the day): Moses descended the mountain holding the ten commandments with instructions mainly about *actions*. The rules had to be made because it was recognized that people had urges to do things they were now being asked not to do. Only later were people told they must suppress aggressive *thoughts* and *feelings*. The outcome of this suppression has been fairly disastrous for children in their relationship with parents. It's much more frightening and disturbing to be on the receiving end of a person's unconscious aggression than to have to deal with an openly displayed loss of temper. But while I'm suggesting it's healthier for people to be aware of their real feelings,

I'm certainly not suggesting that aggressive feelings should be acted out. On the contrary, control must be rigorously imposed on actions. It is relatively easy to control consciously motivated actions. If we lose our guilt about our feelings of aggression, these can be openly experienced and dealt with in a controlled way. It is impossible to control reactions which never reach consciousness, which are experienced unconsciously and which motivate behaviour unconsciously. It is essential to understand that an aggressive response, as I've said earlier, is a logical, inevitable response to a stimulus. There's no way we can eliminate that response. It is no different to, say, the way we'd pull our hand away if we touched a burning object, like a hot stove.

The stimuli producing the aggressive response are non-stop when it comes to bringing up children. All day and sometimes all night long children provoke their parents. In these days, parents are often exhausted. When a three-year-old climbs out of bed for the tenth time and comes blundering into its parents' bedroom to ask for its tenth glass of water, rage inevitably results. But rage need not be acted upon – must not be acted upon. Those parents who have actually lost control to the extent of injuring or even murdering their children have felt provoked out of their normal minds. One husband, who killed his wife's baby by another man, told the court the baby had cried and cried, without stopping, hour after hour and in the end he lost his head and picked the child up and bashed it against the wall.

The provocation might be less intense if we recognized and accepted that aggression was the natural response to children's provocation. Perhaps if one could contact an institution like the Samaritans where parents could telephone and receive help without feeling guilty, a good deal of damage to children might be avoided. (In the UK, the organization Parents Anonymous can help. See Useful Addresses, page 234.)

There are two aspects of parental aggression which may affect children. The first is aggression itself – anger, hate, jealousy, a wish to harm, hurt, destroy or simply eliminate the child. This aggression may be experienced consciously or it may be unconscious. Here anxiety or guilt about aggression may be absent.

The second aspect is a fear about being aggressive – a definite conscious wish *not* to harm, but an anxiety that by accident, by neglect, by commission or omission the parent *will* harm, or hurt or destroy the child. The parent wouldn't have this fear if somewhere within him or her there were not already some feelings of aggression to the child. These aggressive feelings, usually hidden and suppressed, may be present for a number of possible reasons. For example:

1: The parent is exhausted, the child is a burden.
2: The child is 'difficult', cries, won't eat, won't sleep.
3: The child is naughty and disobedient.
4: The child is ill.
5: The parent was a rejected child and has an unconscious impulse to re-enact the experience with his or her own child.

But in this second aspect of aggression, there is no direct and unambiguous wish to hurt the child – in fact, there is horror at the possibility of hurting the child and genuine distress if the child is hurt. Here a parent feels greatly reassured if the child is smiling, fit and well. Direct and positive aggressive feelings occur when a parent really does want to hurt or damage and is pleased, or at least satisfied, if the child is hurt or disabled.

Aggression does, in fact, evaporate following an act of destruction. A parent may feel kind and affectionate once the child is 'damaged'. But aggression can also evaporate if it's accepted and conscious. If a parent could recognize a profound wish, say to 'eliminate' the child, to be free of all the child's demands and irritations, toleration of the child would seem mysteriously easier.

Some people believe that aggression may be exorcized by watching violence without taking part in violent action. The circuses of the Romans when Christians and others were torn to death by lions in an arena, the Greek Theatre, where fathers and mothers murdered their children on stage and vice versa, bull-fighting, boxing, violence on the screen – all these are said by some to exorcize aggression. Others believe they may incite aggressive behaviour. We don't know which view is correct. In some psychiatric hospitals patients are encouraged to act out aggression in dramas and plays in a theatre. This might be a more beneficial way of dealing with aggression than simply by watching scenes of violence.

Very often, parents concerned for the welfare of their child are faced with two seemingly opposite choices for the management of the child. These parents are, on the whole, anxious not to be aggressive to the child. They may fail to take a course of action because it seems aggressive to the child – but, in fact, that action may in the long run be beneficial to the child, although immediately upsetting.

The parents must say no to passionate requests for, say, more sweets or ice cream. The parents must put children to bed even though the children long to stay up late. The parents must demand that a room be tidied or homework done when the child wants only to play. In all these examples, although the parents must commit a minor act of immediate aggression the child will benefit in the long term. If the parents let the child have its way, they're actually committing a far greater aggression which will make itself felt in the long term.

If the child eats too many sweets, it will be sick, fat, have bad teeth and so on. If the child stays up too late it will be tired next day at school. If a child doesn't do its homework it will be punished next day or fall behind the rest of the class and so on. Letting a child have its way has various additional complications:

1. The child is managing the parents and not vice versa, a situation which makes children nervous since they need to feel a parent is stronger and more capable than themselves.

2: The parents are showing the child their fear about being aggressive, thus leaving open the possibility that their aggressive intention is more severe than it may actually be. The child may sense the fear and the possibility of unlimited aggression.

The solution for the parents, when their aggression is necessary in bringing up their children, is to make a considered decision about which course of action will involve the greater aggression, which will be best for the child in the long term. Of course, there are ways and ways of restraining or disciplining children. An attempt to reason and explain may, if one has a good relationship with one's child, produce the same effects as shouting and screaming.

A minor act of immediate aggression, a major act of long term but less visible aggression – these choices are often before us.

Many parents opt shortsightedly for avoiding the immediate aggressive action because it's easier to do so, because many people find their own aggression unbearable, because we are all trained to feel so guilty about our aggression. (And I must repeat again, that we *should* feel guilty about aggressive behaviour – less so about aggressive feelings.)

Avoiding overt aggression, that is being passive over major issues, affects nations and societies. It may be better to be aggressive to families of this generation – limit the number of children they should have, as do the Chinese, than overpopulate the world, so causing immense hardship, starvation, pollution and poverty to billions. So the passivity is really an immense aggression. Passivity is only one of the many faces of aggression.

Open and overt aggression is familiar to us all. But unconscious aggression, rationalized aggression, masked aggression can be expressed in mysterious and disturbing ways – innumerable ways.

A child – or an adult – on the receiving end of repressed or masked aggression is totally confused. What seems like a kindness may in fact be an act of hostility.

A mother who feeds her child on huge quantities of sugar and butter is arranging for her child to be overweight and ill. But the child can only see a mother who gives it as many sweets and cakes as it can eat. A father who allows or even encourages his young child to climb trees and jump off walls with the rationalized idea that freedom is healthy for him is actually asking for broken limbs.

Rationalization about aggressive feelings and behaviour is very common – virtually all of us rationalize about our aggression from time to time. If we are kept waiting for an appointment with a friend, standing for some time on the pavement outside the shop or restaurant, after a while we begin to think that Jane has had an accident and after another quarter of an hour we imagine her dead. The truth is we are so angry at having been kept waiting, we unconsciously want to punish Jane, injure her or, as anger mounts, kill her. These aggressive feelings are kept well under the level of conscious thinking but rise to the surface in the form of anxiety and concern. The reality here is that the least likely cause of Jane's non-appearance is an accident; the most likely reasons are she's forgotten, or perhaps been held up in the traffic, or as often happens with Jane, she's just late.

Over-anxiety acts like a form of aggression. A parent who hovers over his or her child and can't let the child do things on his or her own, go out alone, ride a bicycle in case he or she falls, communicates to the child a fear that he or she will be damaged. This situation is subtly different to the parent who believes that he or she will be or might be responsible for damaging the child. In the case of the over-anxious parent, the anxiety is about the world being a dangerous place. The parent finds the world dangerous and passes this fearful attitude on to the child – which is aggressive to the child – indirectly. The child may, in addition, begin to feel incapable and incompetent, a state of affairs which will remain with him or her for life.

Money is often used as an instrument of aggression. I remember my Uncle Bob, a comfortably-off man, slowly counting out a small bundle of notes from a sheaf in his pocket, to hand to my Aunt Maisie, each week, while she stood silently by, feeling humiliated, her anger mounting to the boil. The performance took place when she asked him for the weekly housekeeping money. She was forced to make the request. He never offered the money voluntarily. Aunt Maisie was a strong tall woman and Uncle Bob was slightly shorter and very dependent on her, which he resented. The act with the notes was his sweet revenge. She didn't have a penny of her own. Apart from the housekeeping money, she could have what she wanted in the way of clothes, being allowed to use charge accounts. But he never gave her any jewelry. It was known in the family that she'd always longed for a pearl necklace. The first thing she did when he died was to buy herself one. She wore her pearls triumphantly every day after this for all to see. One form of aggression was met by another.

Sometimes the aggressive act is committed so as to make the aggressor feel noble, the aggressee guilty. Simon K. loved his garden. He spent all his leisure time working in it. When Christmas arrived, his wife and children proposed giving him a tree from the local nursery which he was delighted to accept. 'But it must be a poplar or a beech', he said. On Christmas Day he was presented with a willow tree which he particularly hadn't wanted and said so.

'How ungrateful can you be?' he was asked, in deeply reproachful tones.

'We took so much trouble to get this for you!'

'But there's nowhere to put this willow. Willow trees don't do well here – it'll die!'

Tears were shed. Simon K. felt terribly guilty.

He apologized. He said how kind they'd been. Feeling depressed and gloomy he went out to plant the willow – which did indeed slowly wilt and die over the next months.

To give Simon K. a tree he didn't want, to fail to find a tree he did want – this is unconscious aggression. But Simon was made to feel the aggressor. There were reasons why other members of the family felt hostile to him. During the previous year he'd fallen in love with his secretary – a brief affair which had passed – but the family had been very disturbed. When the affair was over, he'd been ostensibly 'forgiven' by his wife, but the gift of the willow showed that unconscious resentment still lingered.

Here's another example of aggression made to look like kindness where the aggressee felt guilty.

Mrs Lavender M had always felt unconsciously hostile to her son Martin. When he was grown up he married another hostile woman and had a family. He never suspected that his mother had been and still was hostile to him. She seemed effusively loving and caring. On his birthday, she gave a party for him and his family. The food was lavish. Martin M. had suffered a coronary thrombosis in the last year before the party and was instructed by his doctors not to eat animal fats. Lavender had provided a glorious birthday cake thick with cream. When the time came for Martin to cut it, he gave himself a very thin slice.

Lavender said, 'Martin, is that all you're going to have?'

'Yes mother,' he replied. 'I have to be careful you know!'

'On your birthday! Just this once – after all the trouble I've been to, I had that cake specially made for you . . .'

'Well' – reluctantly he took another sliver.

Lavender burst into tears.

'You're rejecting me. You're rejecting me and my cake!' was what she more or less sobbed.

'Go on, Martin!' said Martin's wife sharply. 'Have another piece of death! That's what your mother evidently wants!'

So the party ended in miserable disorder. Martin K. drove his family home in a gloomy mood.

'You needn't have been unkind to Mother!' he said reproachfully to his wife, who gave a hard and brittle laugh.

'You'll never accept, Martin, will you, that she really hates us?'

Here's another example of unconsciously motivated aggressive behaviour which seems, falsely, like kindness and consideration.

Earlier I mentioned a young man who was able to make women fall in love with him, after which he arranged to hurt them by slowly withdrawing from the relationship. In the following story the same kind of behaviour is described, but with a slightly different edge to it and the reasons for the aggression are shown.

Jack was the son of Lena. She'd been widowed not long after the birth of Jack's younger brother, Dominic. Lena had helped her husband run his business and when he died she took over the whole responsibility for it – and was very successful. But in doing this, she had no time for her children and handed them over to a nanny. Lena didn't particularly like Jack, whom she identified with her younger brother in her childhood. She much preferred Dominic, a sunny, cheerful little boy whom she found 'easy'. She thought Jack was withdrawn and difficult, as did the nanny, who was in complete charge of the children while Lena worked. Jack was not consciously aware of his mother's hostility to him – nor of his hostility towards her. Everyone was always saying what a wonderful woman she was. He went along with the general view – and couldn't do otherwise as a small child. He knew his nanny didn't like him and he knew he often hated her for her unfairness and unkindness. He felt miserable and lonely during a great deal of his childhood and believed that he was unattractive and stupid. He didn't do well at his lessons – the teachers considered him 'lazy' – but he was good at certain sports.

When he grew up, he found to his surprise that he was attractive to many women. He could turn on the charm and also certain women liked to mother him, seeing in him a 'lost little boy'. He began to have love affairs – not only one at a time but several simultaneously. He always managed to encourage these lovers to become deeply involved with him – although he skirted around the edge of the relationship, feeling detached. Somehow dodging dangerously from one to the next, he let each woman feel she was the only one, the truly loved one, in his life. Each woman began to think of weddings and homes and babies, all of which he encouraged. Then, after a while, he began to grow tired of one or another. He rationalized his wish to withdraw by saying he was always looking for a perfect wife – and this woman or that one lacked this or that quality. But he didn't let the women know he wanted to end the relationship. On the contrary, although less enthusiastic than before and with longer gaps between telephone calls and lovemaking, he continued to make it plain to the women that he was really committed to each in turn.

He couldn't bring himself to say, 'It's over', because, he said, it would be so hurtful to them. He kept telling his friends in martyred tones how difficult life had become for him because Vera and Marion and Lilac were so much in love with him, and how painful it was for him as *he* didn't love *them*. But above all he didn't want to hurt them so he thought it was kinder to let them have some hope. His more sensible friends told him it would be kinder to them to tell them the truth and let them get over the break instead of stringing them along. But he couldn't bring himself to do that. So the women did go on hoping and they had an apologetic bunch of flowers every now and then just to encourage them – or suddenly they'd be invited to a weekend in Paris or a night in Jack's country house – because now he was rather well off, his mother having died and left him the business, which he ran surprisingly well. Jack would make love to them once again – because they'd be so hurt if he didn't. There would then follow a longish, gradual withdrawal on his part, during which there'd be tears, scenes and threats of suicide – all of which left him unmoved – and just as each woman decided she'd finally had enough, he'd be back with champagne and red roses and talk of holidays in the sun and the whole affair would roll on once again.

Jack was, of course, unconsciously deeply satisfied at the pain and bewilderment he inflicted on all these women. This was his revenge, unconsciously arranged, his punishment of those women of his childhood who'd inflicted such pain on him. But if anyone had told him that without awareness of what he was doing, he enjoyed making women suffer, he'd have been shocked and furious. He would have denied utterly that he felt the slightest need to punish his mother, who, he would have said, did her best in difficult circumstances.

Both mother and son would have been far better off had the culture, the emotional climate, allowed them to admit to their real feelings for one another. Lena would not have been burdened with a load of unconscious guilt – the latter intensifying her hostility to Jack. She would not have needed to go through all the unconvincing and confusing games of pretence of love – nor the subtle and devastating little knife thrusts of aggression towards him – which she rationalized for both their sakes.

For example, she wouldn't allow him to cry – although he was only four years old – when he lost his father.

'Boys don't cry!' she'd say threateningly.

If, for example, he fell and grazed his knee, at the first sight of a tear she'd mock and jeer. But Dominic could cry as much as he wished because he was the 'baby'.

If Jack for once did well at school and came home proudly to tell her, she'd deflate him immediately. 'No better than I expect of you,' she'd say. 'Anyway, it's not a terribly good mark. Why can't you come top?'

The truth was she was angry and upset when he did well. She felt that Dominic was threatened by Jack's success, as she herself had felt threatened by her elder brother's successes when she was a child.

The solution for her and also Jack would have been her recognition and acceptance of her hostility to him in a society which calmly took for granted the not uncommon phenomenon of parent/child hostility.

Then Lena should have been able to go to some kind of counsellor who should have been readily and quickly available. Had she wished, it should have been possible for her to have some therapy so that she might understand and modify her feelings about Jack. But in any case, he, a child without a father, with a mother who was hostile to him, should have been allowed to form a relationship with a skilled and sympathetic professional outside the family. That person could have helped Jack to recognize his abilities and his identity in his own right – not as a reflection of his mother's and nanny's feelings about him. Jack could have recognized his anger towards these women and the anger could have been confined to them and not directed towards womankind in general. Later he might have discovered he could love a woman and so might have married and had children of his own.

There are many, many men like Jack taking revenge on women for the miseries inflicted by women on them in childhood and many women too, who punish men for the same kind of reason. It would perhaps be shocking for the neighbours if a woman announced 'I can't stand my children and I know why. But I'm doing my best to care for them and supply their needs.' Surprisingly, it is less shocking to hear, 'I adore my little boys but I was in such a hurry today I forgot to get any food'. Our public image must be seen to be unaggressive, however aggressive we actually are in the home.

I remember a patient telling me this: 'My mother was always thought to be a saint. Everyone in our neighbourhood adored her. She was always doing good and kind things for other people. But I don't remember her being kind to us children. She was cold and distant. We couldn't ever get her attention. There's an incident that stands out in my mind. We children had a very loved dog – a big Airedale puppy. He was called Tim. We adored him. One day we were playing in the garden and suddenly we heard a frightful, long-drawn-out scream in the road. It was Timmy run over by a car. The next minute the driver of the car, a chauffeur in uniform, appeared at the gate carrying Timmy's limp body. We were devastated. Tim was unconscious. He died before the vet could come. We children rushed upstairs. We were howling, lying on the floor of my room. Meanwhile, the owner of the car had appeared in the garden, shocked and upset, to say how sorry she was. My mother discovered she was an acquaintance. She invited her in and gave her a cup of tea. We howled and howled. My mother came upstairs. She said, "Children stop this. You're upsetting Mrs X. Stop crying at once." When we were quiet – she always terrorized us – she went downstairs again and played the saint to Mrs X.

It hurts me here – now – to think of that terrible scream in the road. Our poor Timmy, poor puppy . . .' The patient put a soft hand to her heart.

'She was so good to everyone except us,' she said sadly. 'And another thing I remember – there was a pretty, silly woman in the neighbourhood who could play the piano quite well. She was in difficulties. Her husband had left her. She had no money. My mother decided to help her. She was to give us piano lessons. My mother's bright idea – kill two birds with one stone. Those lessons were a nightmare. She had no idea how to teach children. We had half an hour each with her twice a week while she snapped, snarled and tried to make us play pieces that were much too difficult. I couldn't even read the notes. Any possible chance I might have had of playing any musical instrument was ruined for life. My mother never asked us how we were getting on. She never listened to what we were trying to play. But she spent a lot of time with Mrs Busby who thought she was an angel from heaven.'

Aggression is often acted out in the home towards nearest and dearest – and in public, an image of benign good manners may be maintained. Our public image, in the matter of aggression, seems to be more important than our private one. Men and women may shout at and abuse spouses – or children – in a way they'd never dare to use in board rooms or offices or any place in the presence of friends and colleagues. Perhaps reticence about public displays of aggression is a national characteristic – particularly part of the British culture. In France aggression may be more openly and publicly acted out.

Not long ago I went into our local bank in France, to find a small crowd of people gathered at the counter. Beyond the panel of safety glass meant to prevent more violent aggression in the form of robbery, Marie-Louise, one of the tellers, was having an impassioned conversation on the telephone. Her audience watched and listened in respectful silence, some nodding in agreement from time to time with the arguments she noisily put forward. She shouted, she wept, she sobbed, she pleaded, she roared. Finally she replaced the receiver, wiped her eyes and returned to duty. 'It's not fair,' she explained, 'not to give me the morning off after the bank holiday. After all I have my children, my mother-in-law, my life to consider. I haven't had a day off for months.' Members of the audience nodded again and commented in her favour. Nobody cringed. Nobody laughed. Nobody winced. Nobody shrank. A normal argument.

But while this open acceptance of trivial aggressive behaviour between people is probably healthy, the French tend to allow themselves to commit acts of major aggression which are disastrous. The most notable example is in their driving of cars and lorries, with a higher accident and death rate than most other Western countries.

Which brings us to another interesting aspect of the human mind and human feelings. An act of aggression only makes a feeling impact on a person if it is immediately perceived – an on-the-spot, naked, unambiguous injury of some kind. Aggression committed from behind the steel and glass protection of a motor car somehow fails to be meaningful to the driver, who could probably never bring himself to take an axe and mutilate his victim in a hand-to-hand combat. Similarly atom bombs exploding in Pacific Islands or famines in Ethiopia are easily brushed aside.

Not long ago, a great party was given aboard an American aircraft carrier, in harbour in a Mediterranean port, to celebrate the Fourth of July. Champagne followed. A band specially flown from Naples played nostalgic music. Pretty girls floated across the deck with handsome shining young naval officers in immaculate white uniforms.

Little groups of guests were taken on a tour of the aircraft. Each aeroplane was described in terms of the amount of destruction it could achieve. Only one member of our group was upset. He said to us, 'You're all going on as if you were at the Chelsea Flower Show – looking at the roses. "Oh yes? How very pretty! How interesting!" "And this aircraft is capable of carrying a nuclear warhead which will travel so many miles at the speed of so much . . . flattening cities, killing and maiming and blinding and burning so many thousands of human beings, among them children" . . . "Really? How interesting!" '

He was right. The elegant guests murmured and twittered around these horrific instruments of devastation as remote from the comprehension of murder by atom bombs as the Earth from Mars. Acts of aggression are almost meaningless to us unless they happen now, under our very eyes.

Nevertheless, we may be very affected by symbols of aggression. There are those who can't tolerate the sight of sharp knives or pairs of scissors or broken glass, people who faint at the sight of blood or go green at the sight of surgical needles stitching wounds. Here again, we're dealing with reminders and – or – memory provokers.

The reminders may be of one's own or other people's potential aggression, the memories of cruelties earlier experienced. My own mother couldn't bear to see baby clothes with little strings to fasten at the neck, being no doubt obsessed with thoughts or fears, conscious or unconscious, of strangling her babies.

It's worth noting also that there are some people who can't bear to be ill. The symbolic or real helplessness returns them to the childhood situation of a weak creature being in the power of great monsters (as they must have experienced aggression from parents when very young).

I've skimmed lightly across an immense subject with huge complexities but the essence of aggression is this. The ability to be aggressive evolved – in the Darwinian meaning of the term evolution – as an attribute of the fittest, who survive. Since the ability to be aggressive is shared by so many other animals, it's clearly a useful attribute in relation to survival. Aggression is aroused when survival is threatened.

Seen in this context we must assume that our violent societies of today include a large number of people who feel their survival threatened. The solution to crime, delinquency and violence must be by removing the threat, not by trying to help people disperse their aggressive feelings in spectator sports or running or yoga or watching violence on the television.

Constructive Aggression

In the last section, I discussed mainly the disadvantages of the aggressive drive and the problems aggression creates for people in the modern Western society. But aggression has also a positive aspect. Aggression promotes energy and action. Not all aggression need be harmful. Aggression is the fuel for ambition, for going forward, building, throwing off the old ways and developing the new.

Aggression is also necessary in our daily life. In an ideal world, humanity might manage to survive without the aggressive drive. But human societies are emotionally just as 'red in tooth and claw' as are the jungles of the rest of the natural world. If we can't allow ourselves to be aggressive, we tend to 'go under', to become the victims of those people who don't have any scruples about aggressive behaviour. Our ability to be aggressive depends on what we were taught as children and on our view of ourselves, our 'rights'.

Many of us have been indoctrinated, as children, to abhor our aggressive drive. Selfishness was looked on as wicked, we were taught to share, violent behaviour was punished. We were made to understand that we were more acceptable if we suppressed aggressive behaviour and also aggressive feelings.

But if our aggression is wholly suppressed we become slaves of other people's needs. (The outcome may be that we become ill, as I'll describe later.) We must in our daily life be able to say 'No!', a refusal which we may believe is regarded as an act of aggression by the person making a request or demand. But 'No!' is sometimes a life-saving refusal – and we must *mean* 'No!' when we say the word. We must be able to give instructions. We must allow ourselves to accept kindnesses offered to us – or gifts, or the generosity of others – all of which may feel to the recipient like aggressive 'taking'. But 'taking' is often not aggressive at all. Sometimes it's more unkind to others to refuse gifts or offers of help than to accept them. We must be able to say 'No' to those who want something from us which we don't want to give. For example, if a man wants to have sexual intercourse with a woman who doesn't want him, she must be able to refuse him convincingly without being overwhelmed by feelings of guilt.

With aggressive behaviour, there's often a question of 'them' or 'me', whose needs shall come first. The self-preservation of 'me' is usually more important than the trivial needs of another. But here, we have to use our judgement and our sense of morality. Are we doing harm by being 'selfish'? Whose needs are more seriously important, theirs or ours? There are, of course, situations when we should 'rightly' sacrifice our own needs to the needs of others. But the decision to do so should be a conscious one, with all the relevant emotions experienced consciously.

The problem with allowing ourselves to act, justifiably and moderately, in an aggressive way is that, more often than not, our scruples about being aggressive are unconscious. If we've been taught as children that aggression equals wickedness we won't even know, on a conscious level, that aggression is necessary, even vital, in certain situations. We'll act like helpless idiots because aggressive thoughts and behaviour will be barred from, excluded from, our conscious awareness. Automatically, we'll play the rôle of victim in a face-to-face confrontation, only long afterwards cursing at having allowed others to take advantage of us.

The 'l'esprit de l'escalier', the witty riposte thought up after leaving the confrontation, is familiar to many of us. We only return to normal mental functioning when the paralysis caused by unconscious fear of being aggressive wears off. As I mentioned earlier, our ability to feel consciously aggressive and to act deliberately and consciously in an aggressive way depends both on childhood indoctrination and also on our sense of worthiness, our 'rights'. Those who've been rejected in childhood, who feel unworthy and unvaluable, find it hard to assert themselves, to make demands, to reject and refuse.

The more confident we are, the more we value ourselves, the easier it is for us to recognize our 'rights' and to insist on good treatment from others. In other words, the healthy self-confident members of our society, those who've been respected and cared for as children, are those who are able to use their potential for aggression when necessary. Other people quickly sense those who are wholly submissive, who won't be able to be aggressive no matter what the circumstances. The girl behind the counter in the shop will recognize at once those customers she can safely neglect. She'll go on chatting to her friend without fear that the manager will be sent for. Meekness is despised in our society. Gentleness and an inability to say 'boo!' aren't admired. Strength and power and even ruthlessness are admired – although also hated.

Just as important as our ability to use our aggression when it's needed is our conscious understanding of when we *ought* to be feeling aggressive – that is, when our 'rights' are threatened, when we're being neglected or rejected, when people are trying to take advantage of us, do us down. And equally important, we should be able to experience aggressive *feelings* at those times when aggression is appropriate. Finally, if we are able to recognize instantly and on the spot when aggression is appropriate, and experience our logical aggressive *feelings*, then we ought to be able to *act* aggressively if our conscious moral judgment approves of such action.

If our aggressive drive is wholly suppressed, a variety of symptoms may occur. First, we may feel very tired. Suppressing aggression when it's provoked, when it's logical, appropriate (and that's often, in our daily lives) is tiring, even exhausting. As I've mentioned earlier, our aggressive drive is a source of energy. It feeds our daily activities. If we're not busy holding it down we move more quickly, more deftly. Children who unconsciously forbid themselves to be aggressive are bumbling, clumsy creatures, slow and inept at games and gymnastics during which they need to throw their limbs and bodies about. They tend to droop and stoop, shoulders hunched, head bent forward. They find it hard to stare others straight in the eye, shrinking from this symbolic challenge. They drop things, they stumble, they are dazed.

Second, depression and depressive illness sometimes occur when aggression is suppressed, as described in the chapter on depression. Third, pains in tense muscles may occur, giving rise to back and neck aches. Fourth, phobic illnesses sometimes develop. Attacks of panic and fear are extraordinarily unpleasant. Claustrophobia and agoraphobia are very disabling. People suffering from claustrophobia will do anything rather than be enclosed and imprisoned in a small space, or a large space for that matter, such as lifts, ski lifts, the cabins of aeroplanes, hovercraft, ships. So travel is restricted; but in addition, people suffering from claustrophobia have to take elaborate and exhausting precautions to avoid situations which the rest of us hardly notice. I remember one mother whose child was ill on the top floor of a London hospital. The poor woman had to climb twelve flights of stairs each time she went to visit him – sometimes several times a day – because the lift was intolerable for her. Lifts that are wholly enclosed with walls of metal – and most modern ones are like that – feel worse, to a claustrophobic person, than a lift with open gates. The same woman dreaded the prospect of visiting certain friends for the weekend, because she knew the house would be shut up at night and a burglar alarm set to function so that there was no way she could leave the house without sirens shrieking. The essence of the problem is this: there's no possible means of escaping from lifts and ski-lift cabins once they're moving – or from aeroplanes in flight or hovercraft. Any place that feels like a prison will bring on a dreaded panic. Sufferers from claustrophobia seem terrified at 'being at the mercy of . . .' What? Were they, as very small children, at the mercy of cruel adults? Or are they terrified of their own aggression, rather than the aggression of others? Very often, people with this profoundly disturbing condition are in a situation of helplessness, seemingly trapped by circumstances and equally held down by their own inability to feel and act aggressively. Were they able to recognize and use their aggressive drive, they could, as a rule, free themselves.

Interestingly, if patients suffering from claustrophobia and similar panic attacks can be helped to be aware of the fact they have reason to be angry, helped to *feel* angry, the claustrophobia improves rapidly. I've always found that treatment of the attacks with sedatives or sedating antidepressants is much less effective than treating the patients with stimulating substances which help them release feelings.

Here's an example of claustrophobia: Lilian C. was the only child of a powerful, successful leader of industry. She had a very good relationship with her father, but a poor one with her mother, who was a difficult, jealous woman. Her father doted on her, but he was a very possessive dominating man. He needed to have his own way, and he determinedly set about getting his own way, both at home and in his office. He ran Lily's life for her from a very early age. She meekly went along with her darling daddy's view of things, his attitudes and foibles and his possessiveness, until she was about seventeen years old. She was, in fact, a chip off the old block and although small and delicate and feminine, she had her father's strong, driving temperament. At the age of seventeen, having been as good as gold, she suddenly went wild. She fell in love with daring and unsuitable young men, with whom she had daring and dashing adventures travelling far and wide, leading a life as different from the genteel, protected circumstances of her childhood as is possible to imagine.

Her father was distraught; he loathed the young men and he found her behaviour unbearable, but he hung on grimly, waiting for the phase to pass. And it did pass. One night on a beach in Greece, Lily and the young man of the time, who was Greek, were attacked by hooligans and robbers. Lily suddenly panicked. Very quickly she made for home and fell into her father's triumphant arms. There followed a period when Lily was shocked and quiet. Daddy looked after her, was patient and gentle and never once said 'I told you so'. Lily leaned on him once more. And then he decided that Lily should be married – to a man of *his* choice, *his* kind of man.

Within a year Lily was married to a kind, gentlemanly, well-bred divorcé twice her age, who quickly became impotent as he unconsciously recognized that he was competing for Lily with Lily's father. And Lily began to suffer from claustrophobia.

She felt herself at the inescapable mercy of two men, mainly her father, but also her husband, although this was not something she consciously recognized. The life she was leading satisfied others but she herself had no satisfaction whatever; on the contrary, she was utterly frustrated. It was very much a 'them' rather than 'me' situation. But Lily, in fact, didn't realize how trapped and unhappy she was. She'd been brought up to be a very 'nice' girl, who said and felt and thought only 'nice' things about other people.

She told me frequently about how wonderful her father was and how kind and good her husband was. It was true that her father was generous, kind, honest, successful and so on, but it was also true that he wanted to lead Lily's life for her. This was intolerable, and as she gradually realized how dominating he was, she felt it was intolerable. She became angry with him.

Similarly, her husband, a gentle and equally generous man, deeply guilty about his sexual failure, did his best to cherish her – but this didn't compensate Lily for her intense frustration. In fact, both Lily's father and her husband were extremely selfish men.

In the end Lily was able to feel and be aggressive to them. She divorced her husband, married another – a young and passionate man (of whom Lily's father was very jealous) – and began to lead her own more exciting life. Her claustrophobia became a thing of the past, although always liable to recur, if her circumstances re-enacted 'trapped helplessness' for her. Now, however, she could be more aware of and make use of her aggression.

Here is another example of phobic symptoms: Miss C was an attractive young woman who had, unfortunately, the pattern of falling in love with very unsuitable, often rejecting men. Some months before she came to see me, she began a relationship with someone she thought was different, a man who seemed ardent, deeply devoted and prepared to settle down with her for life. They made plans for the future. They thought of getting married. Miss C was radiant. Harry lived and worked in Reading, Miss C in London. She often made the journey to and from Reading by train. One day on the return journey, she found herself sitting next to a neighbour of Harry's, an old friend of his. They began to chat.

'I saw Harry's wife the other day,' said this woman innocently.

'His *wife*?'

Miss C thought she was about to faint.

'Yes. Didn't you know? She has a job in Scotland and only comes down occasionally.'

The neighbour saw Miss C's shocked look, was genuinely upset, began 'Oh, oh dear, I'm so sorry . . .'

Miss C got up and walked along the coach of the train. When she reached a door she had, for the first time, an attack of intense panic. She believed she was about to open the door and throw herself on the track – although she had no wish to kill herself. She just felt she'd be compelled by an intractable urge to fall from the fast-moving train. She was overwhelmed by fear. With difficulty she drew herself away from the door and slowly was able to return to her seat. The panic ebbed gradually, but returned in all sorts of mysterious circumstances, and also in circumstances similar to the first attack. She felt she was about to fall from the underground train. She felt she was going to cut her throat with her large kitchen knife. She believed she would fall under a London bus or from the window of her high apartment. The panic which accompanied these ideas of a compelling self-destructive urge was profound.

She confronted Harry who became very confused and slightly belligerent. He'd been going to tell her about his wife at the right time he said. He and his wife had no longer anything in common. They were going to get divorced. Miss C believed him because she wanted to believe him – but in fact Harry was no different from all those other men who'd let her down before. Time went on. There seemed to be no prospect of a divorce between Harry and his wife – and no more talk of marriage between Harry and Miss C. Her attacks of panic, which had abated a little after Harry had talked to her about divorcing his wife, became worse again. They were so bad she began to feel she couldn't travel on the underground, couldn't cross a street full of traffic, could hardly go into her own kitchen where the sight of the knives could bring on an attack.

When I saw her, she was in a wretched state, very much disabled by the attacks themselves and the fear of having them. Our talks helped her to understand that her reaction to the news about Harry's wife had been one of anger. Because she had been brought up to suppress and repress her aggression she could not recognize the fact that she wanted to kill Harry for his betrayal of her. She had also been rejected as a child and so she didn't recognize that she had the 'right' to be angry. Instead, the whole complex of aggressive hostility had been converted into a phobic reaction, and she could only allow herself self-destruction, rather than the destruction of others – namely Harry.

When she was able to recognize the truth of her wish to kill him – or rather, that she was angry enough with him to feel like killing him – the attacks of panic passed. She was furious, she was sad, but she was no longer afraid.

One last example: Mrs G suffered from severe claustrophobia. She was married to a businessman whose work obliged him to entertain businessmen, mostly from abroad. This meant that Mrs G, in a rôle supportive to her husband, had to attend these entertainments when the foreign businessmen brought their wives with

them. The entertaining consisted of dinners in crowded restaurants, visits to theatre and opera and short journeys out of
London to restaurants and hotels in the country. These occasions,
which occurred often, were a nightmare for Mrs G because she felt
locked into the often small restaurants packed with people, locked
into her seat in the theatre – unless by a miracle she could sit on
the gangway – and locked and imprisoned in the cars driving
them to riverside or country hotels. Agonizing before these trips,
suffering profoundly during them, and exhausted afterwards, Mrs
G felt life was hardly worth living. She could only survive at all,
she felt, by swallowing huge doses of heavy tranquillizers her
doctor had given her, which made her dopey but hardly touched
her panic. When I saw her, I discovered her situation was that she
was married to an extremely dominating and severe man, much
older than herself, of whom she was in awe. If he disapproved
of her he was coldly contemptuous, a reaction she dreaded. He
disapproved highly if ever she said she felt she couldn't face the
evening's entertainment – say, taking half-a-dozen Japanese men
and their wives to see *King Lear*, sitting in the middle of a row of
seats in the stalls, and afterwards dining in a fashionable restaurant
in a cellar in Mayfair.

Mr G's great weapon against his wife was a cold, critical stare
which made her feel hopelessly inadequate. As usual in these circumstances, she told me how good and kind he really was, and
that her problem had nothing to do with him. But on going into
the story of her childhood, it became clear that her husband represented her mother for her and that her marriage re-enacted her
childhood. Her mother too had been formidable, cold, dominating.
Mrs G had been very afraid of her – not because she was physically
cruel, but because she was often coolly contemptuous of her little
daughter or laceratingly sarcastic. She was also crushing, not allowing Mrs G to develop her own personality. In her relationship with
her husband, Mrs G felt that, just as in her childhood, her own
needs had to be put aside in favour of her husband's.

Mrs G was, without recognizing the fact, a very angry woman
– or rather she would have been angry, had she allowed herself to
recognize and experience her feelings. In the first place she was of
course angry with her mother; and in the second place, with her
husband. With insight she began to use her aggression and as she
did so, her claustrophobic panics slowly evaporated. She took

up interior decorating and dropped the business entertainments. Nobody died or even fainted. Her husband meekly accepted the new situation. It does seem that as feelings are released, acute anxiety disappears. And, as in Mrs G's case, our fears of being savagely destructive if we are aggressive are ill founded.

I should mention that some people with phobic symptoms find that alcohol helps them. The reason must be the same as with a stimulating medicine – the alcohol allows a release of feelings. There is of course danger in using alcohol in this way, as addiction may ensue.

Agoraphobia, panic at open spaces, is more rare than claustrophobia, which is a comparatively common illness. There are also those who panic at heights – who can't, without severe anxiety, drive over mountain passes, go rock climbing or stand on the edge of canyons and waterfalls. This condition, although inconvenient, isn't seriously disabling in daily life, as heights can be avoided.

Fear is a very primitive emotion. Many animals seem to experience fear more poignantly than we do. It's worth observing that there are animals who are terrified of open spaces – mice, shrews, moles – and animals who fear being enclosed – birds, for example. There are also animals which avoid heights: cattle, pigs or the hippopotamus. And there are many animals which instinctively – that is, by means of an inherited response – fear certain other animals.

We humans also may develop a phobic response to the sight of snakes, spiders, mice or rats. But in human beings, these responses aren't instinctive. The creature we may believe we fear probably symbolizes something else which we do actually fear, for example, a snake may symbolize a penis.

Finally, as with other disabling behaviour patterns, our phobic response may be one we learned from others rather than developed in our own right. The daughter of a woman who is terrified of closed spaces may very well also suffer from claustrophobia. The daughter has simply identified with her mother. In the mother's case she may have developed the phobia because of suppressed aggression. In the daughter's case, there's no such reason, making the condition harder to treat.

One last word about aggressive behaviour. There are some people who are aggressive as a matter of routine. Depressive illness makes people irritable and bad-tempered, as does chronic alcoholism. Inferiority feelings may make people aggressive; and aggression may mask anxiety and sadness. There is a difference between conscious, uncontrolled bad temper and deliberate bullying, and the aggression related to a drive to survive – perhaps a difference in quality of feeling.

As I mentioned elsewhere, our range of feelings is limited and one category of feeling response must serve many purposes.

Sexuality

Sex is fun, exciting, delirious, sex is love, uniting lovers, sex is bawdy, naughty, disgusting, sex is money, sex is prostitution, pornography, sex is beautiful, absurd, forbidden, terrifying, sex is AIDS, sex is sinful, filthy, degrading, sex is for having children, sex is for blackmail, sex is for bondage, transvestitism, masochism, sex is for advertising (from motor cars to yoghurt), sex in our Western societies is, in fact, almost everything except the great, purely procreative drive which motivates all other animals. Sex is certainly a powerful motivation for human beings, but the drive has become distorted and deformed by restrictions and taboos, folklore and customs and cultures and all the confusions and aspects of sex just mentioned. Hundreds of thousands of books have been written about human sexuality and sexual practices.

Here I can only briefly describe some of the problems which the sexual feelings, thoughts and behaviour of parents create for their children. We nowadays recognize that all human beings are to a greater or lesser extent bisexual. Some are stimulated to have overt sexual intercourse with both men and women. Others may be more strongly heterosexual or homosexual, but all of us are potentially able to feel warmth, affection and physical closeness to members of our own sex. In the United Kingdom the atmosphere in men's clubs is strongly homosexual but most members would be outraged to hear this said. Nevertheless, it is true that in male backslapping, intimate jokes, 'men's' talk and other private or sharing activities, there is an element of sexuality.

Women gathered in groups, office staff or hospital nurses, for example, also enjoy a similar cosy closeness and understanding of one another. The human world would be a less agreeable place without this pleasant and harmless friendship and modified sexuality which exist between members of the same sex.

All human beings are potentially capable of sexual feelings, from the very old to the very young. All human beings are potentially able to be physically attracted to one another, 'strangers in the night', mothers and sons, mothers and daughters, fathers and sons, fathers and daughters, uncles, nieces, nephews, brothers and sisters. If all taboos were removed, all and any might be stimulated to have sexual intercourse together, by day and by night, in public or alone. But human sexuality is riddled with taboos, immensely complicated by conceptual notions, religious prohibitions and the laws of the country. Sexual desire must often be ignored or repressed.

The sexual attraction of people for one another is mysterious, almost magical. Since two people who have never met before, standing, for example, in a bus queue, may feel the most potent sexual desire for one another it's not surprising that sexual passions abound in family life, thriving in the hothouse atmosphere of the cloistered home.

Heterosexuality and homosexuality are aroused in the family, mainly, but not always, banned from consciousness and so unrecognized on a conscious level; nevertheless, they make their impact on parent and child.

Sexual feelings between parents and children and brothers and sisters are, of course, entirely normal phenomena. If well contained and restrained and discreetly expressed, these feelings are healthy. But damage to children occurs if sexual desire gets out of control, if sexual feelings are powerful and sustained over a long time and if overt sexual behaviour follows the feelings. Children may become disturbed for a lifetime by a parent's sexual passion even though physical intercourse doesn't take place.

Children may be very aroused by attracting a parent's sexual attention and are able to experience sexual feelings of their own with great intensity. If these are joined to an adult's intense sexual desires, the resulting damaging pattern of a sexual relationship is very stable and hard to alter in later life, even with the help of considerable insight and therapy.

Repeated rape and anal intercourse by fathers of small children cause immense psychological and also physical harm from which children may never recover. Here the law of most civilized countries intervenes, but there must be innumerable cases which never are discovered, just as there are vast numbers of children physically assaulted by their parents about whom no one ever knows outside the family. Apart from physical harm – the lacerating effect of an adult penis on a small fragile body – much emotional harm is caused by parents lusting, uncontrollably, consciously or unconsciously, after their little girls or boys.

Freud heard so often, from his women patients, that they'd been raped by their fathers in childhood, that he decided the stories revealed a commonly occurring fantasy, an aspect of Oedipal longing on the child's part. But the more that's revealed and discovered about sexual activities and feelings in large numbers of homes in our modern societies, the more possible it is to believe that some kind of sexual encounter occurs between fathers and their daughters. There may be consistent fondling, caressing, fumbling and even rubbing of the child's clitoris by the father.

I remember one very disturbed little girl, brought to me by the Child Guidance Clinic because she seemed backward, and unable to play with other children at her nursery school. Her parents had been very unwilling to consult me but her doctor had insisted. At first the child was silent to the point of stupefaction and seemed very depressed. Slowly she began to talk. In the end it was revealed that every now and then her father, in her mother's absence, had a secret sexual session with her, undressing and masturbating her. She was enormously excited by these encounters and at night in bed, masturbated herself. Her mother, a cruel woman, discovered the child was masturbating and punished her violently each time she discovered the little girl was touching herself. In the end the mother constructed a kind of straitjacket and tied the child into this each night so that she couldn't reach her genitals. But the father continued his sexual activities undeterred, until her doctor realized she needed help.

A lonely parent, an abandoned parent, or a parent sexually frustrated in his or her marriage is perhaps more likely to be intensely attracted to a child. But those parents who break the taboos and the laws, who do have overt sexual intercourse with their children, are very seriously emotionally disturbed. They are 'sick', being unrestrained, unable or unwilling to hold in check desires and actions which are forbidden in our societies in the West. Many will have been sexually abused themselves as children. Others (for example, fathers who are attracted to their little girls) will have been 'fixed' in a sexual pattern that related to games played as a child in the nursery with siblings, or 'the little girl next door'. Although such activities are entirely normal, if the games are played with much intensity over a long period there will have been neglect on the part of the parents – or absence, since these games should be restrained, contained to a minimum, for healthy development.

Apart from physical damage and the more severe emotional or mental disturbances which may follow parents' unrestrained sexual behaviour, much harm of a milder nature is done by mothers and fathers lusting consciously or unconsciously after their children. A child's sexual make-up, the ability to experience sexual pleasure 'normally' in adult life, may be forever in disarray.

After a prolonged passionate 'affair' with a parent, a person may, in order to have sexual satisfaction, need some or all the elements of that first sexual encounter. If the parent put the child in a certain position, for example lying on its face, the adult may find that position during sexual intercourse later in life the one most sexually exciting. If the parent always put a glass of water by the bed and gave the child a sweet, the water and the sweet take on a sexual significance. Later, in adult life, that person may need to have a glass of water and a sweet in order to be sexually turned on, and may, in fact, find it difficult to have an orgasm without these ingredients.

Some people – men in particular – are very stimulated sexually by the smell and the texture of rubber sheeting, such as is used to protect mattresses from a young child's bedwetting. It is believed that this 'turn-on' must go back to a man's very early years when perhaps, as he was put to bed, his mother or nurse played with his penis, giving him intense pleasure but also a catastrophic 'complex'.

Another example is where perhaps a child was regularly spanked by a parent in a sexually exciting situation; the sexual 'turn-on' will be a spanking, or even a whipping, in adult life. The excitement may be such that the adult needs the spanking – or the rubber – in order to function sexually at all, that is, in order to have an erection. This state of affairs may have a disastrous effect on a marriage. For instance, take the case of Henry and Mina. This couple were married, happily it seemed. Sexual intercourse was always a problem because Harry tended to be impotent. They had children, however, and all seemed well. Then, one day after a particularly disastrous attempt at sexual intercourse, Henry felt driven to prove his virility with a prostitute. The latter, efficient at her business, realized that Henry needed some additional stimulation, dressed herself in a rubber mackintosh and gently spanked him with a slipper. Henry became wildly excited, and extremely potent. He realized that mackintoshes and slippers were what was missing in his marriage, but felt too ashamed to tell Mina. One day, however, he felt compelled to confess. Mina was alarmed, disgusted and contemptuous. Realizing, however, that her marriage was at stake and because she was kind and intelligent, she made an effort. She too wore a rubber mac, put on boots and wielded a slipper. This worked initially for Henry – but Mina herself became very put off the whole performance. She no longer felt attracted to Henry, lost interest in sex with him, gave up the ritualized performance, which she detested, and their marriage collapsed. Henry returned more and more frequently to the prostitute. Mina found a lover. They left one another and their children suffered severely.

There are other quirks and eccentricities of sexual behaviour which can wreck 'normal' marriages. Bob C was, as the age of three and four, very attracted, sexually, to his mother. She had wanted a girl and sometimes dressed Bob in little girls' clothes and cuddled him with intense affection. Recognizing her need – unconsciously – Bob began to dress himself in female attire, finding clothes in his mother's cupboards. When he appeared, looking ridiculous but charming, in some garment of hers, she hugged him ecstatically. It became routine that if he went through this performance he'd receive a great deal of physical love from his mother.

In adult life, poor Bob was a transvestite, but only over the matter of sexual intercourse. His wife, on their honeymoon, was thunderstruck and horrified to see Bob approaching her bed dressed in a ravishing negligée and 'shortie' nightdress. She tried to laugh and be tolerant, but found she couldn't accept the situation.

There are understanding and wise women who might tolerate a transvestite husband knowing that he was strongly heterosexual but sexually stimulated by putting on women's clothes – harmless enough, one might think. But a man in woman's clothes is not a masculine figure and most women expect and need a strongly male image for husband or lover. Our culture demands an aggressive view of maleness.

In the child–parent sexual relationship both parent and child might be sexually excited. Alternatively, a parent is sometimes sexually attracted to a child, but the child may be neutral and passive. Or a child may be more excited by a parent than the parent is by the child.

It's believed that all children go through an 'Oedipal' phase in their sexual development. Oedipus, you'll remember, was the son of Larus, King of Thebes. When he was born, the oracle at Delphi predicted that he would kill his father and marry his mother. The king ordered the infant to be taken to the hills and left to die but a shepherd found him and took him to the court of the King of Corinth where he was brought up.

Journeying towards Thebes as a young man, he had an encounter at a crossroads with an older man and in the course of an argument, Oedipus killed this man. Later, as the result of solving the riddle of the sphinx, he married the widowed Queen of Thebes, Jocasta. Later, of course, it was discovered she was his mother and he'd killed his father at the crossroads, so fulfilling the prophecy. Oedipus blinded himself and Jocasta committed suicide.

The Oedipal phase in childhood signifies the attraction of a young child for his or her parent of the opposite sex with the simultaneous jealousy and hostility towards the parent of the same sex. So little boys are sexually attracted to their mothers and try to elbow their fathers out of the role of husband. And little girls are in love with their fathers and jealous and hostile to their mothers. This latter state of affairs is also loosely called Oedipal – or otherwise, the Electra complex. This is, as I've said, a phase which in normal circumstances passes, leaving the child free to continue developing towards heterosexuality (after, perhaps, a phase of homosexuality) with men and women, outside the family circle.

But many problems may occur, getting in the way of the ultimate 'normal' falling in love with a suitable person of the opposite sex. Children are, of course, unaware that during the Oedipal phase their feelings for the parent of the opposite sex are of a specifically sexual nature. They are normally aware only of a longing to be physically close to that parent and a wish, perhaps, to intervene in the relationship of both parents with one another.

If, for instance, the parents are lying together in the same bed, it's not unusual for the child, unconsciously motivated, to try to separate them by climbing into the bed, getting between the parents and snuggling up to the object of affection. As a rule, however, the child is not deeply serious about wanting to get rid of the rival parent. The child unconsciously recognizes its need to have the 'affair' with the parent controlled and supervised by the other parent – i.e. the father, in the case of an Oedipal fling with his mother – and mother in the case of a daughter involved with her father. It is often in the absence of a 'controlling' parent that the relationship between the 'lovers', for example, mother and son, gets out of hand. The child may become unconsciously 'fixated', glued emotionally and sexually to the parent for a lifetime.

If parents are happily married and it's clear to the Oedipal child that his or her father or mother will not allow the child to possess the other parent, the Oedipal phase passes slowly, leaving the child free to form other relationships. But even happy parents may overdo the demonstration of physical affection to a child during the Oedipal phase, may overexcite him or her to heightened sexual feelings, may 'seduce' the child, emotionally and even physically.

While overt sexual activity of a parent with a child no doubt causes grave damage, there are dozens of other ways of causing permanent hurt and harm in a child in a less direct way, for example: Vivienne was beautiful, irresponsible, and, it must be said, a cruel mother. She was divorced. Her husband had left her when her children were young (Quentin was nine, Lucy six and Deirdre four years old). Her husband left, after many rows, to live with another woman, and didn't take much interest in his children. Vivienne, angry and punishing, began to have a series of lovers, sometimes more than one at a time. She behaved flamboyantly, having these men in the house, making love almost under the eyes of her children, walking about half naked, losing all restraint.

Quentin felt both repelled and fascinated – but he was, in fact, immensely stimulated sexually by his mother's enticing behaviour towards her lovers and her open sexual activities and conversations, all of which went on for several years. He became fixed in the sexual pattern involving an older woman, physically very available, but not available for marriage or even a long-term relationship. He was profoundly attracted also to women who were in positions of authority or symbolically 'top' women – well-known film stars or actresses, business women, princesses, models and so on. In sleep, his dreams were often about having a relationship with 'the queen', symbolizing his mother.

The outcome was that all his relationships failed. Many of the women to whom he was attracted were married, and although they were prepared to have a secret affair with him, were not interested in a long-term relationship. An additional problem for Quentin was that he suffered intermittently from impotence. A man is forbidden to make love with his mother – look what happened to Oedipus – and Quentin's loves were always mother figures, symbolic mothers. Impotence is a common occurrence for these men who, unconsciously, see their lovers as 'forbidden'. Quentin drifted through a lonely life with lover after lover, becoming older and so less attractive to older women. He had the additional misery of having been abandoned by his father so he had little sense of his own worth. His end was a tragic suicide.

Vivienne's daughters were also damaged. One identified with her mother, followed exactly in her mother's footsteps, married, divorced and had endless lovers. The other, the youngest child, took the very opposite path. She was frightened of and repelled by both men and women. She lived a lonely life with a number of domestic animals whom she could love. But she couldn't love, nor allow herself to be loved by, any human being.

Seductive mothers may damage their children without going to the lengths that Vivienne did. The important factor is a mother's attitude rather than her actions (although it's better for the children to have a mother who behaves discreetly rather than outrageously). If a mother indulges in strong sexual feelings towards her children or wants them to be sexually attracted by her, children will respond accordingly. It is believed that boys who are stuck with their Oedipal feelings or patterns have only certain courses open to them in adult life when trying to have relationships with other people: first, they may be attracted only to parent figures, symbolic of the father or mother – that is, older men and women. Second, they may be attracted to married people, so re-enacting their parents' married state. Third, men may go to great lengths to avoid the 'crime' or an act resembling incest, that is sexual intercourse with a woman symbolic of mother. This symbolism doesn't mean the woman must be older, necessarily. She must be of the same 'category' – socially, educationally, morally. That is, she must be a 'decent' or 'pure' woman in order to symbolize a mother figure. In such cases, the man unconsciously trying to avoid 'incest' will either avoid 'good' and 'decent' women altogether or be impotent with such a woman. A man may find he can only function sexually with an 'indecent' or 'bad' woman, that is, a prostitute or call girl. In any case, even if he can manage to function with a 'good' woman, he's likely to find sex infinitely more exciting and satisfactory with a non-mother woman, a mistress, prostitute, and so on. Fourth, they may be homosexual. Expressed very simply, the element of fear of 'betrayal' of the original love – that is, mother – enters the picture. To have a love affair with another woman would unconsciously be regarded as a crime against the woman to whom one betrothed oneself in childhood. Fifth, they may allow themselves to love only people as different from the mother as possible – different in race, class, colour, religion, appearance, character. For example, dark-haired people will fall in love only with blonds. White Anglo-Saxon Protestants will fall in love with black women or Greeks or members of the Latin race.

What I've described about mothers and sons applies equally to fathers and daughters.

Sometimes children are unconsciously motivated to escape from the clutches of a lusting parent. I remember seeing an extremely distressed adolescent girl who was very overweight. She wept a great deal while she was telling me her story. She simply couldn't stop eating, however hard she tried. She was getting fatter and fatter. Until a year or two before she'd been sylph-like and had had no problem with over-eating.

In the course of our talk she told me over and over again that her being overweight was particularly upsetting because her father hated fat women. It became slowly clear during our hour together that M.'s father had been enormously attracted to her physically. She'd been 'Daddy's girl'. He'd fussed over her and petted and cuddled and kissed her and hugged her at every opportunity (but he probably didn't consciously recognize the sexual aspect of his love). All this had been all right as long as she was a little girl, but as she began to grow up, and became a woman, she found his attentions overwhelming and disturbing – although she didn't acknowledge this fact on a conscious level. How to escape without catastrophic aggression towards him? Her unconscious mind found her a solution. 'Get fat. He's turned off by fat women.'

So fat she became. Father withdrew, complaining she looked disgusting. And disgusting she felt, much to her distress – but it was either that or a love affair with her dad. Not that she understood consciously what I've just described. On a conscious level all she knew was she was overweight and that however hard she tried, she couldn't find the strength to diet. And it was all worse because her dad couldn't stand fat women.

Older girls sometimes manage to tell their fathers they don't want any more of the sexual relationship. It's well known that small children seldom protest or talk about a parent's sexual 'attack' on them. This must be due partly to the parent emanating the message that the relationship is profoundly secret, not to be discussed with others. The child responds to this message. In addition, small children have, of course, no idea of the rights and wrongs of any situation in relation to their parents. They're completely in the parents' power, used to accepting meekly whatever the parents do with them.

Parents sometimes do, of course, openly threaten children whom they abuse with awful punishment or awful consequences if the child should tell another person about what's happening: 'If you tell your mother she'll divorce me and you'll never see me again'; or 'If you tell your mother I'll throw your puppy in the river'; or 'If you tell, someone will come in the night and take you away.'

The child may find one parent's sexual behaviour – anything from play to intercourse – distasteful or terrifying but it will seldom tell the other parent.

It's believed that mothers often sense or know or are half aware of a father's sexual affair with their daughter, but seldom act to stop what's going on. The mother is a kind of accomplice – perhaps because she's anyway hostile to the child, perhaps because she's afraid of the father or afraid to articulate a horrifying truth. Or perhaps the mother is thankful that the daughter is satisfying the father's sexual urge since she's had enough of it.

Whatever the reason, it's a fact that mothers generally don't accuse husbands of incest – or any other sexual game – with their daughters and don't protect the children.

In this connection, I've talked about fathers and daughters rather than mothers and sons. Sexual intercourse between mothers and sons is probably a great deal rarer than between fathers and daughters – or fathers and sons. Overt homosexual sexual activities do, of course, also occur in family homes. Perhaps the most poignant aspect of sexual relationships between parents and children is that small children accept meekly, trustingly, sufferingly, whatever a parent chooses to inflict on them. They have no alternative and they have no way of knowing what is 'right' and 'wrong' in a parent's behaviour. In our societies, parents have absolute and deadly secret power over children. Unless they break the law and someone outside the family proves they have broken the law, they can do what they like with their children.

A hundred years ago, Lord Shaftesbury was trying to improve conditions for children at work, in factories and other places, but he was unwilling to tackle the problem of child abuse at home: 'The evils are enormous and indisputable but they are of so private, internal and domestic a character as to be beyond the reach of legislation . . .' Can we be sure his words don't still hold true today?

Sex may be used by men and women to bolster a flagging sense of worth and value. Children who've been rejected by parents may suddenly discover in late adolescence that they are able to attract sexually. This is sometimes an intoxicating discovery; 'come and get me' becomes a very attractive game for those with an inadequate sense of self. The person who attracts probably remains cool and uninvolved. The person who is attracted may be violently passionate.

Having attracted, the attractor moves on, leaving behind a bewildered and suffering lover. The attractor is unconscious of the true reasons for wanting to attract, but there is often great satisfaction in seeing the attracted person desperate over the broken love affairs.

On the other hand, there are those who attract only because they are unconsciously repeating the love affair with the parent. These people may find the resulting relationships with, as a rule, elderly parent figures, a great burden. They extricate themselves with difficulty, are distressed about the hurt caused – and move on.

Sex may also be used as a means of reward and punishment. Sometimes this is a conscious performance. I've known women who were able to be warm and available sexually as the result of a gift from a man – a piece of jewelry or something similar. But if no gift was forthcoming, no sex was available.

In addition to conscious withdrawal of sexual availability, there may also be an unconscious blocking of sexual feelings in some circumstances. This 'block' occurs mainly in women, although some men are similarly affected.

The block is the result of being hurt or offended or distressed. Frigidity may result. The users of sex as a weapon have often been profoundly disturbed as children. They may have had several advances made by a parent. They may have been rejected and ill-treated emotionally or physically. Having been helpless as children, forced to accept and receive, they slowly discover, as they grow up, that they too have power over others. They may unconsciously be having their revenge on parents. They are probably so damaged as to be unable to experience sexual feelings themselves, which accounts for their detachment.

Masturbation

Masturbation – stimulation of the sexual organs by oneself, so as to produce an orgasm – is an entirely normal activity. Humans masturbate naturally from early childhood into old age. Masturbation is one of the most successful ways of ensuring orgasm.

Masturbation was for centuries regarded as an evil, wicked and dangerous activity. Even today many people feel some guilt at masturbating. It used to be believed that masturbation could cause insanity, blindness and other physical degenerations. The origins of this weird condemnation of a natural phenomenon are buried in folklore and superstition. If small children masturbate excessively, they have some emotional problem, some anxiety which should be investigated which is probably not sexual in origin. The child is using masturbation to disperse stress and tension.

Frigidity and impotence

Frigidity usually has its origins in emotional disturbance.

In order to allow themselves to have an orgasm during homosexual or heterosexual intercourse, women must have been given permission, as it were, by parents to enjoy sex. Frigid mothers who hate sexual intercourse or who hate men for their own reasons emanate a message of distrust and dislike of sex to their daughters.

Sex may be thought of as 'wrong', sinful, nasty, dirty and so on, depending on the attitude of mothers – and grandmothers and great grandmothers. The message is handed down from generation to generation. As a rule, a woman must be able to trust her partner completely in order to have an orgasm. She must feel relaxed, unselfconscious, wanted and enjoyed.

Those who have a poor image of themselves find it harder to 'let go' sexually. The rejection of a girl by her father particularly predisposes her to frigidity. There is also frigidity due to the feeling that sex is 'forbidden' for all the reasons relating to parents described earlier.

A woman who has had sexual intercourse with her father as a small child is likely to dread pain as an accompaniment of penetration. Many women do fear that intercourse will be painful – sometimes it is – for physical or psychosomatic reasons.

Many young men also fear sexual intercourse. One fear is that they do physical damage to a woman; another that the woman will damage – or castrate – them. A further fear is that sex is 'dirty', and that by having sexual intercourse with a 'pure' and 'good' woman, they will sully her and she will reject them. Potency is then available for the less 'good' woman, that is, prostitute or mistress.

Some men are impotent if they feel that they are betraying another woman – a wife or fiancée, by having intercourse. Guilt often causes impotence.

Apart from impotence which has a physical cause, most men's failure to have an erection is largely derived from the notions of parents transmitted during childhood. The culture and custom of any particular society also have some impact. Sexual intercourse is probably less fraught with difficulties for young people in the present liberated day than it used to be for their parents and grandparents.

Love

In the previous chapters I've mentioned again and again the fact that the loved child feels valuable and worthy and as a result, confident and secure all through life.

This is true – but parents' love should be, as far as possible, a little detached, giving the child space to form its own identity. Over-intense, possessive love may be suffocating for the child, and the child may then withdraw emotionally, finding it hard to love in return.

I'll never forget the description of a very wise psychotherapist whom I knew years ago. He said: 'If you go into Richmond Park and want to feed the deer, it's no use tracking them down, following them around, holding out your sandwiches. Every step forward you take, they'll move one step away from you. The best plan is to sit down, put the sandwiches on the ground near you and then read your book. You'll soon find the deer coming up, to nibble at the sandwiches. Loving is the same. Love, but stand back a little and let the loved one come towards you.'

Most parents who love their children expect the children to love them in return and are disappointed, hurt and angry if the children are rejecting and hostile: 'After all I've done for you . . .'; 'I didn't ask to be born . . .' are two commonplace cries from the heart.

Too much love directed towards a child makes a burden for that child. Very often, single children have to carry, for their parent, the sum of their hopes and expectations. In China, where single children are the rule, it's said that there are major emotional problems in the child population on this account. So, while limiting the number of children in any family is very beneficial to the human race as a whole, it may be damaging to an only child. (In the animal world, as Darwin described, an individual of a species may often have to suffer while the group benefits.) But if parents depended less on their children for their own emotional satisfaction, single children would have fewer problems.

'Over'-loved children may feel a tremendous pressure on them to succeed because loving parents long for their child to do well for its own sake as well as for theirs – just as they enjoy seeing their child healthy and happy. But the parent's expectation of success, health and happiness might be overwhelming, too much for a child to bear.

And, perverse though this may seem, such a child might fail, or develop a psychosomatic illness or be delinquent as a kind of protest.

Overwhelming love, 'obsessional' love, and possessive love are often the result of loneliness and sadness in parents. A bereaved husband or wife, a deserted or deeply deprived parent, may turn to the children for comfort and fulfilment.

Mrs M. J. was widowed when her child Thomas was three years old. Her husband, who'd been very close to her, died suddenly when travelling abroad on a business trip. He had a heart attack, having never been ill or shown any symptoms until that moment of death. The shock for Mrs M. J. was tremendous. She went into a deep depression, her only consolation being Thomas. From that time on, he became, in a sense, responsible for his mother's peace of mind, happiness and emotional fulfilment. Although, of course, there's always a sexual element in a relationship between mother and son, in their case this was not strong. Mrs M. J. turned to her son as she might have done to a father or mother for comfort in her distress. Had she had a dog, say, instead of a child, she might have developed a deeply dependent relationship with that animal.

Mrs M. J. was a shy and sensitive woman who found it hard to make friends and so she was isolated, particularly as her home in the English countryside was in a fairly remote position far from the nearest village. Kind friends and neighbours did try to help her but she had no one really close to her except her son. In these circumstances it's easy to understand that her son seemed almost a source of life to her and she loved and needed him in the most profound way.

Thomas found her love very disturbing. He sensed that she needed an enormous amount from him emotionally speaking and he felt inadequate and incapable – feelings which were to haunt him all his life where women were concerned. In his early years he tried to be what his mother needed. He was her close companion.

From the age of six or seven, she took him to the theatre with her, to concerts, to exhibitions of paintings, abroad on holidays. He did his best to be responsible and agreeable – but he was, in fact, lonely and withdrawn. His own ability to love was repressed, because, like the deer, he needed to be allowed to approach rather than feel hounded.

His mother sent him to a day school because she couldn't bear him to go away to a boarding school. There he did his best to be friendly and acceptable although he found it hard to mix with other children and he was bullied and victimized.

When he was about thirteen, Tom's mother re-married. His new stepfather began to resent him, feeling that his wife was too deeply involved with her son. Thomas thus found himself in the middle of a war between them. In the end he was sent away to a tough boys' boarding school where he coped as best he could for five unhappy years. He wasn't well equipped to deal with other boys, but some of the masters liked him. In those years he slowly became homosexual although, had he been exposed to a different set of formative influences, including the company of attractive girls and women, he might have developed into a heterosexual instead. Thomas unconsciously felt that women could overwhelm him, submerge him, make him incapable. Yet he longed to please them. He was haunted by guilt. He was afraid of hurting his mother, terrified she'd find out about his homosexuality; he began to believe he was dying, first of cancer, then AIDS. He punished himself remorselessly. He came close to suicide – and so into the care of a psychiatrist.

Thus parental love (or any love) can be a destructive force as well as a magically supportive one.

Sometimes when mothers – or fathers – are neglected by their spouses, they invest their emotions in their children instead. Children are quite often used as substitute objects of love. The love is genuine – but too much, in terms of responsibility, for the child, as in this case I've just described.

And the same can be said of parents who dislike or hate a husband or wife. They may fix instead on their children.

The child's alternative to turning away from the over-loving parent is to accept the rôle that's been thrust on it. There are children who do try to be for the parent what the parent needs. Such children become chained to the parents – sometimes for a lifetime.

Mrs Paula D. had a husband who had endless affairs. Again and again she found that when he said he had to go away on a business trip, he was actually in Brighton with his secretary. When he said he had a dinner in the city, on the way home he'd spend a few hours with another woman. When he said he wanted to take a walk alone in the park to clear his mind, he had nipped into a hotel near the park for yet another fling. He was unrepentant and unmanageable. Paula despaired. They had a child, their daughter Mirabelle. Mirabelle was a beautiful and charming little girl and Paula found great comfort in her relationship with her daughter.

The two grew increasingly close. As Mirabelle became a little older – but not really old enough to understand and cope – Paula used her as her confidante. She told Mirabelle about her husband's affairs; it was very disturbing for a child to hear such news about her father. Together they wept, together they cheered up. But Mirabelle was really acting as a mother or elder sister to her mother – a rôle she wasn't sufficiently equipped to play. She became a strange, withdrawn girl, totally locked into her relationship with Paula, who didn't seem to grasp what she was doing to her daughter. On the contrary, she was proud and pleased about Mirabelle's devotion to her and would say, 'We're like sisters, aren't we?'

Mr D. eventually left his family and went to live with another woman, isolating Paula and Mirabelle even more. They never separated. Although Mirabelle grew up and took a job, she and her mother continued to live together and, to the end of her mother's life, Mirabelle looked after her. On her mother's death she was, of course, bereft. Middle-aged, emotionally drained and sad – Mirabelle is now a lonely woman.

There are many men and women in Western societies today who are in Mirabelle's position, having devoted their lives to the care of a loving parent who never realized the harm he or she was doing to the child.

Another kind of parental love which is dangerous to a child is the love of an obsessional person. Obsessional people are perfectionists, as I described earlier, and obsessional parents look for perfection in their children. They may try to achieve impeccable, immaculate little boys and girls with never a hair out of place and never a stain on a pinafore. The children of unrestrained obsessionals tend either to be perfectly groomed obsessionals themselves or go the other way and are the untidiest, most unkempt people. To go to the extreme in the opposite direction is just as unhelpful to a person as to live with the strain of the constant need for perfection. Chaos, disorder and total disorganization may be highly destructive in a person's life, but the rigid over-controlled and over-controlling attitudes of the unbridled perfectionist are also damaging. The obsessional parent doesn't like mess, noise, wild behaviour; the child must quickly learn to control bladder and bowels, often before that child is ready for such control. Guilt is of a high order. Dirt is disgraceful. Meek obedience is praised. In the end a highly conforming, law-abiding, emotionally impoverished, good citizen is produced – or a violent, undisciplined rebel against society. Extremes breed extremes.

What is needed, if a parent has an obsessional nature, is an effort not to try to turn a child into a little paragon. However difficult for the parent, mess, noise and the utter disorganization of the very young must be tolerated. A brake must be put on the urge to control. The parent should look away and let the child get into little difficulties, shriek, suffer little injuries, splash its food about and play with mud. Easier said than done – but it can be done with an effort on the part of an obsessional parent, who is often a very caring parent.

An equally disturbing parent is the utterly chaotic one. Extreme untidiness, late meals, a lack of organization, unpunctuality in other ways, and no system to daily life makes children insecure and anxious. Children, like domestic animals, like and need routine, familiarity and a repetition of the same. However warm and affectionate, it upsets a child to see its mother working in a garden in a skimpy dressing gown when the first guests arrive for a dinner party. Or being asked a thousand times to help look for lost keys, lost spectacles, lost handbags, missing screwdrivers and so on. Once again, the child unconsciously makes a choice between identifying with and so repeating the life of the parent, or may do the opposite and become a highly organized obsessional – or alternate between the two modes of behaviour and feeling.

Too much love between the members of a family may imprison its members within that family. I once came across a family where every member loved every other member with joyful intensity. The parents adored one another and adored their children. And the children doted on their parents and on their siblings. This was a charmed and closed circle. No stranger dared intrude. On the wedding day of one of the boys his bride to be ran away, feeling, rightly, she could never belong to his close-knit family nor establish an independent home beyond its influence.

Another love which may be dangerous and harmful is between siblings. Here again there may be a sexual element, but often the major part of the relationship is love born of loneliness, interdependence and mutual suffering.

Here the parents are likely to be neglectful or uncaring or even aggressive and cruel. The children may be pushed away while the parents are busy with their own lives. Because there is a lack of proper parental care, one child in the family may unconsciously try to act as mother or father to the others – or other. Or children may cling to one another in an excess of mutual childish love because there is no parent to be loved.

Tamara and Vincent were the last two children to be born in a large family. By the time they arrived their mother, a beautiful woman who enjoyed a very social life, was tired and bored by children. She already had four much older children with whom she had a good relationship.

She pushed Tamara and Vincent into the care of a rather indifferent nanny and withdrew. The children had a little wing of the house where they lived with their nurse and every now and then one or other of their parents and perhaps their brothers and sisters would visit them. They were strangely isolated – and remained so until they were old enough to go to school and join the other grown-up members of the family.

They were unhappy little children who felt very rejected, not 'good' enough to be accepted in the main part of the house. Their love was directed towards one another since the parents weren't sufficiently visible or loving themselves to be the objects of the little children's love. They grew up deeply attached to one another – but the profound roots of the attachment became unconscious. Each went his or her way. They rarely met although when they did, it was a joyful reunion – but Tamara went to Canada to work and Vincent to France. Neither married. Tamara, highly promiscuous, searched always for the non-existent ideal man.

In what seemed an extraordinary set of coincidences, Tamara found herself very often involved with a man who was really homosexual – or bisexual. Were these men shadowy images of her brother in childhood? For Vincent became, in adult life, frankly homosexual – perhaps his unconsciously motivated technique for remaining faithful to the childhood love of his little sister.

Yet another form of parental love which may disturb children is one which involves the parents' suffering in the cause of looking after the child. In a child's early years a good parent is inevitably self-sacrificing. But when the child is old enough to recognize its parents' identity and its parents' needs, it's important for the mother or father to show and prove that he or she loves him or her self as well as loving the child. This demonstration of self-valuing provides a model with which the child may identify. And also it helps the child not to feel guilty about damaging the parent.

If a parent makes it plain that he or she is deprived, so as to give the child more, the child feels 'bad'. Very few children will enjoy privileges received at the cost of a parent's obvious deprivation. Loving parents do often go without things so as to give their children important benefits, but this the child need never know.

In minor matters, it's helpful to children to see the parents sharing in treats or luxuries. I remember being impressed once by a Swiss mother on an Alpine walk. All the walkers were tired and sat down to rest. This mother, with two young children, took a bar of chocolate from her handbag and meticulously divided it into three equal parts, one each for the children, one for her. They then all ate with great enjoyment. A trivial incident – but a lesson in admirable parenthood.

Having pointed out the disadvantage of some aspects of loving I must emphasize again that nothing in its life is more helpful and constructive to a child than the temperate genuine love and affection and care of its parents. Loving parents create loving children. Those who've never learned about love in childhood because they weren't themselves loved find it hard or impossible to love in adult life. And to love – to have the ability to love – is perhaps just as marvellous as being loved.

Aggression and love

Mrs S. was a patient I saw only once, many years ago, but the impact of our meeting was so strong, I've never forgotten her – nor her story. She was sent to me as an emergency, a patient who needed to be seen at once. Her doctor, who'd already spoken to me on the telephone, sent also a letter which Mrs S. held out to me in a thin shaky hand:

> Mrs S. aged thirty-seven years was living in Kuwait with her husband. Came to the UK for the birth of her first child – a little girl, born five weeks ago . . . all well with mother and child but mother recently very agitated and yesterday asked to see a psychiatrist . . . suspect post-natal depressive illness . . . won't tell me the problem . . . on her own . . . husband called away . . . grateful to you, etc.

Mrs S. was a small, neat woman, tidily dressed, hair in order, make-up accurately applied. (Very ill people usually can't be bothered how they look, wearing any old clothes and hardly putting a comb through their hair. Also, very depressed women tend to put on make-up – if at all – chaotically, with uneven eyebrows, eyeshadow plastered on, and smudged lipstick.) This woman had taken trouble to look fastidiously normal. She even tried to smile politely as she sat down carefully on the edge of the sofa.

She looked very tired in spite of the careful appearance – black smudges of exhaustion under weary and anxious eyes. She was dumb to begin with. What she needed to tell me was too awful, it seemed, to be put into words, to be spoken aloud between two people. To get us going, I asked about her husband. She could talk about him. She said that he worked on oil rigs as a sort of trouble shooter: 'When there's a problem they send for him and he has to go, that's his job – he can't say no.'

I asked, 'Was he here for the baby's birth?'

'Yes,' she replied, 'just . . . he had to go immediately after.'

'Where's the baby now?' I asked.

'Dr. N [the GP] arranged for his nurse to look after her,' she said.

She looked haunted.

'Is the trouble to do with the baby?' I wondered.

'Yes.' An almost whispered word.

Eventually it came out. 'I'm afraid I'm going to kill her . . . I'm afraid . . . I don't want to – I love her – I wanted her so much. But I keep thinking of . . .'

There was silence between us for a moment . . .

'Tell me about it.'

She was living in a furnished flat. It was cold, rather dreary. There was this gas fire. It had to be lit because otherwise it was so cold for the baby. . . . a big fire with blue flames. 'I keep thinking,' she said, tears beginning to stream down her face, 'I keep thinking – I keep having these thoughts I'm going to throw the baby on the fire . . . I can't stop them,' she said, tears raining down. 'They go on and on – I'm going to throw the baby on the fire . . . I feel I'm going to throw the baby on the fire . . .'

Silence again.

'What if there wasn't a fire?'

'I've thought. I won't light the fire . . . but there's the window – there's always the window – we're on the fifth floor.'

'I love my baby,' she said. 'I love her. I'm afraid . . . Am I going to kill her?'

'No,' I said. 'Of course you're not going to kill her. You seem very exhausted. It sounds as if the baby's too much for you. Tell me more about the baby. What's her name? Is she well?'

'Angela.'

The baby wasn't well – nothing serious, she had a cold, she snuffled and cried, she wouldn't take her feeds, wouldn't sleep, she got more and more tired, and the tireder she got the more she cried . . .

Mrs S hadn't slept herself for three nights or longer. The more difficult the baby became, the more anxious Mrs S felt.

'You're all on your own?'

'Yes.'

'Haven't you got any family?'

'I come from the north, Sheffield. I still have my mother – she's old of course – and a sister. That's all. I don't know anybody in London.'

'Couldn't they help you? You could go to them or perhaps your sister could come down here?'

'Not really, my mother lives with my sister. It's a small house. My sister has her family . . .'

I thought perhaps Mrs S didn't get on very well with her mother and sister.

'When will your husband come back?'

'We can't tell. It depends on the job.'

'I suppose we could always get him back.'

She wept again. 'I'm so ashamed . . . I'm so afraid . . .'

I had to make up my mind as to whether Mrs S was suffering from a post-natal depressive illness or whether she was simply at the end of her tether. She was rather old to have a first child. I asked many more questions.

If she was suffering from depressive illness the situation was much more dangerous. She might reach a point of anguish when she could, perhaps, kill her child. We should have to take her into hospital at once. If she was a danger to her baby we'd have to separate them. I asked, 'Are you afraid of touching Angela – to handle her – bath her, change her – all that?' I wanted to know if she felt as if her very touch might damage the child.

'No,' she said, 'I can do all that – except I've always been a bit nervous of her – I'm not sure I'm doing the right thing – she's so tiny . . . I'm not accustomed to babies . . . before I was married I worked. I've only been married three years . . .'

'Did you play with dolls when you were a little child?'

'No. . . . funnily enough I don't think I ever did. I can't remem-

ber any dolls. I had other toys – a duck, I remember and a teddy
bear . . .'

Her reply tended to confirm my earlier impression that Mrs S
hadn't had a very good relationship with her mother.

Little girls who are secure and happy in their relationship with
their mothers like to re-enact the mother/child situation with their
dolls. But if the mother/child relationship causes tension and
misery for the child she won't want to play mother to her doll.

'When will your husband come back?'

'I don't know – as soon as he's finished the job. It could be any
time . . .'

'What are your plans? Will you go back to Kuwait?'

'We don't know. With the baby it's more difficult . . .'

She'd settled down while we had talked but now became anxious
again.

'Couldn't you make some firm plans? Does your husband have
to be in Kuwait most of the time?'

'No – not always . . . there are other places he's sent to. We'd
thought we'd come back here, perhaps – and live in the country
not too far from the airport . . .'

The uncertainty of their future must have added to her difficulties but there was nothing to be done about that for the moment.
I said gently, 'You don't really mean you think you might throw
the baby on the fire?'

'I'd do anything rather than that – but it's the thought of doing
it that keeps coming back – and back . . .'

'Would you rather not have had her?'

'No! No! I love her, of course I don't want to be rid of her.'

'Some people don't want their babies . . .'

'But I do want mine. I love her – and Ken – that's my husband
– he's so thrilled – we both are . . .'

She began to cry again.

'It's just these thoughts that have taken over – they've taken
over my mind and I can't stop them . . . The more frightened I
get the more she cries – and the more she cries – the worse it
gets . . .'

I pictured Mrs S in her rather cold furnished apartment, alone
in strange surroundings – the gas fire lit . . . the baby screaming.
I imagined her struggling with the frantic little creature, terrified

of hurting her – the two of them locked together and almost demented with fatigue.

And another scene came into my mind. It was the middle of the night in the cabin of a huge aircraft on a journey halfway round the world. The lights had been dimmed. Shadowy forms of people, huddled under blankets, shifted restlessly, hoping in vain for sleep. In a row ahead a tiny baby screamed and screamed, desperate, endless, searing screams, which cut the edge of sanity. Beside its aircraft cot sat a young couple, clinging to one another. Tears poured down the mother's face; the young man's face was grey. Helplessly, they held one another while the baby screamed and screamed. They'd done all they could to soothe their child, fed it, changed its nappy, held it up to get the wind out of its stomach, rocked it, picked it up, put it down. Nothing was any good. 'He's overtired,' said the mother, wiping her tears. 'He's overtired and can't get to sleep.'

'Mother,' said a strong and cheerful voice – and a strong and cheerful woman had come forward. 'Would you let me hold him please? I might be able to quiet him. I'm a maternity nurse – I'm used to them screaming – May I pick him up? It's a bit of a knack – getting them to sleep . . .'

Not very long afterwards silence reigned in the cabin and everyone dozed in blissful relief. It was as if an angel had stepped into the Boeing from the starry skies around us.

I decided that Mrs S needed another human angel to come to her rescue. She wasn't suffering from depressive illness, I thought, but from utter exhaustion – total tiredness, which must have made her angry with her baby for its being so difficult – but it was an anger she couldn't allow herself to recognize. Her unconscious mind took over, sending messages to conscious mind, suggesting the baby should be destroyed.

When there is an unconscious dispute between survival – or self-preservation – and destruction resulting from excessively demanding care of others, our own survival seems to be the more important to us. That is, in unconscious mind. Consciously, if they recognize the dispute, the choice between their own survival and that of others, men and women seem capable of heroic acts of self-sacrifice. Mrs S, like many another mother, couldn't bring herself to recognize her fury with her baby for causing her physical and mental suffering.

Anger is a frequently aroused emotion in those taking care of the helpless, the invalid, the dependent. But those who love the people who are also a burden to them are often horrified at what they believe is an ugly and unworthy emotion. It requires courage to recognize and deal with anger when caring for a loved, dependent person. The anger seems the more dangerous the more fragile the creature who provokes it.

The *behaviour* towards the provoker of the anger – who provokes by reason of dependence, helplessness, demandingness – needs special and extra control. But we could allow ourselves to recognize the feelings of anger – since in recognition, the feelings tend to disperse.

I explained some of this to Mrs S. I told her very definitely I thought there was little danger she would actually throw her baby on the fire – but she was so worn out, so drained by her child, that her own need to survive was coming to the forefront of her mind. I said she needed a third party to intervene between them – she and the baby – for a time, since strangers or professional helpers don't have the doubts and guilt which parents feel. Mrs S needed to be able to sleep and to have a little time to herself. Dr B and I would try to arrange all this for her. Perhaps a day or two in a hospital or clinic, then someone to come in each day and make sure mother and child were all right until her husband came home.

This scheme worked. Mrs S's dreadful thoughts of murder subsided and vanished as she was restored to her normal state, and control of herself and the baby and the environment was slowly regained.

There are, of course, mothers who do kill their babies and a certain percentage of deaths in infancy are due for example to suffocation, or beating of the baby by the mother or father or both parents together. I've had patients who put a plastic bag over their infant's head, or held a pillow on his or her face. These people are extremely ill, mentally and emotionally. They enter a nightmare world where it seems to them that the only solution to their total anguish involves the death of their child. There are many other solutions in normal everyday life for those who would rather be without their child. Adoption by other parents who long for children but can't have their own is very, very easy to arrange.

This simple solution doesn't come into the minds of those who kill their infants. I recall one patient who eventually suffocated her baby; she had entered a sleepless, haunted world when she believed the baby was the cause of her husband's abandonment of her – he had indeed left her when the baby was born for reasons connected with his own childhood. The mother had had many experiences in her own infancy and childhood of being abandoned by her parents, who had no interest in their child, and who left her in the care of a brutal and cruel nurse. The parents, to be fair, had had no idea of the savage nature of the nurse until this was revealed years later. In a sense, these parents set the example to my patient. They felt their baby was a nuisance and got rid of it to the nurse so as to be able to lead their own lives. Their daughter felt the same about her baby but 'got rid of it' in the most tragic and horrifying way.

Not only babies but ill people, or invalids or dependent relatives like ageing mothers provoke anger in those who look after them, as I've mentioned earlier. Sometimes a dependent mother or mother-in-law who lives with her family brings out the worst in everybody and results in the break-up of marriages and so on, as is well known. Vulnerable creatures bring out all our anxieties about our possible destructiveness. Should we be carried away by irritation or anger, should we be so greatly provoked that we 'lose control', we might do serious damage, we fear. We might carry out, put into action some monstrous fantasy of savage harm. People do hit out in the heat of anger and people do commit murder in anger.

These facts don't minimize the complex fears, fantasies, self-destructive tendencies, psychosomatic illnesses, insomnia and phobic states sometimes experienced by those caring for loved (and hated) invalids. Here's a typical example of what might happen: Ms P was a brilliant and charming businesswoman. She reached the top ranks of the 'executives' in the firm for which she worked and, because her career meant so much to her, resisted all offers of marriage until the age of thirty-three when she met an almost ideal partner. He was a businessman also, but had inherited great wealth and had no need to work. He owned the family home, a great house in Yorkshire with farms and estates where he had to be in order to supervise his employees. He was a man of gentleness and wit and he adored Ms P. The only drawback to their marriage was she'd have to give up her work – but, he promised her, she could help him in the running of his estates.

Torn between her love of Rupert and her love of her job, she chose Rupert, telling herself she'd soon be too old for marriage and children if she didn't now 'take the plunge'. They went on a honeymoon to Switzerland. On a certain day they'd planned to join a party of people at the hotel who had decided to undertake a long climbing walk up the mountain nearby. The expedition was due to set off early in the morning. Mrs P, feeling lazy, decided to stay at the hotel and Rupert went alone with the rest of the party. Towards the late afternoon, Mrs P became restive and set off along the path the party had taken. A long way ahead, on a much steeper slope above her, she saw the members of the party coming slowly down. It looked as if one of them was being carried on a stretcher – and indeed, as she hurried towards them, there was a man on a stretcher carried by guides – Rupert!

He'd had a heart attack on the steepest part of the climb. Members of the party had gone for help, a doctor arrived and guides with the stretcher. He survived and lived in fact for some years afterwards. But within one year he'd had another heart attack and later a third. His condition was thus very fragile. Mrs P found she'd married an invalid rather than the thriving owner of a huge estate. One of his brothers took over the running of the farms and lands and Mr and Mrs P moved into a smaller, more easily managed house on one of the farms. But the house was ancient, with heavy old doors and casement windows, hard to open and shut. They would have been better off in a modern house, built with lighter smooth materials. The garden was large and very beautiful but it had a fair sized stream running through it and a pond. I mention these features of the house and the garden because they became significant in the lives of Mr and Mrs P.

In the few years of her marriage, Mrs P grew more and more attached to her husband. In the years before his second coronary thrombosis, they had a very agreeable time together – going sometimes to London, sometimes abroad visiting friends. After the second attack however, the trips were very rare. They were more or less confined to their house. Instead of the exciting, active life she'd had before her marriage, Mrs P became nurse, housekeeper, supervisor of cleaners, gardeners, shopper at the local supermarket. She minded all this a good deal. She missed her London life – but she loved her husband and they were good companions. Nevertheless, she began to suffer from severe and disabling headaches, from pains in various parts of her body, and from an intense and increasing anxiety which finally reached fever pitch. She hovered over her husband like a hawk. She kept watching him covertly to see if his breathing and colour were normal. Every time he opened or shut one of those heavy casement windows, she waited for him to collapse. Every time he took a stroll alone in the garden, especially at night, she imagined him lying face down in the water of stream or pond, felled by another heart attack.

Because she was an intelligent and sensitive woman, she tried not to let Rupert become aware of her anxiety. She worried in silence, never saying, 'Don't open the window, please, it's too heavy for you!' or 'Do you think it's really wise going out in this cold wind and rain?' She thought, 'If he has to be careful about every move he makes, his life won't be worth living.' So, silently consumed by intolerable fears, she told her doctor she wanted to see a psychiatrist.

What had happened, of course, was that she'd become extremely angry with her husband. She was angry that he'd 'tricked' her into leaving her job, angry that he'd gone up the mountain to have his first heart attack, angry that he'd put them into this awkward isolated farm house, angry that he opened windows, angry that he went for walks alone, angry that she was stuck in the country and angry that he made her suffer anxiety.

Since her anger seemed to be utterly unreasonable and wicked – of course none of it was his deliberate doing or his fault – she couldn't allow herself to recognize it. The anger manifested itself only in visions of him dead, in the way she experienced headaches, insomnia and indigestion.

The possibility that she might be angry was presented to Mrs P by the psychiatrist. Unpleasing as she found this image of herself, Mrs P was able to accept the suggestion. The solution for her was to get away from home at least one day a week – to have some excitement in life, some external stimulus which could balance the inward-looking, enclosed life in the farmhouse. A day and a night once a week in London, perhaps some part-time work, or work she could do at home, and she'd find her anxiety and impatience decreasing, together with the headaches and other pains. This proved to be the case.

These cases illustrate a fact about human beings. Our own needs are of fundamental importance to us. Unless we nourish ourselves, we cannot indefinitely nourish others without some sort of break-

down. Perhaps this 'selfish' mind has to do with our make-up –
the manner in which we've evolved. Our individual survival is of
paramount importance – whatever the reason, the fact must be
accepted: we can all do a much better job when caring for others
if we ourselves are cared for.

There are, of course, legendary figures, and many ordinary
people, who devote themselves entirely to the care of others, with
utter self-sacrifice. The reward for them, the self-nourishing, comes
to them by way of or through the help and care they give to other
people or creatures. They are made satisfied and happy by seeing
the gratitude of the people they help; by seeing relief and calm in
a face previously distorted by pain and discomfort; by alleviating
hurt – or on a larger scale, by knowing that starving people will
eat because of their efforts or that no child in Africa will die of
smallpox this year. But most of us do find the very demanding
care of others exhausting and draining. Our reserves of good will
need to be 'topped up' regularly. We are, above all, individuals
with a powerful interest in our own survival.

Cruelty

Human beings have an exceptional ability to be cruel. One could
cite an infinite list of man's horrifying acts of inflicting hideous
suffering on other human beings or on other animals. These acts
are often rationalized. The Inquisition existed in the name of Chris-
tianity. Many appalling experiments on animals take place in the
name of 'science'. Brutal tortures are performed for the sake of
Democracy, or Communism, or Fascism. But no human being
could perform these frightful acts unless there were in that individual an unconscious need to be cruel.

How can we explain human cruelty? The natural world is, of
course, to our eyes hideously cruel. Many animals depend for
survival on the killing of other animals. The victims often have to
go through horrible suffering. Yet no animals except ourselves
choose deliberately to cause pain in others. No other animal attacks
another except in response to instinctively motivated attempts to
survive. Human satisfaction or pleasure in causing suffering is
missing in the rest of the animal world.

Many children in our 'normal' Western societies are daily subjected to vicious cruelty by their parents. One mother in recent

times picked up her baby girl and sat the child deliberately on the red-hot plate of an electric stove. Sometimes children are seen in hospital with multiple burn marks from lighted cigarettes, firmly pressed into the skin. Bones are broken, not once in anger, but one after another, time after time. Eyes are blackened in babies' faces. Small screaming children, terrified, are locked in dark cupboards for hours or pushed into drawers which are then shut so that they almost suffocate. Children are starved, deliberately beaten, tormented, often by those, it has to be said, who've been given the same treatment in their own childhood. In exceptional circumstances, children have been tortured for freakish pleasure as have other helpless creatures.

Helplessness on the part of the victim seems an essential ingredient of cruelty. People don't try to be physically cruel to others who are stronger and more powerful than themselves. So is there an element of cowardice in cruelty – or does helplessness excite cruelty?

There's no doubt that 'victims' attract cruelty. A person who's been tormented in childhood tends to attract tormentors all through life.

Cruelly treated children are usually confused and very disturbed. They have difficulty in admitting to a stranger – or even a friend – that a parent has been cruel. They might even deny that cruelty has taken place, in spite of bruises and lacerations. And for some strange reason, people in the outside world are reluctant to interfere.

Nowadays, there's a move to help children by asking teachers to try to act as substitute parents so that they might use their relationship with their little pupils at school to talk about abuses at home. In one school in France recently, seven-year-olds were asked to write about home life. One child wrote, 'The mother loves the father. The father loves the mother. The child loves the parents. How it is then that such things happen?' 'Such things' turned out to be systematic cruelty on the part of the mother to her child. The child was tied to her bed for hours on end on any minor excuse, in such a position so that she couldn't move. If she wanted to empty her bladder she wasn't allowed to go to the lavatory. If she urinated, in despair, where she lay, she was beaten. The father accepted his wife's actions, a passive collaborator. The confusion on the child's part is shown in her little essay. Parents are supposed to love their child. They are supposed to love one another. How could the mother behave like this? How could the father not rescue the child?

'Rescue' is the first immediate solution for the child of cruel parents. Rescue often doesn't take place for one of two reasons. Firstly, as I've described, the child is reluctant to talk about parents' cruelty – even to admit such cruelty to itself. Secondly, neighbours, bystanders, and even spouses are reluctant to interfere, reluctant to call in the authorities to help the child. People in our Western societies tend to deny that parents are often cruel, often abuse their children. Of course, the cruelty has to be of a major nature before the 'authorities', that is, the law, can be brought in. But even in ordinary circumstances, making a parent face exactly what he or she is doing tends to arouse guilt, which may prevent further cruelty; the fact that other people know is sometimes enough to stop a parent's physical cruelty to a child.

The more subtle cruelties are hard to define and hard to stop. Lacerating sarcasm routinely used, mockery, devastating contempt, brutal language – these are often the weapons of cruel parents. The essence of cruelty is a wish to inflict pain or suffering. There is a desire to hurt or even destroy, and a satisfaction in achieving the hurt. Children are easy to hurt, as are prisoners, people tied up with ropes or chains, animals in cages. So how are we to explain that man deliberately chooses to hurt the helpless? And that human beings deliberately think up the most monstrous methods of inflicting pain?

Cruelty is a distortion of aggressive feelings, driven into unconscious mind because of taboo. But all we know for sure is that cruelty and brutality are handed down from generation to generation in one form or other.

A kind man I once knew, a doctor, was savagely treated in his childhood by his father. He was severely beaten for the slightest mistake or naughtiness – over and over again. He grew up vowing that he'd never do the same with his own children. He became a compassionate and caring doctor, married with three sons. The youngest child wet his bed – a condition which most doctors look on as due either to emotional disturbance or congenitally weak muscles of the bladder. Whichever way we look at this problem we don't consider it's the child's deliberate fault. Yet this doctor decided the only way to cure his son of wetting the bed at night was to beat him. And beat him he did, night after night. He told me about this, one day.

'But Bob,' I said in horror. 'You're doing exactly what your father did to you.'

'It's not the same,' he said doggedly. 'The boy's got to learn and I intend to make him dry at night if it kills him.'

And he wouldn't listen to anything else I might have had to say.

But even though the children of brutal and cruel parents sometimes re-enact the cruelty with their own children, there is no excuse for this behaviour. Unlike aggression which is a 'survival' response, cruelty is a conception, a deliberately thought-up plan of how to hurt. The wish to be cruel can be consciously controlled. But cruel parents and cruel people don't very often suffer guilt. They turn away – repress, suppress, rationalize.

Not everyone is capable of great cruelty. Not everyone could administer electric shocks to tied-up prisoners, or beat them up as they stand bound and naked and helpless. Or push their fists into the eyes of babies. But we're all collaborators. We accept the cruelties of others without a protest. We see on the television screen thousands of children and their parents dying of starvation because cruel men won't let the lorries with supplies of food reach these people. Civilized humanity shouldn't allow this. We do.

And sometimes, hearing a neighbour's child screaming frantically, we turn away.

Jealousy

Quite early in my career as a psychotherapist, I remember an occasion when I'd asked to see the father of a disturbed and unhappy child. The main problems for the child were the unrelenting harshness of his father, nagging criticisms, mockery. I'd been making a plea for a greater understanding and tolerance of his son, to which Mr G listened with a gloomy and sour expression. Then, without any warning, he jumped up, crashed his fist down on my desk and shouted: 'I was brought up the hard way! Why should it be any different for him?'

At the time, I was shocked and surprised. Surely fathers fight their way up in life partly in order to give their children a better time than they themselves have had, more privileges, less hardship? But I realized that there are fathers who can't bear the fact that their sons are better off, in childhood, than they were themselves. A few weeks after I'd seen Mr G I asked another father to visit me. This time, the man was much smoother, a company director, a self-made man, a 'whizz kid' of his generation. He heard what I had to say about his frightened, immature and physically fragile adolescent son. Then he went on insisting, against my advice, that the boy must spend a year on the foundry floor as soon as he left school. No, he wasn't to go to university ('I didn't go and I don't see the point of it . . .'). A year working with the men in the steel works was what he needed. 'I had to do it,' said Sir X calmly, 'so why shouldn't he? It'll do him good,' he added with gentle vindictiveness.

I then had to accept that there are parents who are jealous of their children in the same way that we're all jealous of people who are having a better time in life than we ourselves are having – or have had. Naturally, the under-privileged envy the wealthy, the unattractive envy the beautiful, the unsuccessful envy the achievers and so on. These facts apply equally to certain parents. They envy their children for the reasons described. They did not, when young, have the benefits which their children enjoy. Lacking a compensating love and pride in their children, they feel mainly rivalry.

But there are reasons other than sheer envy which make parents jealous of their children. These reasons are to do with a parent's childhood, and his or her experiences of jealousy as a child in relation to his or her siblings. In having children, we re-enact our own childhood. We identify with one or other of our children – the one who seems most to resemble us in looks or temperament, or who has the position in the family which we ourselves held – eldest child, or middle, or youngest, and so on. We might, if we ourselves were nervous or timid as children, identify with the most nervous and timid of our own children.

And if, as children, we were jealous of one of our brothers or sisters, then we assume, unconsciously, that our own child, with whom we've identified, will also be jealous of a brother or sister. For example, if we were the eldest child jealous of the youngest, we'll assume our own eldest child, with whom we've identified, is jealous of his or her youngest sibling. Because, unconsciously, we're reliving our own childhood through the child with whom we've identified, we'll feel hostile and jealous on his or her behalf towards the relevant member of the family. We'll tend to cosset and protect our 'second self' and feel hostile to the 'next generation' sibling. The reasons for our feelings are almost always unconscious. We may even be particularly unpleasant to the child representing the sibling of whom we, as children, were jealous, paying off old scores for painful experiences in the past.

Here's an illustration of what might be called second-hand jealousy. Joyce B was the eldest child in her family, the cherished daughter. For many years, she was the only child, the central figure in the family, adored by her father, spoilt by her mother. But when she was eight years old, her mother became unexpectedly pregnant and gave birth to a splendid son.

Within a few months, Joyce's father died of a heart attack. Joyce's mother, mourning and lonely, began to focus all her love and attention on Peter, the little boy. Joyce was of course at school all day but even when she was at home she found herself brushed aside in favour of Peter. She grew to hate Peter with a fervent and vehement jealousy.

Many years later, Joyce married and had her own children. She was delighted with the first, a pretty girl. After a couple of years, she had another child. Even while pregnant she began to dread the birth and felt aggressive to the creature in her womb. When the child was born – another girl – she developed a quite violent dislike of her. Later she had a third child, a meek little boy, and felt the same angry hostility as she did for the second girl.

We must assume that she'd identified unconsciously with the elder girl, reliving her own role in childhood. The second daughter received the hostility she'd felt for her brother Peter X. Even though this child was a girl it took on the rôle of usurper of the eldest child's position.

Joyce's attitude to her two younger children was cruel and bitter. Her feelings of jealousy were partly on her own account and partly for Cynthia, the eldest child. She managed to make Cynthia feel extremely threatened by her younger sister and brother. Joyce stood calmly by while Cynthia ill-treated her siblings, feeling rather pleased if the little ones suffered.

Joyce had no insight as to the origin of her feelings. All she knew was that if either of the younger children did well at anything, she felt a sick anger. She found it unbearable if a friend or a neighbour praised one or the other. The younger children had to share all privileges with Cynthia. Neither could be given a present or even a bar of chocolate unless Cynthia had one too. Joyce's whole life in relation to her children was acted out as if she were Cynthia and the younger children were Peter.

I've described an extreme case of childhood emotions being activated when a parent has her own children. But it's normal for people to identify, unconsciously, with the child or children who represent their own role in early life. This may have no serious consequences for the children – but if there have been problems of jealousy in the parent's childhood, they're likely to be repeated the 'second time around'.

Another reason for a parent's jealousy of a child is related to sexual feelings. If a daughter is adored like a lover by her father and the mother feels she's taking second place, the mother is bound to feel jealous of her child. The same, of course, applies to fathers, who might be jealous of a special relationship between sons and mothers. Mother/son sexual relationships and similarly father/daughter relationships are known as oedipal, because of Oedipus, who killed his father and married his mother. The Oedipus legend focuses on the mother–son love affair – but it begins with the King, father of Oedipus, having heard the soothsayer's warnings, ordering that his baby should be taken out on the hills and left to die. Paternal jealousy on account of the son–mother relationship is very common. I discussed this in greater detail on pages 88–90.

Fathers are also jealous of their children because the children take up their mother's time and energy. A father coming home at night after a hard day's work may want his wife to himself, but finds he has to share her with squalling infants, or howling two-year-olds, or sick five-year-olds. And usually, the children come first, which is bound to irritate the breadwinner and arouse in him an angry jealousy: 'Why aren't the children in bed by the time I get home?'

But neither sexual jealousy nor the jealousy of fathers pushed out of the limelight have such an enveloping, devastating effect as simple but intense envy. Both sexual jealousy and the jealousy caused by a mother putting the children first allow room for a parent to love at the same time as feel jealous of his children.

Children are, of course, sensitive to parental jealousy, just as they perceive, usually unconsciously, the hostility of parents for reasons other than jealousy. The jealousy is usually perceived unconsciously because the parent normally is not fully aware of the fact that he or she feels jealous of the child. The notion that a parent is jealous of his or her children is repugnant in our society. Parents aren't supposed to have such feelings – and so, as a rule, the parent tries to suppress jealousy for children. Thus the jealousy becomes unconscious and the messages from parents to child pass from unconscious mind to unconscious mind. How can a child cope with intense jealousy on the part of one of its parents? One way is to try to diminish the parent's jealousy by reducing the need for jealousy. That's to say, if a child's excellence excites jealousy, the child must stop being excellent. The child tries not to excite jealousy by keeping a low profile, making sure never to outshine the parent.

If a child's beauty excites a parent's jealousy, the child must become less beautiful. Beauty can be diminished by putting on excess weight – or by starving so as to look a haggard skeleton. We are also able to disfigure ourselves by causing infections in the skin, pulling at hairs on the face with dirty tweezers, scratching, rubbing. Sometimes a child will pull out, hair by hair, the eyebrows and the hair on the head. A child may be accident-prone, falling, breaking bones, maiming itself. By disabling itself, the child is able to dispel, temporarily, a parent's jealousy.

Here's the story of one such child, Charles B. It illustrates a response to parental jealousy which is not unusual in its theme, although details vary of course from person to person. The doctor on duty in the accident ward of the district hospital at once recognized the name of Charles B, the man who was taken out of the ambulance, because every now and then his name appeared in the newspapers. Take-over bids, the Queen's Award for Industry, astronomical exports, it was in connection with these he was mentioned. Everyone knew he'd started with nothing and was a millionaire by the time he was forty.

Charles B had had a lucky escape. Driving too fast at night along a dark country road with three times the legal limit of alcohol in his blood, he'd lost control of his car and crashed into a tree. He was shocked and dazed and had some fractured ribs, but was otherwise not seriously hurt. In addition to the drink, he'd taken a number of tranquillizers to calm him from cocaine-induced agitation. What with alcohol and the drugs his licence to drive was later withdrawn for a year. What with that and the pain in his broken ribs he decided to accept his doctor's advice and see a psychiatrist, something he'd always refused in the past.

He was asked if he had any special worries. Immediately, he was upset and anxious because his wife and his mother were having a series of dreadful rows. His wife couldn't stand his mother, he said, which he found very disturbing and she – the wife – was always trying to pick a quarrel with his mother. This made Charles B extremely anxious.

Anything else? Yes – funnily enough the same kind of thing was happening with his old cat, Sheila. They'd bought a new puppy – a big bouncing retriever – and Sheila kept snarling and spitting. Charles B was afraid the dog would lose its cool and savage Sheila. There were no other immediate worries – the usual business things but nothing, he felt, that was out of control.

He agreed that he'd been drinking rather heavily for years – and sniffing coke in the last few years. He'd tried to give it up when he got married – but couldn't manage it. He and his wife had a child – a little girl. He adored her. He thought it just as well that it was a girl – he wasn't sure how he'd feel about a son.

His story was that he was an only child. His parents weren't well off (he'd now made them very comfortable), but in his childhood they hadn't been impoverished. His father worked in a bank but had never really succeeded in improving his position, although he was an intelligent man. His mother didn't go out to work; she looked after the home. She was, however, stronger and tougher than his father, mentally as well as physically. 'She wore the pants,' said Charles B, with a rather nervous smile.

Charles thought he took after his mother rather than his father – but he didn't think he was as bossy and dominating as she was. When he was a child you did what she told you – his father did the same. If she said wear your thick underwear, you did it even if it was a warm day and you'd suffer. You changed your socks and had a bath when she said, all that kind of thing. 'Yes,' he said, 'I suppose I was a bit afraid of her – maybe I still am. Yes – perhaps that's why I get so upset when my wife upsets her . . .'

What had been disappointing was that his father hadn't supported him against her. His father just wasn't interested in him – never had been from the start – even when his mother was being really unreasonable. He couldn't remember his father ever playing games with him; he had never taken him to football or cricket like other fathers did. As a child Charles B had spent most of his leisure time alone, kicking a ball around the back yard, wishing he had a brother or a sister.

While we were talking, various forgotten incidents came into his mind. When he was eleven years old, one of his school teachers must have realized what was going on at home. She made Charles do a test. She sent for his parents and showed them, in front of Charles, the result of the test and told them they had a very clever son. If they encouraged him to work hard he might go far. She thought he ought to try for a scholarship at one of the best schools in the district. His parents had listened in silence until she mentioned the scholarship, when they'd exclaimed, 'We don't particularly want him to get a scholarship. We don't think he should be bothered with exams. All we want,' they said, 'is for him to be happy.' He could go in the bank like his father had and that was good enough.

He remembered that this father had never, ever, given him a present. His mother had been the one to buy and give the present on Christmas and birthdays. She had tended to give Charles useful things like shirts and socks, and not things that were fun.

He remembered that she'd once given him a doll for his birthday. He didn't know what to make of it. Maybe she really wanted it for herself, he had thought, bought it and then decided to give it to him.

It dawned on him when he was a bit older that if he was going to get anywhere he'd have to do it under his own steam. They weren't going to help him. He began to work hard and managed to get himself to university, though they made him feel quite guilty about not earning money to help them out. Still – he'd stuck to his guns and now, of course, he was looking after them. Financially, that was.

He remembered when he'd done his first big deal – in South America it was; he'd come home very excited and he went to see them straight off the aeroplane. He found his Dad reading the football news in front of the living-room fire. 'Dad,' he said, 'I've just come back from Brazil. I've done a deal which will make me half a million dollars.' His father didn't look up from the paper. 'Oh yes?' he said, 'I see Arsenal lost their match on Saturday . . .' Charles went into the kitchen where his mother was making the tea.

'I've just finished a deal in South America,' he said. 'I've made 500,000 dollars.'

She looked angry. 'You'll be getting too big for your boots, then, won't you Charlie?' Then she said, 'Here, take this to your father,' as she handed him the tray with the cups. No more was said; no questions, no applause.

He didn't mention the matter again and decided not to tell them about his successes. Yes, he'd been drinking for a long time – since he was at university, he thought looking back on it. 'But at least I don't smoke,' he added with a placatory smile as if he fully understood that alcohol had a destructive if not lethal effect. Recently, since the rows between his wife and his mother, he'd been drinking more. He felt very agitated and the drink seemed to calm him. And he worried about the cat . . . although that might seem absurd. . . .

It's perhaps obvious that Charles B was unconsciously trying to deflect his parents' jealousy. His father was particularly envious of him; his mother angry. It transpired, in the course of his therapy, that she had longed for a girl and was deeply disappointed at Charles's birth. Throughout his childhood Charles had hoped, unconsciously, that by being very good and very meek and passive he might keep his parents' hostility at a low level. By doing only moderately well at school, by being 'good' and by making no demands he had found a strategy which allayed vengeful behaviour on his father's part.

When he realized on a conscious level that, if he wanted to improve his lot, he'd have to make efforts on his own behalf and managed to get himself to university, an unconscious fear made him try to damage himself by drinking. It's as if he'd been passing a message to his father which read: 'I may be doing well in one way, but in another I'm destroying myself so you don't have to be jealous . . .' This compensatory self-destruction is not uncommon in children anxious not to arouse a jealous parent's hostility. There were, in fact, other ways in which Charles had hoped to reassure his parents that he wasn't doing very well, even though successful at his business.

He didn't marry until a comparatively late age, instead being careful to visit his parents extremely regularly, bringing them presents and attending to their needs. As soon as he was able, he bought them a comfortable house, installed them in it, and gave them a substantial income. Everything he had he shared with them. When he did marry, they found a hundred reasons to object to his fiancée and almost refused to attend the wedding.

Now that there was trouble between his wife and his mother, that is, now that his mother was incited to rage by his wife, he felt inwardly terrified, and he identified with the cat, who by being provocative to the dog, might be savagely done to death. People who seem to be doing well in one direction but very badly in others may have, or have had, the problem of a jealous parent. Sometimes illness is offered as a sop, sometimes an accident is unconsciously planned, but the underlying theme is always the same: 'You don't need to be jealous – there's nothing to be jealous of – look at me – I'm a wreck . . .'

A parent's jealousy may be unconscious. In the case of Charles B's parents, his father might almost have had a glimmering of insight about his feelings. He might have thought, 'Why can't Charles be satisfied doing the same thing I've done? I've always had a steady job, earned enough for the family; why should he want more?' But there are some parents who are so guilty about jealousy they'd never allow such a notion to surface. In them, their depriving or hostile behaviour to their children must be rationalized. For example:

Mrs Linda G refused to allow her pretty daughter to wear lipstick and other make-up when every other girl in the form was doing so. She refused to let her have fashionable clothes and fashionable shoes. She said in defence of her attitude: 'Cindy's got her whole life ahead of her. She's got years and years when she can wear make-up. If I let her start now it cuts short her childhood.' Mrs Linda G may have been right about this – or not as the case may be. But the point was that all Cindy's contemporaries were allowed make-up. Cindy was the odd one out, felt foolish, ugly, and ill-treated. She was, in fact, thoroughly unhappy over what seemed, perhaps, a trivial matter. But the trivial matter had its roots in Mrs G's jealousy, which Cindy sensed, feeling she was a victim. Mrs G was really holding Cindy back from changing from a child to a young woman – an extremely attractive young woman, far prettier than Linda G had ever been herself.

It's not uncommon to hear it said by mothers about their daughters, 'We're like sisters', which may sometimes (not always) indicate a buried jealousy. A mother may find it hard to acknowledge the generation difference, and may be reluctant to take on the role of ageing mother to her daughter's brilliant youthfulness.

Lack of success (or fading beauty) aren't the only reasons for a parent's jealousy. Many a parent who's reached a high peak of success is reluctant to allow a child to enter the field of his or her own talent, fearing that the child, in competition with themselves, might do better than they've done. Writers of bestsellers, world-famous musicians and artists, lawyers, administrators, explorers. . . . there have been those who have felt hostile to children 'following in their footsteps'. They may try to dissuade a child from a career similar to their own on spurious grounds – how hard it is, how difficult to make a living, and so on. The truth is perhaps that no one likes to share the limelight. The star wants to remain the star. The lion, even though ageing, wants to be the only lion.

PART THREE

Adverse Circumstances in a Child's Life

Disadvantages, accidents and emotional deprivations are common in our world. There are many occurrences in family life when children are damaged by parents involuntarily – parents who haven't the slightest wish or need to hurt their children. But parents have their own lives to lead. Parents feel the need to extricate themselves from unhappy marriages. Parents may become ill, mentally or physically, or die through illness or accident. Parents may be unemployed or disabled. Parents may need to be absent from home because their work takes them away. Such situations and the ensuing effects on children are described in the following chapters.

NINE

Loss of a Parent

'My mother died when I was four . . .'

'My mother died when I was two . . .'

'My parents were divorced when I was six . . .'

'My father remarried three times . . . so I had several step-mothers and lots of half-brothers and sisters . . .'

'My father left us when I was five . . .'

'My mother went off with another man when I was nine and I never saw her again . . . I think she wanted to see us after a few years but I believe my father wouldn't let her . . .'

'My mother died when I was two. My father couldn't cope with us five children. We were all put in a home. He went off. I didn't see him again till I was seventeen . . .'

'My father died when I was four; my brother was three. My mother didn't want to be saddled with young children. She put us in a boarding school for orphans . . .'

'My parents were divorced. I don't remember my father. I was too young when it happened. He went away and married again, I was told . . .'

'My parents lived in India. They didn't think it was a good idea to bring us up there – illness – the climate – I don't know why. We were sent back to England. I was four, my brother seven. We stayed in a kind of boarding school for children whose parents were abroad. The other children were all older than I was. I didn't see my parents again for two years, when they came home on leave . . .'

'My mother brought me up. I never knew my father . . .'

These and similar stories are commonplace in any psychiatric consulting room. Loss of a parent often results in long-term or recurrent emotional instability. Our modern Western societies, with small families living in comparatively isolated one-family

houses or apartments, make children very dependent on the continuing presence of two parents, father and mother. The more
extended style of family life, such as still exists in Asia or Africa,
includes grandparents, uncles, aunts, cousins, who may all take
part in the care and bringing up of small children. A child has
then a collection of parent-like people with whom to relate. But in
the West a child must go through all the phases of its emotional
development interacting with only its two parents – and sometimes,
a single parent. The concept holds in our societies that the two
'real' parents are the most suitable people to care for a child. This
concept may be based on false premises. It's possible that foster
parents, grandparents, friends or relations might make excellent
substitutes for parents – and certainly do so, often, when 'real'
parents are absent or are cruel and damaging to their children. If
the notion that substitute parents could do as well as 'real' parents
for children were generally accepted, life would be made easier for
many children – and many parents.

As it is, the concept holds in our Western societies that every
child has the right to have two 'real' or natural parents. If a parent
is missing, the child feels 'bad', 'losing out', different to others,
'deprived'.

The concept that 'real' parents are the best parents also tends to
make people who adopt a child feel, consciously or unconsciously,
uneasy, perhaps even slightly guilty. This may be reflected in the
way they manage the child and their feelings may be unconsciously
transmitted to the child, unconsciously received.

Every child does need male and female figures around it, to
whom to attach its love, its sexual feelings, its anger and other
emotions – and with whom to identify. But perhaps a collection of
such figures would fulfil these needs, a child taking from or giving
to each and all those who surround it.

As it is, parents in our society – and particularly single parents
– bear tremendous responsibility for the physical and mental needs
of their children – a wearing and often disturbing state of affairs.
In these circumstances, if a child loses a parent by death or divorce,
or because a parent or parents abandon the child or children, the
result is devastating.

Death

Apart from the shattering grief and the sense of insecurity which follow the loss of a parent, a very young child who can't understand death, or any other reason for parent's disappearance, concludes the parent didn't want to stay. So logically the child has to believe that he or she wasn't sufficiently attractive, beautiful, valuable – or any other rationalized notion of self – to hold the parent. The child is left, then, with a sense of inadequacy which remains with it for life.

The sorrow and uncertainty may be aggravated and complicated by the parent disappearing at a crucial, critical moment in a child's life. At that moment there may be a particular need for the parent to help the child resolve a transitory emotional phase, a mood, say of hostility, or a period of intense sexual attachment which would normally pass and give way to other feelings and attachments.

The death of a parent removes, of course, all possibilities of ever coming to terms with, or resolving, an emotional crisis. A temporary anger, a mood of aggression – parent to child, or child to parent – which would have come to an end, remains for ever in the child's mind, entombed like a fly in amber, to give pain for a lifetime.

I can think of three cases when death of a parent – or of both parents – left children with an intolerable load of guilt which very nearly wrecked their lives. The first was a ten-year-old girl who, in a row with her mother, who was frustrating her, screamed, as children often do, 'I wish you were dead!' Horrifically, her mother did die, very suddenly, shortly after this quarrel. Her death was caused by a haemorrhage in her brain due to an abnormality in an artery, which she'd had since birth. Her daughter felt, of course, that she'd murdered her mother. We all have a tendency to believe in magic, in the supernatural power of feelings or words, and children are particularly liable to believe that feelings of aggression can kill. Had the mother lived on, of course, she and her daughter would certainly have resolved the row, which would have brought peace to the child.

The second case was of two small boys, nine and eleven years old. The parents had decided to take a short weekend trip to Paris – just to be on their own together for once. The children were to be left with an aunt whom they didn't like. There was a row. The children were angry. The parents, feeling a little guilty, were angry in return. The general mood as they left the house was of mutual hostility. The parents had meant to telephone on arrival in Paris but there'd been difficulties in timing the call and, as they were due to return the next day, they'd decided to leave it.

The aircraft in which they were travelling on the return journey crashed, killing all passengers and crew. The children were left with an unresolved quarrel and they, too, half believed their angry feelings had been responsible for the parents' deaths.

The hostility in both the cases I've described was not of course only the anger of the immediate quarrel. It was deeper and older, mingled with love and sexual feelings, oedipal jealousies and passions in the children. Death made it impossible for the children to come to terms with their feelings about their parents. They were left in a highly disturbed state, agitated, grief-stricken, bereft – and guilty, full of remorse for their anger before the parents went away. They both became severely depressed – a depression which was likely to recur later in their lives.

The third person to suffer a devastating loss of her parents was a child of the Hitler era. Her parents were Czechoslovakian Jews. Her father had died when she was five. She and her mother lived together in difficult circumstances. The apartment was small. The mother hoped to remarry, found the child a burden, was often rejecting, impatient and irritable. The child in response was, of course, unhappy, cried a great deal, sulked and was angry with the mother. Hitler's army invaded Czechoslovakia. The Germans herded the Jews to the concentration camps. They were driven in lorries, like cattle, crowded together rocking and swaying as the lorries lurched. Some fell, were trampled upon by the others, and died. One of these was the child's mother. Did the child also trample on her mother's body? She was terrified she might have done. So not only did she have to survive the horror of the concentration camp – but also the horror that she might have helped to kill her mother. She did survive, but deep depression blackened her life for years.

The cases described may seem extreme, but the essential event, the loss of a parent at a crucial moment, is not uncommon. Children begin to be very vulnerable to the departure of parents at about the age of six months – a time when permanent emotional damage may be done a child by the absence of parents for any length of time – even a holiday.

Every phase of a child's development has different needs – but all phases require the presence of parents or parent figures. If a parent vanishes, there's a strong tendency on the part of the abandoned child to search, unconsciously or consciously, for parent substitutes. Sometimes little children try to 'take over' the parents of their friends, embarrassingly climbing on laps, holding hands, clinging to parent figures who appeal to them. The process may go on for a lifetime, children and adults searching endlessly for parent figures. So young girls fall in love with old men, young men marry women old enough to be their mothers. Like Orpheus in the underworld, bereaved children search among ghosts and shadows for the image of the lost loved ones.

Divorce

If children find it hard to survive the death of a parent, they sometimes find it even harder to survive their parents' divorce. Many, many divorcing parents, who are filled with hate and anger and longing for revenge, use their children to punish their spouses. The children are dragged into the quarrels and the courts and are made to take sides. Being forced to take the side of one parent or the other happens to children quite often, of course, in ordinary domestic quarrels. Sometimes parents fight bitterly with one another throughout a long, wretched marriage without ever divorcing. Children are inevitably involved and are inevitably damaged. But the side-taking in divorce has an official, legal stamp to it. Parents battle in the courts as to who should have custody of the children, who should have care and control.

Older children are sometimes taken to a court official and asked to say with which parent they'd rather live – or whether or not they wish to visit one parent or the other of separated parents – and to give their reasons for their wishes. Mothers sometimes lock the door against fathers who've come to fetch their children for the legally permitted weekend. Fathers sometimes refuse to return children to the mother (who has 'care' and 'control') after the permitted weekend or holiday. Parents 'kidnap' their children from the divorced or separated spouses. Parents go back again and again to solicitors complaining about the spouse and his or her behaviour to the children during the permitted time they had together. Children are always aware of the tug-of-war – and war it is. One particular case of this kind of battle stands out in my mind. A famous actress, Electra G, went through a divorce with an equally famous whizzkid businessman who'd fallen in love with another woman. Sunny G, the businessman, was very fond of his children, but he hated his ex-wife. She used her three children (all girls) to torment and enrage Sunny, while he used his power and wealth to try to lure the children away from Electra.

Electra's main aim in life was to persuade her daughters to refuse to see their father and to get a court order forbidding him to see them. She came to see me in the hopes that, after hearing her story which included lurid details about Sunny's sex life, I'd write a report to say he was an unsuitable father and it was harmful for his daughters to have any contact with him. (In fact, very few parents are 'unsuitable' or harmful or dangerous for their children to the point of being forbidden by law to have any contact with them.)

Electra's story included descriptions of how ill the children were after they'd been to stay with Sunny and his new wife, how nervous they'd become, how their schoolwork had deteriorated and how unhappy they were when they knew they had to see their father.

I asked to see the children. They came. I saw them first all together. They sat in a row on the sofa and stared at me. I looked at those three young faces, uncertain, troubled, innocent and defiant. They knew what they were supposed to say and we all knew they'd been heavily primed by their mother before leaving home. My heart sank for them. We talked – generally at first, then about the crucial subject. There were conflicting views. Gradually they became animated. It seemed the middle daughter was the most opposed to seeing her father.

'Daddy was very unkind to Betty on our last visit,' explained Samantha, the eldest, in serious tones.

'How unkind?'

'Well, you see, he wanted us to go and see the horses – which I love and so does Dolly [the youngest] but Betty doesn't like them so you see she didn't want to go and they had this argument and then Daddy hit her . . .'

'Hit her?'

'Well, sort of – he sort of pushed her . . .'

'No, he hit me,' said Betty adamantly.

'Well, then she went for a long walk by the lake by herself and then Daddy sulked and in the end none of us went to see the horses, which was sad for Dolly' – she indicated the littlest girl – 'and me . . .'

'Is it really bad enough at Daddy's for you never to go there again, or at least for a long time?'

At this Dolly burst into tears and said she *did* want to see Daddy and go and stay with him.

There was silence while she wiped her tears and the other two looked uncomfortable. I talked with each separately and came to the firm conclusion that things at Sunny's weekend farm weren't so terrible that the children should be deprived of their father and he of them. As a result of which I wrote a report which Electra destroyed. She then refused to pay my bill.

I say that 'things were not so terrible' at Sunny's farm – but I knew perfectly well that while the children were with him he tried to buy their affection and turn them against their mother. To this end he kept Electra, who had given up acting for the last few years, as short of money as he possibly could, so that she seemed like the depriving one when she had to say no to the girls' extravagant demands.

Parents play all sorts of games when using children as weapons in divorce suits, all of them disreputable and very destructive. Even when parents behave in a responsible and civilized way over the divorce, the shuttle backwards and forwards from one parental home to the other is difficult and sometimes painful for little children. Adolescents too, beginning a life of their own, find it boring and disruptive to abandon friends, work and social engagements over the weekend or holidays when they *have* to go and stay with Dad, or Mum as the case may be. 'Have to go' is the operative phrase. Children are sometimes treated like parcels.

'Do I have to go?'

'Yes, you must.'

'Why?'

'Daddy/Mummy expects you. It's his/her weekend.'

'But I'm supposed to go to this party!'

'Never mind. You're going to Daddy/Mummy. There'll be other parties.'

One of the saddest aspects of divorce is the tendency of children of divorced parents to break up their own home by a divorce when, later in life, they marry and have children. Sometimes people who've been through the break-up of their parents' marriage feel a compulsion to divorce even though there's no very serious, conscious reason to do so. Here's an example:

A lawyer asked me to see a young married couple, Edith and Daniel, who'd consulted him because Edith was demanding a divorce. The lawyer was puzzled because he couldn't really understand why Edith felt she must break up her marriage and, in addition, leave her children with Daniel. Very often, when a man or woman suddenly demands a divorce, without any very grave difficulties in the marriage, there's a lover in the background – but here Edith quite definitely had no other man in her life.

So Edith came to see me first. She was a good-looking, well-dressed young woman but she looked confused, lacked confidence, was rather child-like, and half-defiant as if she had her back to the wall. She was absolutely determined to divorce, she told me, and then burst into tears.

When she'd calmed down, we went on talking gently. She was obviously frightened by what she planned to do but somehow felt driven to go ahead. I asked her why she felt so strongly that she must leave Daniel and the children?

She found it hard to say. She rambled on with a few unconvincing complaints about her husband. He was unstable, she thought, had lost some money on the stock exchange, couldn't make up his mind whether they were to live in London or Devon (they'd previously lived in Kenya where he'd had a job lasting several years). Now his firm had given him a choice as to where he wanted to work.

'Any other complaints about Daniel?' I asked.

She thought for a while. 'He's . . . difficult,' she said, rather vaguely.

'What about the children?'

They were fine. There were four of them, the youngest aged three. She intended to leave them with her husband.

'In spite of his being unstable?'

He could give them a much better home than she could, she said.

'Even the youngest?'

She became tearful again.

Daniel was better at looking after them than she was. She wanted to go to work. She longed to go off to work. She desperately needed to have a job.

Couldn't she work without leaving home?

She didn't think so.

As our talk went on, it became clear there were no very good reasons for Edith's wish to leave her husband. He was a kind, sensitive man. There were no serious money problems, no sexual difficulties, no great incompatibilities.

He came to see me. A serious young man, good-looking like his wife, and also a little nervous and under-confident but capable, I thought, and energetic. He was very upset at the prospect of divorce, loved Edith dearly, he said, and couldn't really understand what she was complaining about. It was true that she found the children difficult and that she'd seemed very low in recent times. If she was determined to go, he said, he would cope with the children, whom he also loved very much. But did I think they must be divorced? I said it wasn't for me to decide that, but that I'd see Edith again. Perhaps a separation for six months was a better idea.

He brightened at that possibility and Edith visited me again.

Surely she didn't want to abandon her three-year-old child, I asked her. She became tearful again. It then transpired that that was exactly what her mother had done to her, gone off, when she was three years old, to live elsewhere, abandoned her husband and all her children. Her mother had then started a small business which it seemed was very successful, but she hadn't seen her children again until they were grown up.

'I think she probably wanted to,' said Edith, 'but my father made difficulties. I see her now. We've got quite a good relationship.'

'Are you thinking of not seeing *your* children?' I asked.

'No, no, I want to go on seeing my children,' Edith protested. It was just that she felt now she must get away from home.

'What about a separation?'

'No, it must be a divorce.'

Edith felt compelled to divorce. She was driven by a profound, unconscious need to re-enact her own situation in childhood. Her compulsion was stronger than her conscious reason. Her parents had divorced because her father had been a dominating, almost tyrannical man and her mother, able and creative, had felt stifled by him. Edith's mother had been restless and irresponsible as regards her children during her whole marriage, having had a very bad relationship with *her* mother.

But Edith herself didn't have her mother's reasons for wanting a divorce. She had, in fact, almost no reason, except the unconscious drive to repeat what her mother had done. In the end, it was agreed that Edith would leave home and live in a furnished flat for a while to start a little secretarial agency. Daniel would buy a house with a garden and have the children. Edith would visit them – have one or two of them over at weekends. And they'd all have holidays together. This arrangement was to last six months to a year and then they'd review the situation. A compromise – but better than a violent break-up as far as the children were concerned. At least they'd see both parents, and both parents would try to preserve some harmony in their relationship with one another.

It is very important, when a marriage breaks up, for the parents to try to remain on reasonable terms with one another, for the children's sake. Children do become very disturbed if the parents are at war, if they have to take sides, and if one or other parent looks downtrodden and wretched.

Children have a bad enough time on their own account in the break-up of their home without having to feel deeply sorry for one or other of their parents, as is sometimes the case. A child may identify with the miserable parent and later unconsciously arrange its own life in misery as a re-enactment of the parent's condition.

There is absolutely no way of saving children distress and anxiety when their parents divorce, but the children's plight is made easier if the parents remain friends, remain in a good state of emotional and physical health, and they continue to see their children frequently – and also, if they remain accessible to their children. Those children who are old enough to use a telephone should be given the number of the absent parent. And those who are too young to use the telephone should be helped to do so by an adult so that they may talk to Daddy or Mummy often. If a kind of frame can be created, however rickety, within which relationships between both parents and all the children remain good, children are to some extent saved immediate pain and have a better chance of preserving their own marriages later in life.

Abandonment

Children abandoned by a parent who has gone to live elsewhere, and seems not to want to see the children ever again, have a special problem. Not only is there an intense sense of being 'not good enough' to hold the parent's interest and love, there's an additional tantalizing rationalization that 'there must be some mistake . . .'

Abandoned children have always in their mind – usually buried in unconscious mind – that somewhere in the world there lives a person who is their parent. One day, they'll meet again. Then it will be proved there was some mistake. The parent does, after all, love the child. One marvellous day, walking along the street, or in a foreign city, or somewhere in a crowd, or in a friend's house, a stranger will appear – and coming forward, will embrace the child and say, 'You are my loved child. At last I've found you . . .'

This image haunts many, if not all, abandoned children all their lives. The thought that their fathers or mothers felt so little love for them that they could disappear and never wish to see their children again is unbearable for most people.

This fantasy originates from the widely held, quite false concept that all parents love their children. How much better for abandoned children to allow themselves to feel anger and contempt for parents so utterly lacking in responsibility and decency as to leave helpless small creatures without a scruple as to the harm they're doing. In the course of psychotherapy, abandoned children are helped to see that the parent was the inadequate person, not the child.

But, of course, the parent also had probably been an abandoned child, driven relentlessly by an inner and unconscious compulsion to re-enact the pattern. So the events are repeated, again and again, generation after generation. The patterns hold – more cruelly, more powerfully than conscious love, pity and common sense.

TEN

Separation: Birth and Other Partings

A patient of mine once told me that the only time she felt really at peace, really free of anxiety, was when she was pregnant. From the middle of her pregnancy, when she could feel the child moving in her womb, till the moment of the delivery of the child, she felt safe, contented, marvellously calm. This was a time when mother and child were joined together, each firmly held to the other, when the mother could not escape from the child nor the child from the mother. There was blissful security for the child and the same could be said of the mother in her relationship with her child. In a sense, the child had perfect control of the mother and vice versa.

The moment the child was born, my patient lost her feeling of peace and calm and became again a person suffering almost permanent and severe anxiety and depression. Mother and child were separated for ever. The symbolism of giving birth, the cutting of the umbilical cord was distressing for my patient who was reminded, unconsciously, of the awful difficulties of her childhood.

Shortly after Linda was born, her mother, a highly disturbed and erratic woman, set off on what she called 'a well-deserved holiday'. This separation – which, of course my patient, Linda, couldn't remember, but which must have affected her – was followed by many others, throughout Linda's infancy and childhood.

Not only did her mother disappear fairly frequently on little trips, she was extremely unreliable about coming home from daily outings to see her daughter. Linda was left in the care of an old housekeeper who wasn't very efficient and grumbled a great deal. An only child, she wandered about the house and garden with the old family Labrador as her sole companion. Her mother might often say she'd be home at a certain time but, in fact, could turn up hours late. Linda would go through agonies of anxiety wondering if her mother would ever come back. On occasions her mother would suddenly decide to spend a night with her own mother who lived miles away. She'd telephone the housekeeper who might or might not let Linda know until late in the evening that her mother wasn't coming home. To add to Linda's difficulties her father was a businessman who travelled abroad very often.

Those nights when Linda's mother stayed away were often times when her father was abroad. Linda, a very frightened child, terrified of the dark, would lie awake at night, listening to creaks and rustles in the old house, knowing that the housekeeper, who slept in a room far from hers, couldn't hear her even if she screamed.

One dreadful day, Linda's father died suddenly on a trip to France. Linda was very fond of him although he was a rather remote figure in her life – but he was kind and, when at home, much more reliable than her mother.

It's easy to understand why Linda found such marvellous calm in the re-enactment of the mother–child relationship in terms of pregnancy. Apart from a most unlikely late miscarriage, there was no separating of mother and child until the moment of birth.

Birth is sometimes said to be a severe emotional trauma to the child. The act of being born must, of course, be a physical and mental shock to the baby. The child is pushed and pulled out of the comforting darkness, the calm silence and weightless ease of the warm womb, into a cold and noisy world. In a few moments, every nerve cell must spring into action, ready to deal at once with a bewildering range of physical stimuli of a disturbing kind. Searing air enters its expanding lungs. Strong hands grasp its soft body. It may even be slapped to make it cry so as to increase the depth of its breathing. But the 'trauma' of birth shouldn't be exaggerated. Mammalian birth has taken place on earth for the last seventy million years. In terms of evolution, it's one of the safest and most successful means of producing healthy offspring. Birth might certainly shock a child, but the shock will stimulate body and mind to accommodate themselves to the 'real' world. Emerging from the womb is *Homo sapiens sapiens*, triumphant outcome of four million years of trial and error, latest descendent of hominid ancestors, cousin of the apes. We tend to forget this fact when a baby is born and may underestimate its hardiness, its equipment for survival.

The real trauma of separation has more to do with the emotions and behaviour of mothers – and fathers. Another patient of mine was a woman who had many children. She would have had many more but her husband became adamant after the birth of the fifth. Like Linda, whom I described above, she'd had a very insecure childhood. Her mother had been a businesswoman, hardly ever at home – and even when she was at home she had little time for her daughter. Unlike Linda, Frances found her greatest satisfaction in looking after infants. Pregnancy itself was not comforting to her. She identified with the baby once it was born and her joy came from caring for it marvellously well. She would hang over the cradle, emanating boundless love towards the little creature. However, problems occurred when the child grew older and wanted to develop its own identity. And serious emotional difficulties arose when the child was old enough to go to nursery school. This was a separation Frances found almost unbearable. She communicated unconsciously and silently her anxieties and miseries to her child who, unconsciously receiving her messages, then refused to be left at school, screaming and imploring and clinging to her mother. The child had to be dragged from its mother in the end and the trauma was severe for both of them. Once her children became really independent, Frances's passion for them diminished. Her obsession lay in re-enacting a mother–child relationship in the form of deeply loving and caring mother, helpless and dependent infant.

Separation from parents does sometimes cause huge and almost unbearable anxiety in very insecure children even if the parents are only out for the evening. This is particularly the case if one parent, usually the mother, is hostile to the child, so that the child may feel, unconsciously, that the mother is capable of abandoning it totally. Will the mother ever come home again, the child wonders as the hours go by? And panic grips the child. Once a person has become very sensitive to separation, partings of any kind become deeply disturbing, as they are symbolic of the original appalling partings. Some people find it hard to say 'goodbye' in almost any situation, but particularly to someone of whom they're fond.

Yet once the 'pattern' of separations has been formed by childhood experience, extraordinarily enough, a person might unconsciously arrange to be involved in relationships where separations are inevitable. Women become entangled with married men who are always going back to their wives. Men fall in love with married women who are committed to their husbands, although prepared to have an 'affair'. So the pain of the earlier partings is relived in the present.

There are other relationships where repeated partings must take place. Airline pilots, journalists, actors and actresses, and explorers are often if not always on the move. Such partners are unerringly sought out by those whose early experiences form a pattern of 'separations'.

It's not as if such relationships, once established and fulfilling the pattern, provide satisfaction or happiness. On the contrary, those who suffered from separation from parents in childhood are those who complain most and feel most disturbed by the journeyings of the partner. The present-day separation, usually not very traumatic, symbolizes and re-enacts the childhood separation, bringing back the old anguish.

Unfortunately, those who endured separation from their parents – or a parent – in childhood tend to inflict the same calamity on their children. I knew a man who made a series of marriages quickly followed by divorces. In each marriage he had one or two children – only to leave them in order to move on to the next relationship. His father, too, had left him when he was a very small child.

Separation from parents might be less traumatic for children if this were a generally accepted normal happening. Children should perhaps be conditioned to separations, sent away from home at an early age to other families, grandmothers, aunts, cousins if they exist. Since divorces are so common and ever increasing, and journeys abroad so frequent for many working men and women, a training, a 'survival course' in independence from parents would be very helpful to many children. But everything depends on how secure – or insecure – children are made to feel.

A very secure child feels less threatened, more able to survive on being parted from a parent. What gives security to a child? Unambiguous affection or love (if possible), steadfast and responsible care and attention, respect for his or her needs, detached support – above all, calm and courageous parents.

ELEVEN

Pregnancy

Is it possible that a pregnant woman can influence the mood and temperament of the foetus in her womb? For instance, does a serene and contented pregnancy produce a serene and contented child? And on the other hand, does a troubled and difficult pregnancy produce a fretful, unhappy child?

Some women do believe that their state of mind during pregnancy has an effect on the foetus, but there's no scientific proof that this is the case. In theory, a foetus is able to respond to stimuli from the outside world as soon as its brain and nervous system are sufficiently developed and after it has all the necessary equipment in the way of sensory organs – eyes, ears, nose, tongue and so on. But as the foetus swims in darkness in a thick-walled water-filled capsule, it's doubtful whether it's able to receive sensory information from outside the womb. It's even more doubtful that the child in the womb is able to receive mental messages about its mother's conscious and unconscious feelings.

It's just possible that very tense abdominal muscles might have some effect on the foetus, perhaps restricting its movements. I once saw a pregnant patient whose husband was fiercely opposed to having another child. He was afraid of the chaos, the noise, the demands a baby makes on its parents. He needed peace and quiet for his work as a writer and he only accepted his wife's plea to have a second child on condition that she undertook to keep the child silent and out of sight, totally under control. The poor woman was terrified of upsetting her husband but she very much longed for the child. She was extremely apprehensive throughout the pregnancy.

The result was that the doctors were mystified about the condition of the child in her womb. The foetus seemed to move very little and was believed to be undersized and perhaps malformed.

Repeated scans could give no clear information on whether or not the child was normal. All this, of course, increased the mother's anxiety, but in the end she gave birth to a normal child, of normal size and weight and normally proportioned.

Did she manage to persuade the foetus to keep still and hunched up throughout the pregnancy? She certainly had a very quiet and well-behaved infant later on, after the birth.

Whether or not the mother's emotions can affect the foetus, what is certain is that the chemicals circulating in the mother's bloodstream and body can pass into the foetus's blood and tissues. We know that certain medicines and other substances swallowed by the mother can pass to the foetus. We know that a mother who smokes cigarettes during pregnancy is likely to produce an undersized, unhealthy baby. So it's possible – in fact likely – that abnormal chemicals which occur in the body during depressive illness, anxiety states and other mental disturbances, may be passed to the foetus. These may presumably affect the developing child.

A very large research programme would have to be carried out in order to understand whether or not a mother's state of mind, with accompanying chemical changes in the body, might influence the foetus in the womb. As yet, we don't know much about the change in blood chemistry accompanying moods and emotions of various kinds in normal adults. But what is certain is that until brain and nervous system have reached a certain stage of maturity in the unborn child, neither conscious nor unconscious mind may be said to function.

Women approach pregnancy with very different attitudes – conscious and unconscious. For some, the pregnant state is a blissfully happy experience: 'I've never felt so well, before or since'; 'I always feel marvellous when I'm pregnant.'

For some women, who feel physically ill throughout pregnancy, it's a wretched time that has to be grimly endured. Some feel shy about being pregnant and would like to hide the swelling abdomen. Others glory in the fact they're carrying a child. I remember seeing a charming but rather haunted-looking woman and her husband both of whom longed for a child, but the woman felt deeply apprehensive and mysteriously upset at the thought of being pregnant. She'd put off the, for her, awful prospect of pregnancy for years. Eventually, she and her husband began to worry that she was getting too old for childbearing. Yet the notion of pregnancy still filled her with dread: 'I'd have to go away somewhere and hide for nine months,' she told me, 'I couldn't bear to see anyone.' What she really meant was she couldn't bear anyone to see her.

We talked about her childhood. She was the only daughter of very puritanical parents. Her mother was particularly prudish and bashful. Sex was a forbidden topic in the home. My patient's education on matters related to sex had been painfully embarrassing to her mother and also to herself. 'The facts of life' had been vaguely and stutteringly outlined to her by her mother in one very uncomfortable encounter when the patient was twelve years old. No questions were asked. The whole matter of sex was so awful the girl had unconsciously repressed menstruation for a few years.

I began to understand that Mrs V couldn't bear to be pregnant because then the whole world could know and see that she'd had sexual intercourse. For her, this was a matter for shame and concealment. To walk down the village street for all the neighbours to see her condition was more than she could endure.

I'm glad to say that, with help, she was able to modify her attitude to sexual matters and eventually was able to conceive and carry a child in reasonable emotional comfort.

There may still be many women who are embarrassed by the subject of sex in spite of liberation, sexual freedom and so on. I remember another woman who'd come into hospital with severe lower abdominal pain which we had difficulty in diagnosing. She insisted that her periods had been normal and regular so we didn't suspect any problem to do with pregnancy. But after twenty-four hours she had a severe uterine haemorrhage and passed some pieces of macerated foetus. She'd had a 'back-street abortion', only half completed. We had to take her to the operating theatre to do a curettage and she needed a blood transfusion and antibiotics.

When she was recovering I went to talk to her: 'Why didn't you tell us, Eva, that you'd been pregnant?'

At this she burst into violent tears. 'I wasn't pregnant, I wasn't!' she cried vehemently.

I saw that her horror at the fact that she'd had 'illicit' sexual intercourse was such that I mustn't argue and so we left it at that. But she might have died if she hadn't been able to go into hospital – and all because sex was totally forbidden to her as a result of her upbringing, which I later discovered in subsequent conversations.

Whatever a woman's attitude to sex, all women approach their first pregnancy with certain conscious and unconscious anxieties. There is always fear of the unknown, fear about the delivery and perhaps, for some, fear as to whether the child will be normal or not. These are 'normal' realistic fears, usually experienced consciously. In these days, in Western societies, an abnormality in the foetus is usually detected early enough to have the pregnancy terminated in good time. Other attitudes to pregnancy may be less rational and usually unconscious. These attitudes will depend upon the pregnant woman's experiences in her childhood and her relationship with her own mother. Giving birth is a very complete re-enaction of the mother–child relationship, and a woman who has just delivered a child is both mother and child, emotionally speaking. If all went well in a pregnant woman's own childhood, if she had a good and affectionate relationship with her own mother, she'll expect that her own child will have a good relationship with her and she with it. She can look forward to the birth of the child with joyful anticipation.

But if a pregnant woman had a difficult relationship with her own mother, then having a child can be a disturbing and confusing experience. On a conscious level, the pregnancy and the child to be may be cheerfully welcomed. Unconsciously, there are liable to be anxieties and fears mainly on the matter of aggression – hers to the child and the child's to her.

'Will my child love me?' (If not it's because I might be potentially hostile to it and in return it will be hostile to me).

'Will I do to my child what my mother did to me?'

'Will I be able to be a "good" mother?'

'Will I be able to look after my child properly?'

'Will I die during childbirth?' (That is, 'Will my baby kill me?')

'Will my baby be dead at birth?' (That is, 'Will I kill my baby?')

'Will my baby be healthy and normal at birth or will it be deformed?' (That is 'Will I damage my baby during pregnancy?' or 'Will it be sufficiently hostile to me to be abnormal and deformed?')

'Will my baby be the right (wanted) sex?'

'Will I get my figure back after childbirth?' (That is, 'Will my baby destroy my beautiful figure?')

'Will I be able to feed my baby?'

'Will my baby want to drink my milk? Or will it reject me by refusing to drink my milk?'

I have known some very aggressive mothers who've repeatedly told their child:

'I nearly died giving birth to you.' ('You nearly killed me.')

'I nearly became blind when I was pregnant with you.' ('You nearly blinded me.')

or 'The doctors thought my kidneys had been permanently damaged when I was carrying you.' ('You nearly destroyed my kidneys.')

What is a poor child to reply to these reproaches, these implications that it has seriously attacked and damaged its mother?

Many of the above fears and fantasies of aggression, mother to child and child to mother, are related to the problems each generation had with their own parents – not to realistic, likely disasters.

There are other, more immediate and realistic reasons for a mother to feel hostile to the foetus in her womb. These reasons are connected with the mother's survival.

If a woman feels or becomes very ill during pregnancy she must inevitably have some hostility to the creature who is making her ill. Severe discomfort, vomiting which goes on and on, backache, sleepless nights, with the baby kicking continuously, swollen legs and varicose veins, complete exhaustion, perhaps with other small children clamouring for attention – these are enough to make a pregnant woman aggressive to her baby. But such aggression evaporates with the arrival of a wanted baby.

From what I've said about the wretched lives of unwanted and unloved children it should be clear that in my view no mother need have an unwanted child. This is not the place to discuss the ethics of the termination of pregnancy but only to discuss the feelings and emotions of those who have abortions.

Abortions often cause depression – sometimes of a severe kind. All that I've said earlier about aggression between mother and child relates most vividly to abortion. Here a woman might realistically believe she'd killed her child. A potential child has, of course, been prevented from developing from a fertilized embryo. But every month every woman alive produces a potentially viable ovum and men produce millions of potentially fertilizing spermatozoa. Because a spermatozoon and an ovum have accidentally got together, surely this doesn't mean that a woman has a child in her womb? She has only a fertilized ovum which might be permitted to be cast off just as an *un*fertilized ovum sloughs off the wall of the womb every month.

Nevertheless, there is still a tendency to make women feel wicked, like murderers, if they have a termination of pregnancy. Thus, guilt and depression may easily occur.

There's another facet to this complicated problem. If a woman has been, herself, an unwanted or unloved child, she'll identify with the fertilized ovum and re-enact the misery of her own rejection.

Finally, there's the matter of depression which occurs during pregnancy, often towards the end – and also shortly after the baby has been born. Physical upheavals in the body play some part in the surfacing of this condition but in my experience there are always reasons in childhood to account for depression during and immediately after pregnancy.

Here's an example. I once saw a woman who'd become seriously depressed shortly before her last child was born. She already had two little girls – and was hoping for a son – but in fact she had another daughter. There seemed to be no other good reason for her depressive illness in that she was happily married and lived a comfortable and secure life in a beautiful country house near London. She had, she told me, a good relationship with her mother who was an active committee woman, magistrate, opener of bazaars, a keen traveller and golfer and a very driving, energetic person, the very opposite of her rather frail and easily tired daughter, Dorothy.

Dorothy thought her mother was wonderful and remarkable. She was grateful for the time her mother managed to spare her from her hectic life. The truth was, her mother was fairly indifferent to Dorothy, who was the youngest of four girls. Both parents had desperately wanted a boy to carry on the family name. Unfortunately pregnancy after pregnancy ended with the disappointing birth of a girl. They took their last chance. Three children were more than they'd wanted but they had one final try. Dorothy arrived. Mother and father were bitterly upset. Neither was interested in the child. She was cared for by nannies. One in particular remained with her from the time she was five until she was grown up and married. When she had her own children, she persuaded Nannie to come back and look after them. Her attachment to her Nannie and her dependence on her was the result, of course, of her parents' indifference. She never admitted to herself or anyone else that she'd been rejected. Instead she pretended valiantly to be the loved child of loving parents.

But unconsciously, she knew the truth. With the imminent birth of her own last child, she was thrown back to those times when her parents demonstrated she'd failed them by being a girl rather than a boy – when they were uninterested in her and unconsciously hostile. She couldn't, of course, remember her birth, nor any events in her life until she was about three years old. But since birth she'd lived through depressing rejection which she'd denied and refused to believe existed. Now, in identifying with her own last child, whom perhaps she wanted to reject for the same reasons that had caused her parents to reject her, she vividly experienced deep depression.

There are certain patients for whom analytic psychotherapy does more harm than good, who are best kept with illusions and rationalizations. Dorothy was such a person. She was married to a kind and pleasant man who was a friendly and supportive husband. But he was a professional expert, employed by a highly successful international firm. He spent much of his life away from home endlessly busy, always travelling. When he wasn't in New York or Zurich or Rome, he was in Tokyo, or Bangkok or Hongkong. And when he was in England, he was locked in conference in his office. Inevitably Dorothy and her children saw very little of Martin. He was very like Dorothy's mother, in fact. He had the same absentminded and half-meaningless consideration for her, the same 'I must rush', 'Bless you!' attitude.

But Dorothy had a beautiful and comfortable home, as much domestic help as she needed – and she needed a great deal – and a life free of trivial anxieties. Prolonged and 'in depth' psychotherapy could only help her to see the reality of her relationship with her parents, genuinely and appropriately a cause for depression – and the similarity of her husband to her mother. Would this have helped her to make a different life for herself? Probably not. She was gentle and docile, a vulnerable woman with three very young children. I decided it would be best to give her supportive help and anti-depressant medication. This worked well although there was – and always would be – a tendency for the depression to recur under any kind of stress, mental or physical. Nevertheless, she slowly regained confidence and returned to her quite cheerful self-defended state in which she'd been before her last pregnancy.

At the beginning of this chapter, I described women who felt truly contented and calm when they were pregnant. There are also women who feel the exact opposite. I remember one unhappy woman who suffered from a kind of claustrophobia throughout an unplanned pregnancy. She felt completely at the mercy of a tyrannical monster in her body which she had no wish to sustain. She longed passionately to be free of the inextricable 'locked togetherness' of mother and child. At times she even thought of suicide – although strangely enough, she refused a termination of pregnancy which was offered to her. Grimly, she endured the pregnancy to the end and was utterly thankful to deliver the child.

Her story was she'd been born in South America, an illegitimate child. She had been adopted – but at a late age, six years old. She'd lived with her mother in physically and emotionally miserable conditions. When she was six, her mother married – but one of the conditions of the marriage was that the child was not to be part of the new home. Her mother had signed her away to a good and kind English couple who were her employers, temporarily stationed in the country. They knew the child well and were very fond of her, having no children of their own. They took the little girl back to England with them and she didn't see her mother again. The separation was cruel for her. It took her years to adapt to the new life. She changed from an emotionally stormy, intense extroverted child into a restrained, silent, perfectly mannered girl, beautifully spoken, beautifully dressed and with a heart of stone.

When her little girl was born, she wanted to have the baby adopted instantly. But the man she'd married, much older than herself – the 'father' she hadn't had – persuaded her to keep the child. The story has only a half happy ending. The woman did keep the child but she wouldn't look after her herself. The little girl was brought up by nurses and nannies, and I heard that her elderly father, who was affectionate and kind, died suddenly when she was only a few years old.

Pregnancy is often not an easy time for many women, as I've shown here. There's a tendency for our society to take a 'pull yourself together' attitude towards pregnant women with emotional problems. There are not many obstetricians or general practitioners who'll refer such women to psychiatrists unless they seem seriously disturbed. Pregnancy is thought to be a time when women react and behave 'strangely' and one mustn't take too much notice of their little emotional outbursts and anxieties. But as I've said, a pregnant woman is reliving her relationship with her own mother, re-enacting her own childhood. If there have been problems during that relationship, that childhood, they'll surface now, during the physically, emotionally vulnerable state of pregnancy.

If a woman is allowed to experience her feelings during this time instead of being asked to push them aside, or under cover, she might firstly have a much easier time during the pregnancy and secondly be a much 'better' mother when the child is born. Instead of – or in addition to – classes for exercises and relaxation techniques, there might also exist groups where women are encouraged to express their fears, anxieties, and hostilities, and are given help as to how to deal with these feelings.

Feelings in themselves are relatively harmless. Actions can cause harm. Restraint must be imposed on behaviour. It doesn't necessarily follow that because a person allows him or herself to be in touch with the reality of feelings, damaging behaviour will be put into action.

PART FOUR

Children's Responses to Damage

In the last chapters I've described various ways in which parents may damage their children. Firstly, by means of aggression (consciously or unconsciously acted out). Aggression may take the form of physical violence or of hostility, conscious and unconscious, or overt or concealed cruelty, or of contempt and mockery.

Parents may also damage their children by sexual abuse – actually physically inflicted on their children – or by means of powerful sexual feelings and attitudes towards children, these also being sometimes conscious and sometimes unconscious.

Parents may damage their children by being jealous of them. Here again the jealousy may be consciously experienced and acted upon – or the jealousy may be unconscious and be expressed in a 'rationalized form'.

And again, parents may damage their children by distortions of love and over-possessiveness.

Children are also damaged by disturbances in family life, divorces, separation and abandonment or a parent's illness or a death. Unemployment of a parent and other misfortunes in a family's circumstances are also liable to damage children.

To all these adverse circumstances children may respond in a great variety of ways.

During childhood, most children don't consciously recognize that they are being abused or ill-treated, unless the parents' behaviour is very overt and flagrant. The developing child, from infancy to the end of adolescence, is at the mercy of its parents or those adults surrounding it. The child attempts to survive. If survival becomes threatened by the behaviour or feelings of parents, the child is able to switch off its attention, to lessen its awareness of specific events and behaviour. It may be oblivious, it may perhaps suppress (if there is such a function as repression), it

153

may deny. Each or all of these abilities may be put into action, unconsciously as a rule. The outcome is that the child is in a state of confusion and illusion, almost unaware of what's being done to it. So the child doesn't react to the trauma with appropriate emotions. The child tries to believe and behave as if all was 'normal' in its life – 'normal' being the image of family life promoted by our society and culture, which has reached the child via its surroundings and parental messages. For the child, the ill-treatment is received almost as if it were happening to someone else rather than itself.

But the child does record and does observe, often unconsciously.

Later on in life, under the influence of psychotherapy or for some other reason, events forgotten and buried may become available for conscious examination.

Without such conscious knowledge of past happenings, there are responses which are unconsciously motivated. Blindly, in a sense, people punish parents in an unconscious 'look what you've done to me' state of mind. People become depressed, commit suicide, are delinquent, behave neurotically, have psychosomatic illnesses, are accident prone, drink to excess, are addicted to other drugs – and continue to inflict on their own children the same treatment which they themselves received in childhood. The next chapters describe such responses – not only in children, but in adults who have experienced damage during childhood.

TWELVE

Stoicism

Stoicism in ill-treated children is not uncommon. There is a rugged denial of suffering, an anaesthesia of the spirit, and sometimes the body, which is self-imposed – although not consciously so. The child refuses to admit to experiencing pain, although pain is the logical response to the mental or physical blows it might receive.

I was once working at a neurological hospital in London, very near a famous children's hospital. One afternoon a message came from the paediatric hospital to say they had a child on one of the wards whom they believed had been born without the ability to feel pain. She had seemed not to respond when doctors and nurses had treated – as gently as possible, but inevitably causing pain – some infected wounds and abrasions on her legs. On testing her, she'd again shown no response to painful stimuli. This inability to experience pain had not been seen before at the children's hospital and must be a very rare condition in an apparently otherwise normal child.

We all trooped round, a collection of white-coated doctors from the most senior physician to the lowliest houseman, and gathered around the cot of a hunched-up three-year-old, an expressionless little creature who pretended not to notice us.

The senior physician began to test her response to pain, gently at first, then getting progressively more determined with the sharp point of a pin. There was no sign on the inscrutable face that she'd felt anything at all, and she didn't withdraw the limb that was being punctured.

The pin went deeper, little spots of blood oozed. Quite suddenly, to our dismay, the baby's face crumpled, tears began to fall and the poor child let out a loud heart-wrenching wail. So poignant was this reaction that I can see the whole scene now, a critical moment in human frailty. The child had reached the limit of her ability to endure. We withdrew quickly. It was quite clear that she'd been born with all her abilities to perceive sensations working normally.

We later learned that she'd been treated with savage cruelty all her life. She had gradually reduced the level of her attention to physical stimuli and so survived a little more comfortably.

More usually, anaesthesia may affect the spirit, the mind. It's easier to arrange unconsciously to be numb to emotional pain. Withdrawn, dulled children are commonly seen in disturbed families. The pattern of refusing to respond to emotional stimuli, a kind of flattening of the emotions, remains, once it's been established, even though the painful stimuli have stopped. Adults whose feelings are 'hushed' find this state of affairs unpleasant. Physical effort and physical danger seem temporarily to relieve the sense of stifled emotions. Without realizing why they do this, 'numbed' people tend to drive cars very fast, or ski down icy vertical slopes or parachute jump, or find a way of being intensely stimulated. Alcohol is also sometimes taken in large quantities for the same reason, as are other drugs which excite. It's easy in the circumstances to become an addict. And for certain people, the excitement of gambling with heavy stakes relieves the sense of 'muffledness'. It's possible, also, that people with a subnormal appreciation of 'feelings' live dangerously without recognition of the danger – just as a person with a numb hand might be liable to burn it on the stove because he or she hadn't appreciated the warning heat emanating from the metal surface.

Patients with depressive illness often complain they feel as if there's a glass wall between themselves and the outer world – or between themselves and their feelings. I remember an American painter, normally a man of very intense feelings, who suffered from a depressive illness. He went, in the spring, to the English countryside. Birds sang, daffodils swayed in the bright air, dew lay on the green grass. He said, 'I knew I ought to be enjoying it, but it all stopped just here . . .' and he held his hand about six inches away from his body. Here was a failure in connection. The sensory stimuli were experienced, as seeing, hearing, tasting and so on without an emotional accompaniment.

People suffering in this way struggle to achieve a feeling content to life, as I've explained, and may ask for psychotherapeutic help. It is possible for the emotions to flow again, but because the childhood pain which gave rise to stoicism was so unbearable, there is unconscious reluctance to let go of a kind of armour plating.

It's important for a patient to realize that psychotherapy only manages to achieve very little, very slowly at best. It's not possible to help a 'numbed' person re-experience emotions at the drop of a hat, making him or her instantly vulnerable to hurt. On the contrary, successful treatment will allow the patient to release a little trickle of emotion in a spasmodic fashion. But slowly, a normal ability to 'feel' may be restored.

It's difficult to understand how the switching off of feelings may occur in the first place. Are feelings repressed or is attention withdrawn at the moment of suffering? We cannot tell.

THIRTEEN

Loneliness and Solitude

Loneliness is one of the most sad and most common of human ailments, perhaps shared only by those animals who have been forced out of their herd, sick, disabled or old. Among human beings it's one of the most unnecessary of miseries, since any one of us has the potential ability to relate to others, and people abound on our planet.

Potential ability – but like many of our potential abilities, relating to other people must begin in childhood, a basic pattern formed and consolidated from infancy to adolescence. 'Relating' to others first takes place within the family and is later extended to strangers.

'Relating' involves emotional communication – and particularly demands an ability to feel affection, love, anger, aggression – all those emotions which people normally feel towards one another in an intimate co-existence. Not only must we be able to transmit these feelings, we must also be able to receive them, to accept them. This to and fro of emotions enriches our world, makes life seem meaningful and worthwhile. If for one reason or another we, as children, unconsciously forbid ourselves these feeling experiences, we grow up alone, in a barren world. But, luckily, even though we might spend our childhood in emotional solitude, laying down a pattern which doesn't include true relationships, there's still time to learn to let ourselves feel and relate to others as adults. The process is more difficult in later life, but, with help, we can reach and use the feelings necessary for making relationships.

Many children are lonely. Many parents believe, mistakenly, that they've only to put their child or children in contact with other children and close relationships will be automatically formed. This isn't the case, even with very young children. Lonely children will be lonely even in a group of others if they haven't been able to learn how to make contact, emotionally, with other human beings. In the first place, solitary and unsociable parents don't provide an environment in which a child learns to be sociable. But also, children take on, unconsciously, their parents' attitudes, emotions and problems, as I've so often described in this book. Lonely parents have lonely children. And children may become lonely at any time, from birth to adolescence. Lonely children will be lonely adults.

Single children are often lonely, of course, especially if their parents don't have the time to give them sufficient attention. 'I spent my childhood alone, kicking a ball around the back yard,' one of my patients, an only child, told me . . . a bleak image! But even children in a large family may be isolated and solitary. To be able to relate to others, to make use of our potential ability to relate to others, a child must believe in him or herself – must believe that he or she is a worthwhile creature whom people will accept – even like, or love.

A child who feels unworthy and unlikeable will find it hard to be accepted by other children or other adults and probably won't even try. Those children who hang about on the outskirts of the playground, who spend playtime at school hiding in corners, hoping no one will see how left out they are, the children towards whom other children are hostile, are children rejected by parents. Their loneliness will haunt them all their lives unless help is given to them. Many such children and adults can relate only to animals, who are undemanding, uncritical and give unstinting love. A child who has experienced cruelty, emotional and physical, from parents and others, will fear close relationships and will hesitate or refuse to allow the possibility of further attack and suffering. Such children and adults will feel safety and comfort in emotional and physical solitude. But solitude, which soothes the spirit, saddens the heart. To be deprived of the ability to love is one of the greatest deprivations a human being may experience.

The ability to love, the process of loving are, in a way, more rewarding than the state of being loved. But those children who've been rejected have, early in life, as a rule, loved intensely the parent who relentlessly caused them to withdraw their love, caused them to isolate themselves, to live, in shame, alone. Here's an example:

Marisa's mother hated her. She enjoyed tormenting her child, she enjoyed ridiculing her, she laughed when Marisa fell and hurt herself, she teased and taunted and criticized her without restraint (having had the same treatment from her own mother). She forced fattening food down Marisa's throat, which Marisa loathed, and then she mocked her for being plump. She dressed Marisa in ridiculous, ugly clothes and she made it clear how she despised every aspect of her little girl. Marisa then deeply understood how wretched and loathsome a being she, the child, must be. Marisa spent her childhood in shadows, slinking around, trying to keep out of everyone's way, with only the household dog for a friend.

When she went to school, she continued to slink and cringe, bent double, almost, in an effort to efface herself, not to exist . . . As a result, she attracted the hostility of the other children, who cruelly despised her, just as her mother did. And she also attracted the hostility of certain sadistic schoolmistresses who made her life a private hell. She crawled through her childhood with face averted and eyes cast down. She was extremely pretty and very intelligent, but she believed herself a monster and a fool. As she grew older, she developed a false pretence of confidence. She made a few friends and a few boys began to make advances towards her. But when people came near her, she shrank back. She smiled, she pretended, but within her there was a fortress where her emotions were imprisoned. She went through the motions of relating to people, as if she were able to experience feelings, but she was actually as isolated as if she were living on a desert island. So she remained solitary, escaping forever from emotional contact with other human beings.

Such childhood experiences, perhaps less blatantly miserable than in Marisa's case, account for some of the lonely people who drift on the fringes of our Western societies. We make few allowances for misfits. The outcast of childhood may become the outcast who roams city pavements, sleeping on park benches and under bridges – or who tramps the countryside with a knapsack and a hungry, tired dog; or who lives alone, staring out of a silent apartment into a dark world; or who is the eternal bachelor, the eternal spinster; or who, thriving, successful, dazzling even, makes no real contact with people and suddenly commits suicide in utter loneliness. The outcast of childhood is the man who lives alone at the end of the valley, where no road comes, the woman who goes home after work to a bedsitter, to make supper for one on a gas ring, where no other voice is heard, no telephone rings and no letters arrive with the postman.

There are other reasons for loneliness in childhood. Children don't like difference in other children. Eccentric parents, dressing their children in noticeably bizarre outfits, however attractive, lay the ground for their children to have a difficult time with their fellows. Eccentric children aren't easily accepted any more than are disabled children in a class of 'normal' children, or black children in a class of white children. Being different from the herd brings penalties and loneliness, at least in childhood.

Then, there are parents who don't really relate to their children, however hard they try and however much they might want to do so. Emotionally 'dried-up' parents can't get genuine feelings across to their children, who sense the fundamental lack in their parents and react accordingly. The child's emotions are locked away, just as the parents' are.

There are parents who are absent for long periods, leaving a child in the care of an indifferent nanny or 'au pair', and however joyfully the parents may return, with exciting presents and treats for their child, this can't compensate for the loneliness the child has endured while they were away. Nor can a kitten or puppy provide any alternative to a relationship with another human being. And children may be lonely even in the presence of a parent, if their parent is constantly engrossed in other matters and emotionally 'shuts out' the child. Here's an example:

John was an only child. His mother was a writer who worked at home. She believed that her simple presence was sufficient to prevent her child being lonely. She was wrong. While she was writing in her room, little John was silently crawling about on the floor outside her room, unresponsive to his elderly nanny's attempts to get him to come and play in the garden or nursery.

When he grew a little older, he begged and implored to be allowed to sit in his mother's room while she was writing. This was finally allowed on the understanding he would remain totally quiet and not disturb her in any way. So he sat against the wall, behind her, in her room. He hardly moved, he hardly breathed. He watched that adamant, excluding back of his mother while, utterly absorbed and oblivious of her child, she got on with her book. No one could have felt more lonely, more excluded than this child. He spent hours watching and waiting until the moment she put down her pen, turned around and slowly emerged from her private world to become aware of the existence of her son. At this point, she often hurried to the kitchen, brushing him aside.

John's father was a much older man who'd been married before, who had almost grown-up children by that marriage, and who now had little time and patience for the little boy. In any case, he was often away from home, so was of no help in making John feel accepted and acceptable. John grew up to be a totally solitary person, unconsciously feeling he had no right to emotional intimacy with another human being, unconsciously believing that his rôle in life was to be excluded. Yet his parents hadn't been hostile to him. They simply had no time for him. So his unconscious emotional pattern was that other people had no time for him. Contrary to what might be expected, that John would end up as a sheep farmer in the Australian outback, John grew up with the conscious plan to marry and have lots of children. He fulfilled this plan, twice. Each time his wife complained that she felt she was living with a kind and nice automaton, a gentle iceberg, a polite and sensitive robot. Each time, he married an emotionally intense woman, who acted out her feelings rather dramatically – 'for' him in the way I've described elsewhere in this book. Following the endless complaints about his being withdrawn, his inability to react and interact, he became impotent, and both marriages ended in disaster. So, each time, John returned to exclusion and loneliness.

If feelings aren't available to a person, the business of making and keeping contact with other people becomes a wearing and tiring business. There is a sense that demands are being made by others which can't be fulfilled. Those whose emotions of love and hate are silenced (or squeak rather than roar), find social life a strain. A dinner party becomes an endurance test rather than an amusing and enjoyable entertainment. People with this problem find solitude deeply satisfying.

One such patient who lived in a remote area of the countryside told me he had fantasies that all his neighbours might be away, ill or dead – so reducing, or eliminating, the social demands that they might make on him. But as I've said earlier, while for some people solitude is wonderfully restful, to live in utter loneliness is a desiccating state of affairs, however much one might enjoy natural beauty and animals.

Psychotherapy helps people to experience the emotions needed in relationships. Many solitary people unconsciously resist the idea and the process of psychotherapy because they don't want to return to a state where they might be cruelly hurt. But while children may be disastrously hurt by savage parents and others, adults are much less vulnerable. Grown up, we can laugh at insults – or retaliate vigorously. The rewards of feeling in relationships are huge, the pain of loneliness immense. Courage is needed – and most of us do have the courage to feel emotions. The courage involves treating solitude and loneliness as if they were symptoms of an illness. Many people do make efforts to fight loneliness – many people give in to it. The experience of feelings is better, for most, than walking down the streets alone at night, staring into shop windows, better than going to museums and movies alone on Sundays and better than the terrible sense of being isolated in a crowd, spending Christmas alone with the blinds drawn, the windows shut so that other people won't know you're alone . . .

I started this chapter saying that the world abounds with people. The lonely are those whose childhood patterns haven't included the making and keeping of relationships. It's never too late to learn how to experience feelings towards – and from – other people. Those girls and women who sit on the edge of the dance floor watching the others, praying that someone will come over and ask them to dance – or those men, praying the girls they would like to ask to dance won't say 'no' – don't need to go through such ordeals. There are enough partners. Everyone can dance.

FOURTEEN

Addiction to Alcohol and Other Drugs

If some parents have made life hard for their children, then many children have discovered how to make life hard for their parents. Self destruction is the name of the game. And parents, in return, may use the same self-destructive tactics to call attention to their own hurt. Watching other people suffer, knowing they're suffering because of one's neglect or lack of understanding, is miserable for most human beings. There's guilt and self-searching. Most parents aren't conscious of the harm they may have done to their children. Most harmed children aren't aware either of the causes of their self-destructive behaviour. The reproach to their parents is a silent cry – a cry made by the unconscious mind. But the cry is meant to be heard. Attention to the pain and the wounds is required.

Children use whatever weapons are available to them. Among the many weapons which our societies provide, drugs rank high. Alcohol, cannabis, cocaine, heroin, nicotine . . . 'Look what you've done to me! It's all your fault.' The silent cry goes out.

It's a purely human cry. The state of mind which it proclaims, a despairing, angry, punishing 'cut off my nose to spite my face' attitude, is not to be found in other animals. Animals other than man seem to be more accepting, driven by instinct to make the best of things and to try to survive even in the worst circumstances.

The human concept is of 'wrong' done – by parent to child – and also by child to parent. Once again it could be said that a lack of instinct-motivated behaviour accounts for the self-destructive response of humans to a sense of 'wrong' done to them: 'Look what you've done to me. It's all your fault!' involves two concepts. Those of sadism and masochism.

Sadism and masochism are aspects of aggression, two faces of the same aggressive impulse. 'Sadism' is a term applied to aggression of a direct kind. 'Masochism' is a term used to imply a tendency to arrange for one's own suffering. But, as I mentioned earlier, an individual's suffering causes pain and discomfort in others who observe and are responsible for the suffering. So masochism is an indirect way of being aggressive.

The terms sadism and masochism were originally used to describe aspects of sexual behaviour and both words were derived from the writings of two men. 'Sadism' is derived, of course, from the Marquis de Sade (1740–1814) who wrote novels describing people who experienced sexual pleasure from inflicting pain on others. Sacher Moser (1835–1895) wrote of sexual pleasure experienced by a person as a result of having pain inflicted on him or her.

Thus the two words sadism and masochism were created. Nowadays, these two words are loosely used and have largely lost their sexual connection. 'Masochist' is often used to describe a person who more or less arranges to suffer, who apparently thrives on suffering and who seems to insist on suffering. 'Sadist' is used to describe a person who enjoys being cruel to others. And the two words are often linked. 'Sado-masochism' means a person who inflicts suffering on others perhaps by virtue of inflicting suffering on him or herself.

It's a fact that most people do feel wretched – largely out of guilt – knowing that a child, or a parent, is suffering. Masochism is a weapon, often used without a conscious awareness of the aggression entailed. On a minor level, here's an example: 'Look at us, poor lonely old parents! You should be at home looking after us instead of gallivanting around with your worldly friends, never giving a thought to your father and mother!' – an unspoken but emanated reproach.

Or, 'Here I am all alone on my birthday, lonely and sad. And where are you? After all I've done for you! What would your poor father have said! You can't even be bothered to come back from abroad to give me some hope that life is still worth living! Surely your book could wait!' Again, the above was probably not clearly articulated but mysteriously emanated.

And, 'No, no! This old coat will do. Far be it from me to want you to spend your hard-earned thirty thousand a year on your old mother! You go and buy yourself another pair of earrings (Ferrari, telephoto lens . . . etc., etc).'

Masochism, as just described, may be as aggressive as outright sadism, but the aggression is carried out in such a way as to leave the aggressor feeling free of guilt and virtuous. 'My needs are small. I am frugal, prepared to eat bread and water and dress in these old rags . . .'

Another example: 'Off you go and enjoy yourselves, never mind me. I'm just an old lady. Nobody's interested in me. I'll sit here and peel the potatoes. I take it there's a small electric fire somewhere in the house, just to keep my feet warm – or a rug perhaps. Any old thing will do and I'll find myself something to eat, don't you worry about me – a bit of a sandwich or something. Have a wonderful time. I'll want to know what you had for dinner and what the play was like, if you find me here when you get back – but I may go to bed if I get too cold . . .'

Here the underlying, unspoken theme is: 'How can you be so heartless as to leave me here all alone (at my time of life and with my rheumatism playing up) in this cold and dreary house while you go out for a wonderful evening! I'll teach you. Don't you dare enjoy yourselves! I hope you spend a miserable few hours regretting your disgraceful behaviour!'

But since the spoken words and attitude are innocently meek and altruistic the children cannot blame her for aggression and jealousy. On a more serious level, the attitude, 'Look at what you've done to me' or 'Look at what you're doing to me!' may result in extremely self-destructive behaviour on a grand scale. The need to demonstrate the hurt (unconsciously motivated) is one of the many causes of alcoholism and the widespread addiction to other drugs. Most drug addicts begin by taking small amounts of a particular drug, gradually increase the quantity and finally are psychologically and also physically dependent on the drug.

In the case of alcohol, there seems to be a physical factor in the make-up of the addict which promotes addiction. Alcoholism runs in families. The physical factor might be inherited. There's also always the possibility that the children of alcoholics unconsciously identify with their parents and repeat the pattern of drinking.

Alcohol in small quantities is a marvellous drug, in that it both stimulates and calms. People drinking moderate amounts may feel free of tension and at the same time exhilarated. Grief and anxiety may be numbed and troubles forgotten. But if alcohol is continually taken for a special purpose, to soothe, relax or allay sorrow, there is danger of addiction.

Alcohol disinhibits, of course, and people feel carefree and irresponsible – and behave in irresponsible and often dangerous ways. The truth – sometimes unpleasant – tends to emerge under its influence. Alcoholics are often highly aggressive, irritable, bad-tempered and unreasonable. The families of alcoholics suffer dismally. Yet, amazingly, the partners of many established or potential alcoholics encourage drinking, try to persuade the alcoholic to 'have another one', pouring freely from the bottle and handing over what is virtually a poison. Alcohol is a lethal poison when taken consistently in large quantities, destroying the nervous system and the liver among other viciously harmful effects.

Sometimes an alcoholic is doing the drinking for other members of the family or is being the 'bad' member of the family, as I've described elsewhere in this book, or acts out behaviour for others in a wild, uninhibited way which other members of the family long to do but don't dare. Here's an example not untypical of the way people become alcoholics:

Tamara was the daughter of two alcoholics. Both her parents drank to excess. Her mother was the more cruel and depriving of the two, when she was drunk, which was often. Tamara and her two brothers had a wretched childhood. At the age of nineteen, she married Hamish, charming, dishonest, spoilt, amusing and very destructive. Tamara was meek, crushed and used to suffering.

She had no clear idea of what she should or could expect in terms of loyalty and kindness from her husband, or what her 'rights' as a human being might be. Hamish, perhaps not altogether consciously, took advantage of her undefending, undemanding, unaccusing attitudes and began, very soon after they were married, to have affairs with other women, to spend most of his money on nightclubs – gambling, having a 'good time' in a way which didn't include Tamara. But because somewhere in the depths of him he felt 'bad' about himself, he couldn't altogether get away with his treatment of his wife. He needed, unconsciously, to make her 'bad' and turn himself into a saintly martyr. To this end, he began to help her to become an alcoholic. He said when he came home from the office at nine, ten or eleven o'clock at night, she having prepared dinner for eight o'clock and expected him home at that time, 'Why don't you just sit down and relax instead of getting all hot and bothered? Pour yourself a hefty gin and tonic and switch on the telly.' This Tamara began to do. It certainly was a pleasanter way of waiting for Hamish to come home. One hefty gin became two or three. When Hamish finally appeared, he was carrying bottles of champagne and wine. With these he plied Tamara. She welcomed the stupefying effects of the drugs. She began to drink in the middle of the day, and at intervals through the afternoon.

Then Hamish came home to a sodden, disagreeable, untidy wife, a disorganized, uncared-for home and a crying baby – for at about this time they had their first child, a daughter. No food was prepared. And Tamara, previously so meek and gentle, began to scream at him. Hamish the hero took charge. He pushed another large tumbler of alcohol into Tamara's hand. He fed and bathed and put his daughter to bed. He cooked. Quick meals became his speciality. He was a saint, suffering terribly from his alcoholic wife.

All her friends knew, because Hamish told them, that Tamara was an alcoholic and that Hamish 'had' to take care of home, child and wife when he came home from the office. He often came home very late in the evenings, going on largely as before, meeting girlfriends, having love affairs (which he continued to let Tamara discover by letters left lying about, lipstick marks on his shirts and other obvious signs of treachery).

It can be seen that it may sometimes take two to create and maintain alcoholism – on the one hand a person with the inherited characteristics which promote addiction, on the other, a person who provokes anxiety and pain and who also supplies the drug.

By good luck, in one sense, Tamara developed acute appendicitis, was taken into hospital for surgery and there met a doctor who persuaded her to give up alcohol. So she was admitted to a specialist unit where she was weaned of the addiction, but there followed a long struggle before she completely freed herself from her craving for the drug. She was immensely helped by attending the meetings of Alcoholics Anonymous, which she continues to do to this day. In the course of time she separated from Hamish and in the end divorced him. Until the very day she left him he went on pouring out quarts of gin and handing them to her saying, 'Oh, go on, Tammy! One won't hurt. You're no fun if you don't have just a touch of drink!'

It's interesting that many people try hard, at parties for instance, to persuade non-drinkers to take some alcohol. They feel irritated and, presumably, guilty, if they are drinking and others won't join them. Or is there another reason for a drinker's discomfort in the presence of non drinkers? The disinhibition which alcohol brings about makes drinkers feel that any sober eye is assessing them coldly and critically.

'Do have just one!' 'Just have a drop!' 'Come on – join in!'

Alcoholics who have completely given up alcohol sometimes have a hard time resisting the urging and pleading of 'friends'. Psychotherapy alone is useless, on its own, for the treatment of addicts, no matter what the addiction. The underlying, unconscious or conscious cause of drinking to excess is irrelevant. In the first place, addiction has to be treated by the addict giving up the drug completely. The initial stages of drug withdrawal are very difficult. Horrible symptoms occur. Severely addicted patients giving up alcohol may suffer from hallucinations, 'D.T.'s' (delirium tremens).

Once the physical withdrawal from a drug is over, psychotherapy has a vital part to play in the 'cure'. Many depressed patients drink to excess, in the belief that they feel better from the affects of alcohol. But while alcohol numbs temporarily, it acts largely as a depressant. The day after a heavy bout of drinking – or even a moderate amount of alcohol – a person's depression is intensified. People suffering from depressive illness who have suicidal thoughts tend to kill themselves when under the influence of drink. The combination of the depressant effect and the disinhibiting effect makes those who feel driven to suicide carry out the act.

Addiction to other drugs very often stems from the unconscious 'Look what you've done to me' motivation. Young people, particularly in adolescence and late teens, take cannabis, cocaine and sometimes heroin, for a great number of different reasons. One reason is that which motivates the silent cry – the child who has been ill-treated, neglected or sexually abused.

The masochistic response to ill-treatment, the punishing of others by means of one's own suffering, is one of the most irrational and idiotic of all possible responses. Addicts to alcohol or other drugs usually suffer very much more than the parents they're unconsciously aiming to punish. It's this fact that psychotherapists hope to point out, convincing addicts of the futility of self-destruction as a response to hurt and ill-treatment. But for some people, it seems there's something alluring about self-annihilation. Mysteriously, we may be drawn towards dissolution; in the physical sense, a ghostly hands beckons us, like the Lorelei, along a passage towards death.

I've known patients who were immensely self-destructive whom I tried to turn away from their relentless tendency, who returned again and again, like unarmed citizens into a firing line, to their masochistic behaviour. Again and again I'd see their hurt and bewildered faces after yet another encounter with disaster. Here was hurt and bewilderment on a conscious level, but unconsciously a kind of satisfaction at having demonstrated yet again the damage done to them as children.

On a conscious level, the rationalization is, 'It won't happen to me!' or 'We have to die of something!' Unconsciously, heavy drinkers and smokers are driven by tragic vindictiveness; by dying, they cry, 'Look what you've done to me!'

Some people believe that they function better, mentally and physically, under the influence of drugs. Alcohol, with its depressant action, relaxes tension and so seems to release energy. Cocaine excites. Some cocaine addicts I've known falsely believed they made keener, sharper decisions under the influence of the drug. That is an illusion. The sense of pleasure, change, brilliance of thinking and feeling that people experience when taking cocaine is completely misleading. Tests have shown that instead of functioning better, there is, in fact, a marked impairment of intellect and judgement is faulty. We think we're being witty, incisive, decisive and clever. We're not. Rather the opposite. We're fatuous and foolish as a result of taking cocaine.

'Look at what you've done to me! It's all your fault!' – this attitude is only one reason for taking drugs, but it's a common one. Alternatively, young people want to prove how independent, brave, different, rebellious, adventurous they are and they sometimes do this by smoking, drinking and using other drugs. But in my experience, well cared-for children who are supported, loved and generally emotionally privileged, don't feel the need to join the 'drug culture'.

Why do people seem to want, enjoy and need the effects of drugs in the first place? Drugs of various kinds have been used by people for a very long time. Why do we enjoy the experience of a disorder of perception, which amounts to a disordered function of mind and brain?

Perhaps we long to be freed of the endless activity of conceptualizing – the rigid orderliness of of normal mental and cerebral activity. We try, perhaps, to escape from the imprisoning effects of the functions of that part of our brain which evolved most recently, the part which is so specifically human.

FIFTEEN

Hope

Hope, a feeling hard to describe or define, is a powerful driving force in human beings.

Hope for some specific happening often begins in childhood. For example, a rejected child may begin to hope that one day it will be warmly loved by a parent. If the hope is not fulfilled, it is carried on into adult life, giving rise to often repeated patterns of behaviour and feeling – the driving force behind the pattern being that the longed-for expectation will finally come to pass. In childhood, the longing and expectation may be conscious.

As time goes by, hope drifts into unconscious mind, continuing to motivate behaviour and feelings. Hope may be constructive and may help people to survive. But the hope that has no chance of fulfilment, which gives rise to 'neurotic' patterns of behaviour, is very destructive.

In certain circumstances, hope probably keeps people alive. Prisoners of war, hostages taken by terrorists, parents of desperately ill children, wives of men in danger, shipwrecked sailors . . . hope helps them to survive. But hope can be one of the most futile and destructive of feelings if there's not the slightest chance that what's hoped for will ever come to pass. Better to cut the losses and try something else. Give up hope, if there's no possibility of fulfilment. Sometimes, people's relationships come to a full stop because they're waiting for an event or state of affairs that can never be achieved. For example:

Mr M lived in hopes that his widowed mother would start to love him. She'd been very rejecting towards him when he was a child and much preferred his elder sister. Mr M's mother disliked her son and adored her daughter – a state of affairs which persisted into her children's adult lives.

As a child, Mr M tried many different strategies to attract his mother's attention, without success. He had cried, he had smiled, he'd been ill, he'd been brilliant, he'd failed dismally, he'd developed a twitch of the eyelid of his left eye, he'd started to limp. To no avail.

Mr M's mother remained adamantly indifferent. Mr M's anxiety and depression about his mother's rejection of him in favour of his sister drifted out of his conscious awareness and were absorbed by his unconscious mind. Unconsciously he yearned for and looked forward to the day when his mother would throw her arms around him, tell him it was all a mistake, that he was the one she loved and his sister didn't count.

While waiting for the arrival of this day Mr M got on with his work, but he couldn't manage to make a relationship with anyone else. He was emotionally stuck. He was motivated, unconsciously, to do the things which might have pleased his mother and avoided doing what might have displeased her.

This meant he couldn't allow himself to do terribly well, or at least not better than his sister. He couldn't allow himself to fail either. By chance – accident, almost – he became involved in a business which rocketed to fame. To his pleasure – but it was a pleasure accompanied by anxiety, sleepless nights and indigestion, Mr M found he was due to receive a knighthood in the New Year Honours. On a conscious level he believed that Mother would be pleased and proud. Unconsciously motivated insomnia and peptic ulcers hinted otherwise.

What happened was easily predictable – his mother was cool and offhand about his knighthood, leaving Mr M quite consciously upset and irritated. What he didn't realize was this: that even if his mother had suddenly become very affectionate and pleasant towards him, it wouldn't have helped him. While he would have been consciously delighted, he would have continued with his old pattern of feelings and behaviour: 'Don't do very well – but don't fail. Avoid another relationship until you've worked things out with your mother.'

The reason for this is that patterns are assembled in childhood, as a reaction to events and parental behaviour and attitudes in childhood, as described earlier (see page 16). The pattern is formed at that particular period of our lives and is wholly resistant to change, no matter what happens in adult life. We can't go back to childhood and relive the past in more satisfactory terms. We're stuck with the pattern. At best, with the help of psychotherapy, we can arrive at an understanding of what happened and resign ourselves to the early state of affairs – in Mr M's case, 'my mother didn't love me, she preferred my sister'. We may then make conscious efforts to establish a new pattern.

Mr M needed his mother to make it clear she loved him during his childhood. His hoping and waiting should have ended with the end of his childhood. What happens after childhood can't re-make the past. Many people live under the shadow of destructive hope. All they are doing is a kind of 'vamping till ready', playing for time until the great day dawns. But the only real salvation would be to re-live childhood – and this time round, achieve the reality of what's hoped for: 'Mother does love me'; 'Father is about to marry me'; 'My brother values and respects me', and so on. In other words, there is no salvation and no point in hoping. This fact is never realized in adult life unless unconscious feelings and events can be made available for examination.

Mr M was a little unusual in that the majority of people play the hoping game in a situation once or twice removed from the original – a second incarnation, as it were. They play the game with substitutes, wives or husbands or lovers who represent the original players. Here's an example:

John lost his mother when he was a very young child. His elder sister, dominating, jealous, ruthless, had taken over the management of the family. She made John's life a misery by bullying and tormenting him until the day he went to boarding school – and thereafter during the holidays.

He escaped from home as soon as he could and, at twenty-two, married Samantha. At about the same time, he started his career as a writer and in order to support himself and Samantha bought a bookshop with the money he'd inherited from his mother. Over the next few years he and Samantha had two children, a boy and a girl, and they had a bit of a struggle with money. Samantha was wonderful. She ran the home, she helped in the bookshop, she was lovingly supportive to John and generally was a tower of strength.

Then John began to do well. The bookshop slowly prospered. One of John's novels was a success and sold a great many copies. But as their situation improved, Samantha mysteriously became irritable and impatient with John. The better he did the more unpleasant she was. John found this hard to understand. He began to try to escape from her bitter carping tongue. He had one or two brief affairs with girls who came into the shop to buy books, although they didn't mean very much to him.

One day, Samantha found out about one of these relationships – perhaps John unconsciously intended her to do so. She became unbearable. She wanted a divorce immediately. At this point John developed a duodenal ulcer, and at the same time a business venture failed. John felt himself collapsing.

Mysteriously, Samantha suddenly became gentle, supportive, marvellously helpful and kind. John promised to be a good boy. They were reconciled. But as soon as he started to do well again, with improved health and a new book accepted by his publisher, Samantha once more became angry and bitter, full of reproaches and criticism. This cycle of events was repeated again and again.

In the end, during a 'down' phase, John went to see a psychiatrist who suggested therapy, which John accepted. It became clear that Samantha was jealous of his success (she had her own childhood reasons for doing so). It became clear also, to John, that Samantha represented, for him, his sister in childhood who had been kind to him when he was suffering and vicious when he was thriving.

Feeling better and believing he understood the situation and could cope with it, John decided he'd had enough psychotherapy (mistakenly) and returned to the fray. Samantha, of course, hadn't changed. She had been furious and insulting about the psychiatrist.

John's ulcer started playing up again and the bookshop went through a bad period. Suddenly Samantha became her calm strong 'self'. 'She's marvellous,' said John to his best friend, 'I take back every bit of criticism of her. I'm sure it's all going to be all right now.' But of course, no sooner was John well again and the bookshop once more on course, than the cycle restarted.

The fact was that John had longed to be accepted by his sister when he was a small child, longed to be loved by her after the death of their mother. At such times as he seemed very pathetic, ill, or humble, his sister felt less threatened by him and was able to be affectionate and kind. But when he revived she would lapse into her bullying, terrorizing mood, since her problem was that she was jealous of John's masculinity. When he seemed 'castrated' she could accept him, but she couldn't do this when he seemed a thriving male. But John had lived in hopes that one day it would all come right and they'd have a wonderful relationship.

Of course, it never did come right and as he grew older, his longings became more unconscious. He found and married Samantha. The sensitive antennae of the unconscious had picked up the signals about her. Here was the reincarnation of John's sister.

Now, unconsciously, he felt he had a second chance to work things out with Samantha, as a symbol of his sister. The hope that he might be able to do so was a burning, powerful drive; but of course the pattern was an inexorable 'locking in' to a woman jealous of his masculinity. Like his sister, Samantha had unconscious childhood reasons for her behaviour. Samantha could only tolerate John when he was disabled. What kept the adult John a prisoner of his relationship with Samantha was the hope that one day it would all end happily. She'd love him no matter how well he was doing.

But again and again he had evidence to the contrary. Again and again he'd pick himself up and hope once more. The hope was really about his sister, Jane. If by a miracle (or as a result of psychotherapy) Samantha had changed and accepted and loved him in health as well as in sickness, he would have become restless. He probably would have left her in order to find another woman who fulfilled the pattern. What he wanted was impossible – to go back in time, to be a child again, to reach an understanding with his sister, to be mothered by her when he most needed mothering, when his mother had died.

We see two aspects of human feelings and behaviour in John's case. Firstly, the 'pattern', the re-enactment of the childhood scene, the childhood relationship. Secondly, the power of hope, futile, useless, never-to-be-fulfilled hope, that was damaging and destructive to John's life.

As long as he hoped, unconsciously, to please Samantha/Jane, John could never allow himself to do well in a long-term manner – or even to be healthy. He had to fail at regular intervals, he had to be ill at regular intervals, so that he could reassure himself that he was after all accepted and therefore acceptable, loved and therefore lovable. He unconsciously resisted psychotherapy because he felt that this utterly important, almost ritualized series of events, confrontations, arguments, collapses and revivals helped establish a sense of self-value.

A small child who is abandoned by a parent, whether by death or for any other reason, feels that the parent would have stayed around if the child had been sufficiently important to him or her. The parent's departure clearly indicates to the child that he or she is not a very valuable being. John had had such feelings of inadequacy and inferiority when his mother died, feelings intensified by his sister's rejection of him. The intermittent acceptance gave him hope (although it was at the cost of failure and illness). But it was false and futile hope.

The hope that 'things will change' in a relationship is very common in our societies. People remain glued to the most dreary and destructive relationships, always believing 'it'll get better one day . . .' (meaning, to the unconscious mind, 'mother', 'father', 'sister', 'brother', will one day accept them, unconditionally, unreservedly). Unconditional acceptance . . . to be accepted and loved without conditions of 'good' behaviour, to be loved for one's 'self', without working at it, without 'deserving' it, this is the great dream.

It's an unrealistic dream. The majority of parents love their children more generously when they're 'good' and are exhausted and irritated by their children when they're troublesome and 'bad'. The children who test their parents most severely with 'bad' behaviour are those who already feel doubtful about the parents' acceptance and love of them.

If a parent will love a child when it's behaved badly, that's a real test of love – and a love worth having. Sometimes, if a child can cause a sufficiently major crisis, a parent can, surprisingly, become loving and supportive to the child. Perhaps the parents unconsciously needed the child to arrange a crisis and once this has occurred, the parent is satisfied and can love the child.

Thus, if a child is sufficiently delinquent to be taken to a court of law, a hostile parent might go to the court with the child and become caring and devoted. But the chances are that the affection and support last only as long as the crisis lasts.

How tempting then for the child, having its hope of love temporarily fulfilled, to arrange unconsciously a crisis again and again. And as an adult, be sent to prison for each successive crisis of lawbreaking, again and again. The pattern is unconsciously motivated. Hope, also unconscious, insidious, destructive, a sad hope of successful achievement of love, lives on in the face of reason.

SIXTEEN

'Acting Out' for Parents

People living closely together tend to share their feelings with one another, unconsciously as well as consciously. Feelings are 'catching', unconsciously transmitted from one to another. The more sensitive and vulnerable an adult or child is, the more easily does he or she 'receive' the transmitted messages. Anxiety, for example, may run through a group like the measles, beginning, say, in one parent and very quickly shared by all members of the family. The same may be true of depression – and also elation and pleasure. There may also be more complicated responses to another person's more complicated feelings.

There is a process which we call 'acting out'. 'Acting out' means putting into action behaviour relevant to feelings. We may feel aggressive and then 'act out' aggressive behaviour. A person may 'act out' behaviour related also to unconscious feelings. And, very interestingly, a person in close contact with another may unconsciously act out the other person's unconscious feelings or wishes, or fears.

This happens usually when the first person can't or won't, for moral reasons, 'act out' according to his or her own feelings and when such feelings exist only in unconscious mind. For example, a person, say a parent, may unconsciously long to steal, for some neurotic reason. He or she may be so ashamed of such a longing that the whole idea exists only in unconscious mind. But the longing may be unconsciously transmitted and unconsciously received by another member of the family, say a child. The child might then 'act out' for the parent, unconsciously responding to the parent's unconscious longing. The child may steal without any unconscious reasons and without any conscious wish to steal.

The child is acting out what the parent can't act out (or, indeed, consciously knows he wants to act out). The parent might then be very angry with the child, who, confused and disturbed, has behaved like an automaton in a dream – or nightmare. The angry (but unconsciously satisfied) parent can feel virtuous and free of guilt. The child has taken the responsibility, the blame for the 'badness'.

Sometimes one member of a family, usually a child, takes the responsibility and has to shoulder the blame for 'acting out' for each other member of a family. All the repressed 'wickedness' of the people in the family is unconsciously transmitted to and unconsciously received by the one child, who then becomes the 'black sheep' or 'whipping boy'. That child does the dirty work for the entire family, while the others get off scot-free in terms of guilt or conscience.

This unconscious acceptance of the rôle of 'black sheep' by a child – and later adult – is probably due to an unconscious desire to please, to be accepted and loved by the other members of the family. It's often a rejected or less loved child who becomes the 'black sheep'. Here's an example:

Hedda P came to see me because she was so unhappy about her daughter Cassie, the child of her first marriage. Cassie lived far away from home in another city and her friends were drug addicts (as she was), outcasts of society, prostitutes or call girls, rascally men and women, idle, good-for-nothing parasites – at least that's what Harold, Hedda's present husband, called them. Cassie was born within a year of Hedda's first marriage and Cassie's father left home shortly before Cassie was born.

'The whole idea of having a child seemed too much for him,' Hedda told me. 'That's why I called her Cassandra – she brought bad news. Isn't that what Cassandra did?' Hedda fixed her fifty-year-old child's eyes on mine, questioning uncertainly. Her face was eerily smooth and young and there was a slightly inappropriate youth in her clothes and hairstyle. Hedda, it seemed, was desperately clinging to an image of herself from the past, probably for Harold's needs, I thought.

'Did he come back?' I asked, 'after Cassandra was born? Cassandra's father?'

'No – not really. I went to live with my mother. That didn't work well but I had no alternative. I went to work and she looked after Cassie. Then when Cassie was four I met Harold.'

'And you married him?'

'No – not at once. We lived together for a long while. Harold's such a perfectionist – he couldn't decide whether I was really the right one for him and also, he didn't want another man's child . . .'

'But in the end he did?'

She smiled a little bitterly. 'In the end, yes . . .'

'And did Harold get on well with Cassie?'

'At first, yes. He was sweet to her and she loved him. But afterwards when Jane and Marie-Louise were born, no. Cassie began to get difficult, jealous, I suppose, and I think I was very harsh with her. I have to admit it. I know I was a bad mother even before that . . .' Hedda spoke with sad candour.

'I expected too much of her when she was little. I was too strict, but does that account for everything? Is what she is all my fault? Did I make her a lazy, good-for-nothing dope addict? She says I did. And I think maybe my mother says I did. Do you think so?'

'You must tell me more about your husband's relationship with Cassie. When your other children were born how did he behave with her?'

'He was very – ' she hesitated, searching for the right word, 'dissatisfied with her. She began to do badly at school. She began to whine a lot. Then she wouldn't eat. Then when she got older he didn't like the way she dressed. He said she looked like a tart. He didn't like her make-up. And he didn't like her friends. Now he hates her and he won't let her come to the house . . . Not that she wants to – but she'd like to think she could come home if she felt like it. I say "home". It hasn't been home for years for Cassie. But it's her own fault – she brought it on herself. He's a kind man and a good man really.'

Hedda began to cry, mopping her tears with an immaculate white handkerchief held in a wonderfully jewelled hand.

'Cassie does make me *so* unhappy,' she said, 'I mean, it's not right for a daughter not to want to see her mother.'

Hedda had been telling me about Cassie and Harold ever since her first visit to me. Cassie, it seemed, was extremely pretty and had been much admired by Harold until things started going wrong between them. Harold, I was told, was a very handsome, charming man who liked perfection. The house had to be perfect, the food had to be perfect, Hedda and the two girls Jane and Marie-Louise had to be perfect. When there were lapses from perfection, Harold had headaches and insomnia. Harold had immense self-discipline and self-control. He never touched alcohol and he didn't smoke. He would never in his wildest dreams consider being unfaithful to Hedda and if she even looked at another man, he'd kill her.

'Literally,' said Hedda, 'I mean it. He'd kill me, I know.'

'How can a man with such self-control commit murder?' I asked.

'Ah!' said Hedda. 'There are moments, very rare but I've seen them, when Harold goes wild. It's rare – but it happens – and it's terrifying. He's like a madman . . .'

I wondered if Hedda was really as happy in her marriage as she insisted she was. I wondered if Cassie weren't providing Hedda with other reasons to account for her unhappiness – deflecting Hedda from having to face the fact that she was in a marriage which was over-constraining, over-restraining, suffocating, even. Was Cassie perhaps playing 'black sheep' for Hedda, acting out Hedda's hostility to Harold which Hedda could not allow herself to admit to on a conscious level?

But the whole truth was revealed a little later. One day Hedda announced to me that Harold had said he would like to come and talk to me, if that was allowed, as he felt he had things to say which would be useful in my talks with Hedda. Hedda was very keen that I should talk to Harold – hoping, I wondered, for what outcome?

He came. As Hedda had described him, he was good-looking, thoughtful, seemingly sensitive and kind. He was almost too well dressed, too consciously glossy and fashionable, like a photograph in *Vogue*. He sat down, first glancing to see the state of the cushion onto which he was to lower himself. An enormous tension inside him was concealed by a benign and smooth manner.

After a while he came to the point. He had wanted me to know, he told me, that Hedda's daughter was evil. If ever there was evil to be found in a person it was in Cassandra. She was the devil incarnate. 'After all we've done for her – so nicely brought up – nannies, music lessons – dentist – straight teeth,' he gestured towards his mouth with a manicured hand, 'good girls' school, all the clothes she wanted, dolls, teddy bears, extra French lessons, holidays . . .'

'I understand,' I said, 'that you won't let her come to your house?'

He groaned slightly. 'Do you blame me?' he asked reasonably, 'with those hobos, those queers and dope addicts and gangsters and whores who are her friends? Fine friends I must say – could I let them in the house? Could I let *her* in knowing she was going back to talk about what she'd seen? I mean – it's a very nice house, we have possessions, pictures, objects . . . It's clean, it's free of germs in our house. Do I want her to come in looking like a tramp bringing disease and AIDS? The answer is definitely no I do not. Do you blame me?' he asked again, rather pitifully.

From all this I understood two things. One that Harold had probably been (unconsciously) physically – sexually, that is – attracted to Cassie as she had begun to grow up but had repressed all relevant feelings very vigorously. Secondly, that Cassie was Harold's 'alter ego'. She was acting out for Harold all that Harold might have longed to do but didn't dare, all that Harold was attracted to but would never in a million years admit to. She was careless and idle and unconventional in contrast to his fiercely rigid self-discipline. She was promiscuous, adventurous and wild to his supreme self-control, his restricted and minimalized life style. She had 'let go' *for* him, since he couldn't possibly let himself go and as long as he unconsciously longed for a more violent and vicious life, Cassie would continue to lead it for him. She was the 'bad' one of the family and both parents unconsciously needed her to be bad.

A child who is in that position is irredeemably lost unless insight supervenes. Cassie was old enough to get away from the family psychopathology. Had she allowed herself to have analytical psychotherapy she might have led a happy, constructive life, but when a younger child is in a position like hers in a family, the entire family needs therapy to release the 'black sheep' from his or her rôle.

Many other rôles are taken on by children – and spouses – to act out a parent's unconscious feelings. Anxiety may often be experienced and expressed by a child in response to a parent's unconscious anxiety. When another person is anxious *for* one – that's to say, carries out the expression of the anxiety, it releases the unconsciously anxious person. Many of us have experienced this situation. Here's an example:

Mr B was a very anxious obsessional person who could adopt an unnaturally calm and unflurried manner. But if he had to catch a train or aeroplane alone, he'd be frantically agitated, arriving at the station or airport hours early, constantly re-examining his wallet for ticket and passport, making sure all his possessions were in order. If, however, he was travelling with his wife, she was the one who'd be anxious and frenzied while he was able to say, 'Plenty of time, darling – and if we miss it, we'll just take the next one'; and he'd hang about putting finishing touches to his luggage while his wife became more and more agitated.

Many a child has been desperately anxious while parents made soothing noises, or even laughed.

The same may be said of depression. Sometimes others are able to carry a person's load of depression, allowing that person to feel more cheerful. Sometimes, in a family, there's a seesaw of mood. Cheerfulness and depression alternate from person to person – but someone always has to experience depression at any particular time if one member is actually suffering from a deep depression or depressive illness.

Not infrequently children may 'act out' a parent's unconscious sexual desires. Mr X was a thriving antique dealer. He was married, had two sons and a daughter, and all who knew him well would have said he was a jolly, heterosexual man. At a party he could do a successful song-and-dance turn, with a straw boater and ukelele and a carnation in his button hole. There was just a certain subtle intimacy that seemed to occur when he was dealing with his male clients, that might have given a hint as to Mr X's unconscious homosexual tendencies.

One of his sons was a gentle, sensitive boy, particularly attached to his father; and Mr X might have admitted, very secretly, that this was his favourite boy. He was physically demonstrative towards this son, who enjoyed having his hair ruffled and his cheeks pinched by his father. Mr X's other son, on the other hand, a tall, strong and vigorously heterosexual young man, shrugged off his father's tentative physical gestures.

The favourite boy grew up to be a homosexual. When he found out, Mr X was dismayed, called his son all sorts of names, claimed to be disgusted and had several long talks with him trying to persuade him to find a nice girl instead. When Mr X died suddenly this son discovered that he was deeply dissatisfied with his homosexual way of life. On a friend's advice, he put himself in the hands of a good psychotherapist. Four years later he was happily married and after a further year, found himself the father of a little daughter whom he adores.

Certain homosexuals, if they seriously would prefer to be heterosexual, may, in the course of lengthy psychotherapy, discover that
they are, in fact, able to be sexually attracted to the other sex.
They may then find heterosexuality or, at least, bisexuality, acceptable and agreeable. The possibility of a change in sexual direction
depends largely on the original early influences which may have
produced or reinforced homosexual tendencies. Changing from
homosexuality to heterosexuality is difficult and the motivation for
change must be very strong for the therapy to be successful. But
it is possible.

Richard, very loving and caring of his father, had unconsciously,
in his father's life time, responded to the latter's unconscious sexual
desires. He had not allowed himself to recognize his own needs,
which were different to his father's. Children may act out parents'
sexual longings in other ways – by taking lovers, by being promiscuous and so on. They carefully, but perhaps unconsciously,
let the parent know of their sexual activities and the parent may
then enjoy the child's sexual involvements vicariously.

The child is motivated only by an unconscious response to a
parent's unconscious feelings and has no real wish for the lovers
or the promiscuity. It is extraordinarily difficult to rid oneself of a
parent's unconscious needs, to extricate oneself – to know one's
own real needs – after playing a part during a long association with
a powerful parent – but it can be done. Then, a new life may
begin.

SEVENTEEN

Delinquency and Crime

How bad are the 'bad'? Can people who commit crimes, who murder and steal and assault, really be responsible for what they do? The answer is 'yes', unless they are mentally defective or they are suffering from mental illness.

We are all motivated to act by stimuli arising in unconscious mind. If we've suffered from ill-treatment or deprivation and neglect in childhood we're likely to be motivated to act in an unconstructive or destructive or anti-social way, as I've earlier described. But motivation is one thing, action another. We don't *have* to act according to the motivating impulse. We're not obliged or compelled to be cruel or wicked unless our conscious judgement is at fault. There is a gap between stimulus and action. In the gap, during that interval, we can and must use our ability for conscious, conceptual thinking. Since we are obliged by our make-up to think in conceptual terms, unless we fall into that category of people described as suffering from 'diminished responsibility', we know 'right' from 'wrong'.

We should and must discipline ourselves to *act* in a 'right' rather than a 'wrong' way. This sounds self-righteous. George Bernard Shaw said, 'The poor can't afford to have principles'. But, of course, our societies would collapse if the laws weren't upheld, if there wasn't insistence on people adhering to certain important moral standards. These standards need revision in any society from time to time – and they are revised; laws do change. But the deliberate infliction on others of physical or mental injury is and will always be 'wrong', except in very special circumstances such as war.

Some people find self-discipline harder than others. Some are self-indulgent. Some crimes are committed under intense emotional pressure, hard to resist. Some minor crimes such as petty stealing are committed almost without conscious awareness. But major organized crime, that takes time and planning, is committed by people who are in full possession of the ability to control themselves, in full possession of understanding of the differences between right and wrong, who deliberately consciously choose to do wrong. Drug traffickers, members of the Mafia, terrorists, dictators who wipe out members of the opposition, Stalins, Hitlers – no matter how terrible their childhood experiences – are nevertheless evil men who have consciously chosen to commit crimes of utter savagery whilst in full possession of understanding of 'right' and 'wrong'. Similarly parents who inflict deliberate injury and hurt on their children are wicked and evil no matter how wretched their childhood, no matter whether such harm was inflicted on them as children. Human beings have a choice of action. In this way we have an advantage over other animals.

We may be motivated in the direction of crime and delinquency. We are not obliged to follow our impulses. We can resist them. Having said that, it's a fact that the prisons of Western Europe are overflowing with disturbed, confused, unhappy men and women, misfits of society, most of whom have endured awful deprivation and hardship during childhood. The majority of minor crimes are probably not committed as a result of deliberate strategy. Impulsive stealing, in particular – apart from well-planned, highly organized theft – may often be committed without conscious awareness. Petty stealing is, in fact, accepted in our society, as a symptom of an underlying emotional or mental disturbance.

A person coming up before a magistrate for taking a small article from a shop without paying for it, is often treated leniently and with understanding if he or she can be shown to have been acting under emotional stress. We know that children who steal are usually those who lack love, attention, care or understanding. The lack is liable to be more important from the emotional rather than the material point of view. Little children who take things from others at school – pens, rubbers, pencil sharpeners, pretty objects – take them from children more emotionally privileged than themselves.

I remember the case of one child, John, aged five who kept taking things from his neighbour's child, Bill. John was a very rejected child. Both parents worked; they had little time for either of their two children and anyway preferred the little girl. John

knew that Bill had two caring and devoted parents. In an unconsciously motivated attempt to have some of the love and care which
Bill received, he took objects which symbolized 'love and care'.

Sometimes children steal when a new baby arrives in the family
and they feel they're being pushed aside in favour of the newcomer.
The motivation is entirely unconscious. The 'stealing', usually of
trivial objects, is a kind of compensation, a hope to obtain symbolically, missing love, or to share, as in John's case, the love which
is received by the owner of the objects. A cherished child excites
envy and intensifies the pain of its own deprivation in a rejected
child.

But children also steal, when they're emotionally disturbed, for
other reasons. An eleven-year-old girl was once brought to see me
by the headmistress of a girls' school where the child was a boarder.
She'd been found to have been 'stealing' from a cupboard where
the girls' sweets and biscuits were kept, to be doled out in small
quantities by a teacher each day. Dora had taken sweets from the
cupboard, which was forbidden. Worse still, she'd taken sweets
which belonged to other girls rather than her own. I discovered
that the girl's parents were having an emotional crisis. The mother
had fallen in love with another man. The father was desperate and
violent dramas were being acted out in the home. The little girl
was desperately upset, on her last weekend at home having been
asked by each parent to take his or her side. She was terrified at
the idea of the parents separating and was returned to school after
the weekend not knowing what might happen in her absence.
Perhaps she was unconsciously motivated to 'steal' just to draw
attention to her need for help.

Here's an example of a typical small-time delinquent, Daniel.
When I knew Daniel he was a young man who'd already been in
prison once and to reform school earlier in his life. His story was
that he'd had a reasonably happy childhood until he was eleven
years old, although he'd always been terrified of his bad-tempered
authoritative father who was a schoolteacher. He was close to his
mother, who was protective and supportive. When he was eleven,
she suddenly died. Daniel's father began to drink heavily and
Daniel, as the eldest child, was put in charge of his two siblings,
a girl of nine and a boy of six. He was made to do the housework,
the cooking and cleaning, each day when he came home from
school, and also at the weekends. There was no let-up. His father

thundered at him, often drunk, and sometimes beat him. When Daniel was about fifteen, he rebelled. He got into very bad company, took drugs, became delinquent. He ended up at a reform school. He was seen by a psychiatrist who found he was unusually intelligent but emotionally very immature and he had a poor sense of his own worth.

He was given a training in gardening, as he'd always wanted to be a professional gardener – a garden designer, in fact. He passed exams, had a diploma. But he continued, in a minor way, to be delinquent. He stole. He took possessions from his more privileged friends. Later, he stole from strangers and shops. He had a spell in prison, which had a very bad effect on him, making him more bitter and aggressive and rebellious. His stealing originally probably had an unconscious motive, one that I've already described. He was underprivileged, unloved. He wanted to compensate for this. He wanted to draw attention to his plight.

Later, the stealing may have become a habit – an easy but dangerous way of acquiring things. But he found it easy to obtain employment, enjoyed his gardening work and earned well. There was no really adequate reason for him to continue to steal.

An additional complication was his relationship with his younger sister. Because they had been thrown together so much after their mother's death, he had become emotionally 'fixed' on her. At about the time I saw him, she'd fallen in love with another man, had been abandoned by him and she'd had an illegitimate child. All this disturbed Daniel very much.

For no good conscious reason, he stole from a woman for whom he was working. She was a kind and understanding person, much older than Daniel, and perhaps she'd become a mother figure to him. He took, senselessly, a blanket, some antique silver spoons and some money from her house.

At the same time he became involved with some drug traffickers in the nearby town. The police, searching his room, found the silver spoons wrapped in the blanket, with the stolen money. He went to prison again, this time a 'hardened' criminal in the eyes of the law.

It's easy to understand the motives for Daniel's anti-social behaviour. His was certainly a cry of 'Look what you've done to me!' Also, he tried to get by his own efforts, symbolically, what had been denied him as a child – 'mothering', parental love, understanding and respect for his emotional and physical needs as an adolescent. It's easy to see him as a victim, which he was. But that doesn't mean that he had the licence to withdraw his moral judgement from his actions. He knew very well that he was doing wrong, whatever the unconscious motivation. There's a hair's-breadth line between those of us who are prepared to stop, knowing we are about to do wrong, and those who won't stop.

A famous lawyer once said to me that he thought he was motivated to take on the defence of criminals (for which he'd earned his reputation) because he felt 'There, but for the grace of God . . .' Those of us who keep virtuously on the right side of the law might perhaps all say the same thing.

Kleptomania

Kleptomania is stealing, but it's regarded as a different kind of stealing to that I've described above. It's regarded as an illness. It's described as a pathological impulse to take and perhaps hoard secretly small, usually trivial goods.

Disturbed and distressed women walk out of supermarkets unconscious of the fact that they're carrying a small tin of beans among the shopping, for which they haven't paid, are arrested, and make the headlines. Sometimes this kind of stealing is carried out in a blind despairing way under the influence of a depressive illness.

Here again, there is usually an unconscious need to draw attention to a plight or to compensate for deprivation. People suffering from anorexia nervosa, forbidding themselves delicious foods, sometimes steal food or other objects and fall into the category of the deprived. I once saw a very disturbed woman who had a psychotic mother and who'd married a very rigid, depriving and mean man. The patient suffered from severe anorexia, having the habit of inducing vomiting after any and every meal. This woman was banned from entering the little shops in the village where she lived in Lincolnshire because she stole, non-stop, sweets, ice-creams, cakes, buns, fruit, safety pins, balls of knitting wool, hair clips, sugar or socks. There does seem to be a kind of senseless stealing which is only a half-conscious performance and has its root in unconsciousness.

EIGHTEEN

Depressive Illness

Depressive illness is one of the most awful, hard to endure, commonly occurring illnesses of our time. The illness causes very severe suffering and is long-drawn-out. It's an illness that takes away people's willpower and courage and can make life a great burden. There's a distinction between a depressed mood, which occurs as a reaction to day-to-day problems and difficulties, and the illness which we call depressive. The illness is psychosomatic – that is, it has mental and emotional features and also physical ones. A depressed mood does frequently occur in depressive illness – but the illness can be present without obvious feelings of depression. One of the earliest and most marked symptoms of depressive illness is a disturbance of sleep. The patient can usually fall asleep quickly enough, but tends to sleep lightly and may wake often during the night. Sleep returns however, until the very early morning, when a state of agitated and extremely unpleasant wakefulness takes over. Then there is no possibility of falling asleep again, only a restless mulling over of present causes of anxiety and misery and a tormented recall of incidents in the past which were humiliating or destructive. There's a paranoid flavour to the thoughts flooding the mind – that's to say, patients recall times where they seem to have been badly treated or despised by others. Depressive illness is essentially an illness of people who have a low opinion of themselves, consciously or unconsciously, as I'll explain.

It's also the illness of obsessional people, perfectionists who care about detail, who try desperately to get things right, to have everything under control, clean, tidy, organized. It's the illness of people who are the backbone of society: punctual, responsible, hardworking. It can come on at any age after infancy.

To return to the symptoms: there's usually a loss of appetite and a loss of weight – but over-eating and overweight can occasionally occur with this illness. There are difficulties with concentration and memory. A dark cloud hangs over life – and the patient may feel hopelessly pessimistic about the future. It's impossible to make decisions. Even the smallest task, shopping or doing the washing up, takes on monumental proportions. Sometimes the patient is aware of a deep, unfocused sense of guilt and failure. Sometimes vague physical symptoms abound, like headaches and aching muscles, which may mask the underlying depressive illness. Tiredness is a very common symptom. There are two main types of the illness – one, in which agitation is a major symptom; the other, where apathy takes the patient over. The agitated depressive can't keep still; the apathetic one can hardly bear to move.

The symptoms often improve slowly during the day and the patients may feel better towards evening. As I've said, it's a horribly unpleasant illness – many sufferers say they'd rather have any physical illness. Sometimes people think of suicide as their only solution and sometimes they do actually kill themselves.

It used to be thought that it was an illness of adults only and that children didn't suffer from depressive illness. We now know otherwise. I quote from Dr Dora Black (*British Medical Journal*, vol. 294, 21 February 1987, p. 462–3):

> Until recently most doctors have ignored or denied the possibility of depressive disorder in pre-pubertal children. Those who acknowledged it were either over-inclusive, or suggested that it was masked by other symptoms thus enabling society and its psychiatrists to continue to disbelieve that children could be depressed. The same happened with infantile sexuality. In the past ten years research has shown that pre-pubertal depression is a reality and may continue to become an adult depressive disorder . . .

Depressive illness can come on suddenly, but there's usually a precipitating factor. Something sets it off, either a relatively trivial happening, or perhaps a serious crisis. It tends to affect people when they're physically at their most vulnerable – women at the menopause, or after giving birth – or, in both sexes, following physical exhaustion, or after an illness treated with antibiotics.

Depressive illness improves, as a rule, of its own accord but it usually lasts a minimum of six months to two years, and it may go on for many years. It's a recurring illness. There may be periods of freedom where 'a cloud seems to lift', often quite suddenly. Then the illness may return.

In the days before antidepressants, many people spent a large part of their lives in mental hospitals when suffering from this illness. Nowadays, we mercifully have a wide range of chemicals which relieve the symptoms although they don't shorten the duration of the illness. The medicines must be taken until the illness reaches its natural end.

Sometimes phases of depressive illness are separated by phases of excitement and unusual energy. These phases can be quite pleasant and the patient may feel unusually well. But the energy of the agreeable phase can easily get out of hand and turn into a violently agitated state, which is called 'mania'. When mania regularly intervenes between phases of depression the condition is called 'manic depression'. During mania, people do extraordinary things, like taking off all their clothes and dancing in the streets, or spending all the money they have (and more) on clothes, or paintings, or orphans.

The relations of people suffering from manic depressive illness prefer the depressed stage of the illness, and this is much resented by those in the manic phase. During mania, sleep is usually disturbed – the patient may hardly sleep at all. There is usually marked loss of weight and the mood is feverish. The manic phase may, however, be very mild. Patients will then experience mainly relief at the ending of the depressive phase and find themselves unusually energetic.

The medicines used for depressive illness don't in themselves alter mood. They aren't stimulants or tranquillizers. They're chemicals which alter the body chemistry in a way not fully understood. Possibly they act as an antidote to abnormal substances which the body is making, which cause the symptoms of depressive illness. The illness is, as I've said earlier, psychosomatic – partly of the mind and partly of the body. The very fact that medicines can improve the symptoms of the illness (although not terminate or 'cure' the illness) is a proof of the somatic or physical aspect of the illness.

But the fact that there is a somatic or physical side to the illness doesn't mean that the illness is *caused* by the chemical disturbance. All we really know is that there does exist a physical side to the illness which could be similar to, say, a rash of the skin, brought on by emotional stress.

As to the causes of depressive illness, once again we must turn to childhood and parent–child relationships. I can't remember having seen any patient suffering from this illness who hadn't experienced some form of rejection from parents as a small child. The experiments and observations of ethologists show that depression can occur in primate infants if they are removed from their mothers and held in isolation for varying lengths of time (very cruel experiments). Depending on the length of time the infant primate is separated from its mother and the intensity of the isolation, the animal may be emotionally disturbed for life. It has been shown that primate mothers who have become emotionally disturbed by this experimental separation from *their* mothers may themselves be very hostile to their own young to the point of injuring or destroying the child. Since depression is an emotional mood, and the ability to experience it has evolved, what is the value of depression to survival of the species? The answer must be 'none'! And perhaps depression is caused when survival is threatened. It may be the emotion which results from the failure of some of the multiple interactions and activities which support and enhance survival.

As parents are regarded as all-powerful by the conceptualizing child, when rejection occurs the child then rationalizes to make the rejection logical and finds faults in him or herself. The child sees him- or herself as unworthy, unlovable. The rationalization may take extravagant or simple forms. The child is too tall, small; the colour of his or her eyes is wrong; it's too aggressive; it's not aggressive enough; its sexuality is at fault; if a girl it should have been a boy and vice versa, etc, etc. Whatever the rationalization, what is clear and unambiguous is the child's self-denigration. And the sense of unworthiness remains, even though the reasons for it pass into unconscious mind.

It requires only some trigger to set the depressed mood going. The sense of unworthiness can link itself to some current reasons for self-contempt. For example, middle-aged women in our Western societies are particularly prone to depressive illness. A vulnerable woman, that is, one with a history of rejection in childhood, enters middle age with apprehension.

Our Western culture worships youth and sexual attractiveness.

A middle-aged woman can very easily feel unlovable, undesirable. If this feeling is linked to a forgotten (that is, unconscious) early rejection, it's easy for depression to set in for the slightest reason. Also, the women's 'liberation' movement may create a sense of inadequacy in older women, women too old for a new training and unsuited to any specific work or career. Here again, if these feelings of inadequacy are unconsciously linked to an earlier rejection, any little trigger may set off depressive illness.

Here are some cases of people suffering from depressive illness who experienced trauma during their childhood:

Mrs A. B., fifty-five years old, was found dead by her husband in the early hours, having swallowed boxes and bottles of pills, accumulated over years. She'd been suffering from depressive illness for a long time. On the night she killed herself she was alone. Her husband had gone, as usual, to his work. He was a pianist in a night club, started playing at 10 p.m., and never came home till after 3 a.m. On this night, Mrs A. B. had begged him not to go – but her pleading was not unusual. She hated his hours of work. Used to her moods and indifferent to them, he went. When he came back she was dead.

Mrs A. B.'s father had fallen in love with a younger woman when the patient was about two years old. He'd left home to live with his new love and refused to return. Mrs. A. B.'s mother was extremely angry at being left alone with her child. She tried to make her husband share the responsibility. The method she chose was a strange one – and it never worked, although she tried it over and over again.

In the evening, she'd lift her sleeping child out of her cot, wrap her in a shawl and carry her through the streets to a place where her husband was likely to pass on his way from working in the city. As soon as she saw him, Mrs B's mother would rush forward, thrust her child into his arms and run away. The man invariably followed the same course. He carried the child back to the house where she lived with her mother. He put her carefully to bed, switched out the light in the room and went away. He was not moved by the baby's screams. He didn't mind about leaving her alone in the house. He was adamant.

So the terrified child lay alone in the dark until her mother came home, sometimes an hour or two later. Mrs A. B. didn't remember being taken out of her bed by her mother, nor being put back into bed by her father, nor lying alone in the dark, empty house. All she knew was that her parents had separated because her father had fallen in love with another woman and that she hardly ever saw him after he'd left home. She had been told by her mother about the way her father had carried her home, put her to bed and left her alone.

When her husband went out at night to play in the nightclub, Mrs A. B. was aware of a fearful despair, even before her depressive illness came on. Once she was ill, her horror of being left became a nightmare. They argued, she and her husband. He said, 'This is my job, to play in a club. You knew that when you married me. That's where the money comes from.'

She said, 'But now you could do something else. Are you going to play in a nightclub for the rest of your life?'

He said, 'That's where the jobs are, that's why I do it, and you'd better put up with it, because I'm not going to change.'

He thought her unreasonable and tiresome, and went adamantly on his way. Her depressive illness was triggered off because a young man, whom she had thought was fond of her, suddenly grew tired of flirting with her and made all kinds of excuses not to see her again. She'd met him in the chemist's shop. They'd gone to the cinema together in the afternoon, walked in the park, had tea by the Serpentine and laughed a great deal – rare for her. He had no money but bought her a rose. She was entranced. They met again. And again. And then he vanished. Suddenly the dark clouds drifted down over her. Her husband's evening departures became intolerable. She killed herself.

Here is another example: C. D. was an unmarried woman of forty-eight, whose parents had divorced when she was five years old. Neither parent wanted to care for their child so she was put in the house of a strict and formidable maternal grandmother. She realized she had been an unhappy child but she was not consciously aware that she had felt rejected. She was intelligent and capable. When grown up, she worked in a large organization. An older colleague tried to be kind to her, took her under her wing. One day she realized she felt sexually attracted to the older woman. After a while she couldn't restrain herself from confessing about her feelings to this woman, who reacted with shock and horror. The older woman then withdrew from the relationship, saying she thought they'd better not meet again. The younger woman fell into a depressive illness. One day she tried to telephone the woman who was sharp and coldly hostile. The patient wrote a suicide note, drank a bottle of whisky, and stepped out of a fifth floor window. She had no reasons for depression other than the rejection by her colleague.

In another case, a woman aged forty-three, L. M., was married to a man much younger than herself, a well-known fashion photographer. He began rather noticeably to show a good deal of attention to a few young and beautiful models. The patient was in an uneasy mood when she visited her parents for Christmas. She'd always had a bad relationship with her mother, who was a cold and selfish woman. The mother had a small, bad-tempered terrier whom she cherished. One afternoon the dog bit the patient quite severely as she tried to move him from her seat on a sofa. She went upstairs to bathe and disinfect the wound. When she came downstairs, she found her mother, with a strangely benign expression on her face, feeding chocolates to the dog. The patient brooded long and bitterly on this incident and soon lapsed into a depressive illness.

These cases illustrate how various aspects of the mind are involved in the experience of distress to the point of suicide. First, there is the unconscious aspect of the mind, which recorded the early childhood experiences of rejection and ensuing depression; second, the ability to repress feelings and events from conscious awareness to unconscious mind; third, the ability and tendency to symbolize; fourth, the tendency to link or integrate; and fifth, the ability to experience emotions consciously.

We begin with the past, with childhood. All three patients experienced deep depression in childhood. Mrs A. B. was too young to remember the behaviour of first her mother, then her father, but she had suffered greatly from their rejection and abandonment of her.

C. D. did not allow herself to recognize her parents' rejection of her, repressing the quite obvious truth when she was sent to live with her grandmother. In both cases, the facts and feelings were recorded by the unconscious mind. It required a symbolic rejection to be linked to the old rejection of childhood for the patients to be overwhelmed by the old childhood depression. The latter was re-experienced together with the comparatively trivial upsets of the present day.

The linking or fusing of the present with the past was unconscious and there was no conscious understanding of any reason why the depression was so intense. Very small children are, of course, completely at the mercy of adults and completely at the mercy of their feelings. There's very little they can do to help themselves, unlike adults. The depression of childhood is linked to helplessness. The rejection of the child by adults who seem powerful and wise can only be interpreted by the child as due to a fault in the child – an unworthiness, a huge inadequacy. There is also a fear that since he or she is so unworthy and since the parents or a parent demonstrates how little they care for, or about, the child, the child might be abandoned, left to die. So the feelings that flood into consciousness with the re-enactment of rejection by a symbolic figure are of total despair, helplessness, and inadequacy.

I say symbolic rejection. In the case of Mrs A. B., the young man casually met in the chemist shop with whom she'd walked in the park, who'd given her a rose and vanished, was not really of any great importance to her. She felt flattered, warmed by this brief encounter. But she hardly knew him. In the case of C. D., the older woman represented a mother – and there again, if it hadn't been for the earlier rejection C.D. could easily have survived the shocked coldness with which her colleague received her declaration of love.

Any rejection can be the symbol of earlier rejection. I've known someone overcome by dejection because a dog he met on a beach turned away and refused to allow itself to be patted.

Adults can do a great deal for themselves to overcome depressed moods and rejection by others, provided they do not have to cope with the re-enacted feelings of childhood in addition to present-day distress. Adults can go to the doctor and get some pills if necessary, or get all their friends to support them, or take a trip abroad or find another boy or girl friend.

The child, on the other hand, is like someone pinned against a wall, being beaten. The blows fall and the child can't escape. The adult can escape, but, if unconsciously re-enacting the childhood situation, may not recognize that escape is possible.

One of the methods that people use to escape depression is the drinking of alcohol, which is a form of mini-suicide. Temporarily mitigating depression, a drinking session is followed by even more severe depression next day. In the long run, severe illness is likely to follow steady, regular alcohol intake. The same applies to cocaine, which is often used for the same reason.

Treatment of depressive illness

Drugs

The drugs which alleviate depressive illness are divided into two categories: one kind are called MAOI inhibitors, the others tricyclic antidepressants. MAOI inhibitors require restriction in the diet, because when they are combined with certain foods they can give rise to dangerous symptoms. The tricyclic antidepressants on the other hand are less dangerous and there's no need to eliminate certain foods from the diet.

All drugs take some days or even weeks to have their effect on the illness and the correct dose has to be given to the patient. The dose varies from patient to patient and is often a question of trial and error. Many patients need help with sleep during depressive illness and will need to take a drug which produces sleep. One can never be certain, when prescribing for a patient with depressive illness, that the drugs first chosen will be the most helpful ones. Doctors often have to change the pills and change the dosages, if the best effect from drugs is to be obtained.

Manic phases are treated with tranquillizers. Manic depressive illness may be treated with lithium, which has the effect of moderating both the manic and depressive phases. This is a substance which must be monitored regularly by blood tests, since the concentration in the blood must be of a certain level. The lithium level may go up or down alarmingly even if the same dose is regularly taken.

Psychotherapy and depressive illness

Depressive illness is a dangerous illness because, as we've seen, patients do kill themselves in moments of despair, even when under treatment. This is a tragedy, because the mood of despair is temporary. When the illness lifts, the patient returns to a normal frame of mind. I believe that antidepressant drugs should be given and psychotherapy should be combined with antidepressants. If a patient is very depressed, the therapy should be supportive and not analytical. A very depressed patient is not suited to analytical therapy, which can be reserved until the illness improves. The alternative to depression is anger. There's an old psychiatric saying, 'aggression – or depression'. Anger is extremely therapeutic for a variety of emotional disturbances. But before the ability to be angry can be achieved, the patient needs support.

The difference between supportive psychotherapy and analytical psychotherapy is this: analytical psychotherapy analyses, takes to pieces and examines the pattern of a person's thinking and behaviour. There is, simultaneously, an attempt to understand and bring into conscious awareness circumstances and events which might relate to the formation of this particular pattern. The investigation requires intelligent and attentive co-operation on the patient's part. During the acute phase of a depressive illness, the patient is in no condition to analyse the childhood causes of depression. Confused, unable to concentrate, without hope, exhausted, wanting to die sometimes, a severely depressed patient can't take in explanations and isn't, in fact, remotely interested in them.

Supportive psychotherapy deals with the present crisis. Practical advice is offered and understanding and sympathy. Severely depressed patients must be encouraged to get out of bed rather than lie there all day, go out, eat, talk to friends and so on. All these activities require considerable effort on the part of the patient (and the therapist!).

Returning to those experiments of the ethologists. They discovered, as I've said, that they could cause emotional disturbance by isolating baby primates from their mothers. By returning these depressed and wretched young primates to groups of old and young primates, they were helped by contact with surrogate mothers and peers – acting like siblings. In other words, the disturbed monkeys were given a kind of supportive psychotherapy. The normal monkeys made gentle physical contact with the depressed and agitated 'patients', grooming them, stroking them and slowly restoring them to communal life. These experiments are not conclusive and are controversial. It's not wise to apply them uncritically to the human condition. On the other hand, when I hear the story of rejecting parents endlessly repeated by depressed patients, in one form or another, repeated with such predictable regularity and with such pain, I cannot help feeling that in supporting these emotionally damaged humans, I am acting like a primate surrogate mother, soothing symbolically, with a clumsy primitive hand, trying to restore and lock into position the missing components of some age-old bonding system, determined by evolution. And this, perhaps, is what successful psychotherapy achieves – the completion or restoration of unfinished or broken patterns of feelings and feeling responses. The integrated whole may be necessary for healthy development and mental health in adult life.

Suicide

'May I please speak to Mr Z?'
  'I'm sorry – no . . . who is it?'
  'Is that Yvette?'
  'Oh! Doctor! . . . Victor's . . . dead . . .'
  'Yvette! How? When?'
  'He . . . his pills . . . I found him at midday . . .'
Yvette could say no more and, weeping, put down the receiver.

So he'd done it at last! Something he'd been threatening, every now and then, for the last three years – ever since he'd been my patient in fact. Typical of Yvettte, that even though she knew how depressed and despairing he'd been lately, she'd waited until midday instead of going in to see him early in the morning . . . Typical of their relationship at the present time. She was at the end of her tether, exhausted, resentful and angry with him.

People suffering from long-lasting depressive illness do, in the end, contrive, with unconscious determination, to goad their families, friends, and doctors into indifference and hostility. When this stage has been reached, a person contemplating suicide becomes most vulnerable. What is it that causes a man or woman actually to swallow the pills, to jump beneath the moving train? Perhaps some trivial incident has occurred – someone has said a hurtful thing, someone has failed to keep a promise, or a job has been lost, or a business has had a setback, or there's been a quarrel, or the break-up of a relationship . . . The tragedy of suicide is that it's almost always preventable (except in the case of the calm, deliberate action of a person suffering from an incurable, agonizing illness).

Many people thinking of suicide are looking for a hand held out, a reassurance of love – a saviour. Unfortunately, at the crucial moment, when people have been depressed for a long time, those around them are exhausted. The supportive hands withdraw, the reassurances have been repeated so often, without effect, they're no longer given.

The suicidal person feels compelled to test the patience and love of those around him or her and pushing further and further, provokes in the end rejection which is both dreaded but also believed to be inevitable. The test is, 'Do you love me? Am I lovable? Do you love me however impossible I might be? Am I loved unconditionally?' These are the demands of a child – and it's in childhood the anxieties and depression begin.

In the act of suicide, there is a great cry of reproach, a great cry of despair. There is also, very often, an unconscious wish to punish, a 'Look what you've done to me! It's all your fault'.

Certainly, a person's suicide is a terrible punishment to those close, to the members of the family, companions, friends – and also, to the doctors. Suicide leaves a trail of bitter guilt. I myself felt deeply guilty at Victor's death. He'd telephoned me several times the night before he died, telling me, as he had so often in the past, that he'd reached the end. He no longer had anything to live for and he didn't want to go on. As always, I tried to comfort him and to give him courage – vainly. The last time he'd telephoned I'd promised to call him in the morning. I didn't do this. Rushed and harrassed, I postponed the call until the early afternoon. Too late. Had I telephoned he might have been saved – until the next time. Victor had tried to kill himself many years before and failed. He probably would have tried again at some time in the future when those feelings of utter futility, hopelessness, impasse, overcame him once more.

Suicide is, as a rule, carried out in a very abnormal state of mind, often under the influence of alcohol, and often by people addicted to alcohol or other drugs. But those who kill themselves are those who've been rejected as children and although, at the moment they choose to kill themselves, they feel total despair for some immediate reason (or profound anger), it's the experiences of childhood which are responsible for the death.

It's often said that people who keep threatening that they're going to kill themselves seldom actually do so. This isn't true. People may talk of suicide for months, even years – and suddenly, one day, in a certain mood, at a certain dark hour, an impulse drives them to fulfil the threat. The moment when a man or woman decides to die must be one of the loneliest in human experience.

Victor himself had saved up pills, barbiturates, which he'd persuaded an unwise doctor to give him over a period of many months when his sleep had been very disturbed. He was keeping these pills for the day when he could no longer tolerate living – and he had told me about them. (Many people who attempt suicide have done this, accumulated a store of lethal pills which they secretly hoard in readiness for dying).

Victor had had plans to kill himself from his childhood onwards. He felt he had been an outcast, neglected and despised from his earliest years – and he continued as an outcast all his life. He was born in Germany. He belonged to a distinguished Catholic family. He was the younger by many years of two sons. His father was an important lawyer, his mother an eccentric and beautiful woman who openly opposed the Nazis. His father died before Hitler came to power. His mother was imprisoned during the war and when released also became ill and died. Neither parent had much time for Victor. He was brought up by governesses in a large Berlin apartment. I could picture him, a thin, ascetic, lonely little boy, wandering through empty corridors and huge, silent rooms, suffering even then from extreme boredom and a sense of futility and meaninglessness about his life. Somewhere in the background lurked a formidable governess. Victor had loved his mother passionately from afar, but she was too busy to care for him. And he had only glimpses of her as she rushed through her home. He had almost no contact with his eminent father. Before she had her head-on collision with the Nazis, Victor's mother had sent him to England, where once again he was lonely, outcast and tormented at an English public school.

As soon as he left school, still during the War, he joined the British Army (but being German was only allowed to serve in the Pioneer Corps – humiliating for a proud young man – but he accepted his position since there was no alternative). After the war he started a small business and met Yvette. From time to time he became ill with severe depression. His previous attempt at suicide had been when he heard of his mother's death.

He was referred to me because of his depressive illness. He talked of death often – but there were periods when he was cheerful and optimistic, when he could be witty and charming and energetic. Not long before he died, his business began to fail. Worse still, he was becoming irritated by Yvette and she was growing hostile towards him.

I'd met Yvette. She was a small, graceful woman, rather withdrawn and humourless. She didn't understand Victor's depressive illness and she did very little to help him. Victor must have chosen her for her simplicity, plainness and smallness as a contrast to the heroic scale of his powerful, noisy mother. He had enjoyed her silence, her neat presence, her preoccupation with trivial household details, her flowers, her cat . . . But lately, as his depressive illness closed in on him again, all became meaningless once more.

I saw Yvette some weeks after his death. We faced one another wearily, guilt meeting guilt. Victor's reproach lived on. So it is, with suicide. The man or woman vanishes; those left behind continue self-searching, asking again and again, 'What did I do wrong? What might I have done to prevent this? Why wasn't I there . . . ?'

And, in fact, while the act of suicide is aggressive, both to the person who dies and to those close to him or her, there is often aggression also on the part of those around him or her: 'All right, then, go on, do it!' I didn't telephone. Yvette didn't go into Victor's room until he was dead.

Here is another example. Edward X, a mountaineer, married, between expeditions to Antarctica and the Himalayas, a beautiful but irresponsible and reckless young woman who wasn't capable of managing a home and bringing up children on her own. However, she was forced to do so since Edward was often away climbing peaks or finding his way to the Pole. They had two children, a boy and a girl.

Edward was a glamorous figure and on his rare appearances in the home his children were entranced by their handsome, bronzed father covered in fame and glory and decorations from many nations.

On one of his expeditions he met and became completely infatuated by a woman mountaineer. On his return home he told Joyce, his wife, that he'd fallen in love and wanted to spend the rest of his days with Hedi. He departed with hardly a backward glance at his two children, Gavin and Sheila. Gavin was six at this time, Sheila four years old. They didn't see their father again for some years. Joyce, once she'd got over the shock of the rejection, met and lived with a number of men, and in addition had many casual lovers.

Edward X was often in the news, photographed on mountain tops or trudging through Amazonian forests talking articulately about his achievements on the television in a glare of publicity, fighting for the lives of seals, or whales, or trees. His children couldn't fail to think of him as a hero – and themselves as being insufficiently interesting or worthwhile for this hero to visit them. Their mother, meanwhile, was too busy with her lovers to pay more than transient attention to them. They were largely brought up by their nanny, an elderly Scotswoman, and their maternal grandmother, an ageing version of their mother. No one noticed particularly that they were sad, withdrawn children – apart from the times when they were ferociously difficult, demanding, and delinquent. After one particularly bad row Gavin, now adolescent, took a handful of aspirins he found in Joyce's bathroom cupboard very blatantly, telling Joyce about it at once. He then had to go to the local hospital and have his stomach washed out, and after this the doctor arranged for him to be seen by a psychiatrist. As a result of this drama, unconsciously arranged by Gavin to draw attention to his plight, a letter was written to Edward X and a meeting arranged between him and his children.

He was quite pleasant to them as he might have been towards any two strange children; they behaved politely and further meetings were arranged. Hedi, however, who now quarrelled with Edward X, claimed she didn't like his children, and she regularly snubbed and neglected them on their visits to their father. As Gavin and Sheila grew older, they drifted away, once more, from their father.

Here are two children rejected by both parents. In the case of their father, he was a man admired by the world, so they had to admire him too. His exploits, his courage, his successes were known to all. The children were obliged to think of him as a wonderful man who found them lamentably lacking in value. As regards their mother, although Joyce did in her way love them, she was so casual with them, so careless of their needs that they must have concluded that she too didn't think much of them. Both children grew into two deeply disturbed adults, although, to the outside eye, they were beautiful, intelligent people.

Sheila married very young, a man much older than herself, a

powerful man in industry. He had divorced his wife to make this marriage. He very soon discovered that Sheila was one of the most insecure people in the world. At the slightest problem, she burst into tears, wept and screamed for hours, locked herself into the bedroom, threatened suicide. She was extremely suspicious of her husband, accused him wildly of unfaithfulness, became hysterical if she saw him talking to another woman, and was known to leave a party if he danced with one of his old friends. A year or two after they were married she had a child, a little girl. Shortly after the birth Sheila began to suffer from depressive illness. Serious plans for suicide entered her mind. She began to believe that Henry, her husband, was on the point of leaving her for another woman. She didn't want to look after her child, who was then cared for by a nurse. Henry, desperate, agreed with his doctor that she should have psychiatric treatment. He wasn't reassured when the psychiatrist after several talks with Sheila told him he thought Sheila would be incapable of loving their child – and probably, with her history, incapable of loving any other person.

Henry, who was strong when it came to industry, was not strong in his relationships with women. Confused and distressed at the state of his second marriage, he began to see his first wife again, admitting that perhaps he'd made a terrible mistake in divorcing her and marrying Sheila. His first wife was of course grimly pleased with the news of Sheila's calamitous state. The psychiatrist made only slow progress with Sheila. The scenes with Henry continued. One night when things were particularly terrible, he left the house taking his little daughter with him. He meant to return after an hour or two – and he took the child because he was afraid Sheila might harm her – but when he returned, Sheila was dead, after jumping out of the window of the top floor of their house.

It's easy to understand that poor Sheila, with her great instability, unconsciously feared and arranged a confused re-enactment of her childhood experiences: the father going off with another woman, a deserted child, and in her depression saw only one solution for herself – suicide.

When people think seriously of killing themselves, it seems to them there are no alternatives. The world looks so grey, the future so hopeless they can't conceive of any other way out of their difficulties. There are of course a number of constructive steps which might be taken rather than 'ending it all'. In Sheila's case, long-term psychotherapy, a stay in a pleasant clinic, divorce, later, perhaps and marriage with a man nearer her own age, holidays, a job, and so on.

Sheila's brother, Gavin, also committed suicide but in a different way. He began to drink and gradually became addicted to alcohol. He married and divorced twice (which his father had also done as the marriage with Hedi eventually came to an end). He had many love affairs, like his mother. He had a series of reasonable jobs because, like his father, he was able and intelligent, but one by one he lost them because alcohol made him incapable.

His father, when he died, left him a small income. He lived on this alone in a small house in Wales with a collie dog. One day, a neighbour who'd come to borrow something found the house locked, the dog inside barking and barking. After a while the police were called and on breaking into the cottage found Gavin dead. He'd had a haemorrhage in his stomach – a ruptured vein which occurs as a complication of liver disease which alcohol causes.

Although he had many talents and qualities, he looked on himself as worthless. The pain and self-loathing which such a conviction causes – although often unconscious – leads people to numb themselves with drink, or other drugs, and to slow self-destruction. But dying by degrees is different to the violent aggression of instant suicide. All of us probably know people who killed themselves violently. All, perhaps, feel they might have helped to prevent the tragedy. This is true. Such suicides take place during a mood – and moods are transient, moods change. So, when people kill themselves there's twofold aggression. There's the overt aggression of those who act and the passive aggression of those who observe, indifferent or provocative.

Psychosomatic Disorders

Psychosomatic disorders are related to stress. They are physical disorders believed to be brought on by emotional disturbances. Asthma, eczema and peptic ulcers are examples of psychosomatic illness. Many other illnesses are thought to be related to mental and emotional upheavals, notably cancer of the breast. Recent researches into this last illness indicate that severe stress may not only cause cancer of the breast in the first place but may be related to recurrence of the cancer after surgery or other treatment has taken place.

It's easy to accept that the body responds to emotional upheaval. I remember a surgeon who worked in London during the blitz in the last war telling me about people he'd observed during the air-raids. He said, 'You only had to be sitting in a bus when the sirens began to wail and you could watch instant body–mind reactions. Some of the passengers would go red in the face and neck, others went white. Faces began to sweat, tremor was present in some limbs, others were rigid.'

Flushing, pallor, sweating, muscle tremor or rigidity – these are brought about by the activity of the autonomic nervous system in response to fear. The nervous system has two aspects. There's the central nervous system, the brain and the spinal cord and nerves going to the limbs; and there's the automatic nervous system which carries impulses to and from the heart, lung tissue, blood vessels, the bowel/bladder, the endocrine system and so on. The automatic nervous system is very much influenced by the mind, but it functions largely without our conscious awareness of its activities. Excess hydrochloric acid may be produced by the stomach and duodenum in response to anxiety or anger, as may be a raised blood pressure. Sometimes people in an emotionally tense state feel the need to urinate frequently, or defaecate.

But the way in which people react to emotion depends on certain inborn, that is hereditary, characteristics. Particular physical tendencies – still mysterious to us – determine which system in the body, if any, might be affected by stress. For example, some people develop peptic ulcers during periods of chronic anxiety or frustration. Some respond to stress with skin irritations and rashes, or with migraine or asthma. The inherited physical predisposition to a particular illness waits, as it were, for the moment when emotional factors will precipitate symptoms and cause the illness to spring into being.

Psychosomatic illness is common in children in distress. Digestive troubles, diarrhoea, tension headaches, migraine, and bedwetting may easily occur in anxious or disturbed children. Asthma is another illness very much influenced by the emotions. It's said that asthma may be the response of a child to a parent's hostility.

A friend of mine once remarked, when we were discussing a certain event, 'Oh yes! I remember. It was the year my mother died and my asthma stopped.' The theory is that the hostile mother wants, consciously or unconsciously, to harm her child. The child responds by becoming 'harmed', harming itself one might say, with the attack of asthma – a condition which certainly involves a lot of suffering. In this way the mother's hostility is deflected. As I've explained earlier in this book, aggression tends to evaporate and disperse temporarily once damage has occurred. The parent is able to be free of aggression towards the child for a while. But then, the hostile feelings reassemble and are directed towards the child who promptly produces another attack of asthma.

I used to work in a hospital for diseases of the skin where I carried out a small study on a series of people suffering from sudden alopecia – a falling-out of the hair of the scalp which may be severe enough to produce total baldness. All the people I saw had had an emotional shock before their hair began to fall. Some had had car accidents, one had been in a fire, some had lost a close loved relative or spouse. But some had suffered shock from seemingly trivial happenings – although the emotional pain was severe. One lady, I remember, had had her beloved budgerigar escape through an open window and disappear for ever. And others too had lost pets, through illness or accident.

I also talked to many people with skin lesions of various kinds. The relationship between mind and skin was very obvious. I saw children who began to suffer from eczema when their parents started to have ferocious rows or during the parents' divorce proceedings. Other skin lesions could also be seen to flare up or recur under stress.

Unlike some of the other responses of children – or adults – to disturbing and distressing circumstances, psychosomatic illness is not a protest or an unconscious call for help. It is the body's accompaniment of mental or emotional suffering, an outward indication that the patient is a victim. Some psychosomatic illnesses are close relations of allergies. Allergic people become hypersensitive to certain substances ('allergens'), for example, pollen, dust, or certain foods and, as is well known, when such people encounter these substances, symptoms are produced. The symptoms are skin rashes, hay fever, asthma and so on – in fact, the symptoms which can also be brought on by stress.

There are also illnesses called 'auto-immune' which are brought on by our bodies producing self-damaging substances similar to allergens, to which the body reacts with symptoms: for example, rheumatoid arthritis, lupus erythematosis, possibly thyrotoxicosis and other illnesses. These conditions are not at all understood, at present, but very probably the mind plays a rôle in their development and progress.

One patient of mine, Felice, suffered from a great variety of psychosomatic disorders, skin rashes, rhinitis (an inflammation of the mucous membrane of the nose), migraine, and intermittent attacks of asthma. She was the youngest child in a family of four children, unwanted and unloved. Her mother had disliked her from the moment she was born. Her hostility was suppressed but revealed itself threateningly and unconsciously from time to time. For example, she told Felice, when the child was old enough to understand, that she had 'accidentally' given her a large dose of castor oil when she was only a few days old and Felice had almost died.

Felice, a timid, docile person, spent a terrified childhood, waiting for her mother's next attack. Her body was often involved in these attacks. Felice's mother, aggression masquerading as saintly care, insisted on Felice following a regime of fierce dieting to alleviate rashes and headaches and various punitive forms of rest and exercise. She was also forced to swallow horrible tasting syrups and other medicines. She was never allowed sweets or cakes or almost any food she enjoyed on the grounds that her body would produce symptoms.

As a result of all this, Felice grew up with the belief that her body was ready to grasp the slightest opportunity to be aggressive to her, to attack her. She unconsciously transferred her mother's hostility to the power of her body to do her harm. Instead of being terrified of her mother, she believed, unconsciously, that given a chance her body would destroy her. The conscious expression of this belief was irrational fear of illness. If she cut her finger she panicked and saw herself dying of tetanus or blood poisoning. If she caught a cold, she was afraid she'd go down with pneumonia. As a result of this preoccupation with and fear of her body, her psychosomatic symptoms were aggravated and multiplied. The worse Felice felt, the more anxious she became – a terrible circle of suffering.

Many people fear their bodies. We are more aware, nowadays, of the reasons for diseases and we are warned about our eating habits, sexual behaviour, smoking, alcohol. The fear of illness is, however, often irrational. People continue to smoke and drink and eat animal fats but are afraid of death. We probably, unconsciously, rationalize what was originally a fear of hostile parents, replacing the parents by the body.

From what I've said it can be seen that, unconsciously, we give our bodies an identity – a conceptual notion of a being which has power over us – which is, of course, a replica of our position as children with powerful parents. We may even tend, unconsciously, to endow separate organs of our body with their own identity, particularly if these cause us pain and illness. Those with failing kidneys, for example, may see their kidneys as malevolent dictators of a way of life which must be followed – diets, rest, a weekly visit to a dialysis machine (which also might, in our unconscious minds, assume an identity – a saviour, or a monster).

Our conceptualizing minds cause us to endow even a recurrent pain from which we might suffer with an identity – for example, a backache, or sciatica (It's got me again).

Which brings me to the last point. Emotional stress very easily gives rise to tension in muscles. Very tense muscles and muscles in spasm cause us pain. Many backaches, headaches, neckaches are the result of stress and anxiety. Our minds do have great influence on our bodies. We're only at the beginning of our understanding of how the mind affects the body, but it now seems many more illnesses are mind-influenced than was earlier believed. It may be that people who've had a distressing childhood are more liable to physical illness in later life than others. We'll know more about the mind/body relationship in the years to come.

PART FIVE

Conclusion: Analytical Psychotherapy Reassessed

Analytical psychotherapy is of enormous benefit to many, gives limited help to some, and may be of no help at all to others. To recapitulate, by *analytical* psychotherapy, I mean a therapy which, in the course of conversations and a relationship developing between therapist and patient, investigates the childhood causes, the origins of a person's problems. This is a therapy which takes a problem apart, analyses the elements, follows the threads of present-day feelings and behaviour into childhood.

Here are three examples illustrating when and how analytical psychotherapy may be helpful and to what extent, also showing the limitation and futility of analytical psychotherapy in certain circumstances.

First, the case of Jocelyn, aged forty-five years. She is a nurse and works in the United States. She is very highly qualified and received honours and prizes as she passed through the training to become a nurse. She decided long ago that she particularly wanted to work with children. Recently, she accepted a post at a large children's hospital in a small town on the East coast of America.

When she telephoned me, she told me she'd had a recurrence of her depressive illness – 'but I'm coping with it – I'm dealing with it very well', she said. She also told me she'd moved from the children's hospital to a general hospital. As she told me this, she began to cry, 'I couldn't bear it'. She sounded very agitated. 'All those little children, the *abuse* – a mother who'd stuffed a potato down a child's throat which had to be removed by surgery, a father who'd had sexual intercourse with a one-year-old baby, the broken bones and the bruises and the wounds . . . and all the sexual abuse . . . I couldn't take it . . .'

This was Jocelyn's history. Her mother had died when she was

215

two. Her father, an alcoholic, had ill-treated her terribly. The courts removed her from her father and put her in the care of foster parents. But there too, she was roughly and coldly handled. She said, 'There were too many of us, they couldn't cope – they weren't actually cruel, it was more neglect . . .'

Emotionally, she was deprived until she was old enough to work and live alone. When I met her she had a child-like body and a child-like face and she smiled a great deal. But her eyes had a dazed and stony look; her smile was unconvincing. I knew she'd suffered at times from bouts of severe depressive illness but that she was a survivor who struggled to live and to love.

Her love affairs were abysmal failures. Jocelyn couldn't love and she was always involved with rejecting men. She fought on, became a nurse at a mature age and did very well, as I've said. But it was predictable that she'd have emotional difficulties nursing children, and particularly battered and abused children.

She identified, of course, with those little creatures, infinitely more pathetic than any adult in pain or illness, and she identified especially with the victims of cruel parents. Her own experience of physical and emotional pain, which was considerable, was added to the suffering she saw in the babies and children on the hospital ward. The double burden was too hard for her to bear. Her depression recurred. She had to give up her long-cherished plan of nursing children.

Jocelyn was too severely damaged from the emotional point of view ever to be 'cured'. She was like someone who'd had a severe physical injury early in life and who carried scars, painful limbs and wounds always liable to break open again, only the injury was in terms of feelings and not her body.

The second case was another young woman, an ex-patient who also telephoned me. She apologized for disturbing me but wondered if I could just give her a word of help. She had begun to suffer from claustrophobia and found the long hold-ups in the tunnels of the Underground almost unendurable. But as she lived a little way out of central London and as she had to come into London for her work at least once a week, there was no other means of transport.

The story was she'd had another child four months ago, a second longed-for baby to be a companion to her little girl aged three. Lulu herself had been an only child. As a small girl, she'd been adored by her father but he had died when she was nine. Her mother was a businesswoman, extremely able, efficient and successful who had hardly taken a fortnight off work to have her child and had put the infant in the care of nurses immediately.

Her mother, I knew, had had a very ambivalent attitude towards her daughter. Her love, such as it was, was loaded by an intense unconscious aggression. The child was a nuisance, a burden, and particularly after the death of her husband, Lulu's mother felt increasingly agitated in the presence of her child. Unconsciously, she wanted to be rid of the burden, Lulu was nervous, clinging, cried a great deal, wanted to be with her mother, didn't want to be with the nurse, wouldn't eat, had nightmares and so on. Her mother, caught in a dilemma between her unconscious longing to eliminate Lulu and her conscious wish to love her daughter, began to suffer from fears that Lulu was about to have an accident, an illness, would die. . . . Lulu responded by being rather delicate and prone to mild illnesses and occasional attacks of asthma and, in addition, she developed a severe fear or phobia about objects that she thought could be harmful to her. When her eye fell on such objects, she began to ruminate in an obsessional way and couldn't stop the thoughts. For example, on seeing a packet of safety pins or hair clips she would think, 'What would happen if I swallowed all those? What would happen . . .' Her hand, in fact, would stray towards the pins and she would begin to finger them. 'What would happen if I put them in my mouth . . . would I die?' Or, seeing a nailfile, she would obsessively brood on cutting her wrist with it; or a pair of scissors: 'What would happen if I pushed these in my ear right through my head?'

She also wondered whether she'd kill herself or break her legs if she jumped from a balcony on the upper floor of the house, or if she swallowed a bottle of cleaning liquid, whether she might die of poisoning. These thoughts of damage and death were interminable, often nightmarish and disabling.

When I saw Lulu, she was particularly affected by these thoughts. She had married and was having problems in her relationship with her husband. He drank too much at times and, in company, then flirted noisily and outrageously with other women. In addition, he was doing badly at his job, and although she worked as a competent journalist, they had financial difficulties.

She and I investigated the relationships she had with her mother, her father and her husband. We came to the conclusion that her thoughts and fears about death and destruction and pins and scissors in mouth and ears stemmed partly from her mother's unconscious fears and wishes about death and destruction, partly perhaps from her father's unconscious sexual feelings about her, partly from her own unconscious feelings of aggression towards her husband.

As a result of therapy she was able to express her anger towards her husband, to acknowledge her own aggression and, more reluctantly, to acknowledge her mother's aggression towards her. Her fears diminished very greatly. She was able to have a child, previously dreaded, fearing it would die in her womb, or at birth, or as an infant, because of her inexperience in child care, or whatever. (She had feared also that *she* would die during pregnancy or giving birth.) She continued to work as her mother had done up to the last week of pregnancy, and was very worried at the prospect of having to give up work for a while after the baby was born. But when the time came after an uneventful pregnancy and delivery, she enjoyed her first baby so much that she remained at home for several months.

Later, she was pregnant again. This time the pregnancy was not fraught with anxiety – but, horror of horrors – the baby was born with a congenital defect of the heart. Surgery was essential. The next four months were devoted to caring for and being wildly anxious about the baby. Many weeks were spent in the hospital's cardiac surgery's intensive care unit. She watched many other babies in the same condition die in that unit, and sometimes it was touch and go with her son.

When she telephoned me he'd recovered from successful surgery and the outlook was good. Not long before she'd taken him home from the hospital, the attacks of claustrophobia came on. I came to the conclusion that Lulu's claustrophobia was once again due to suppressed aggression but this time it was the new baby who caused her unconscious hostility. The baby had been born with a heart defect, thus fulfilling the awful apprehension and dread that Lulu would damage her baby in her womb. The baby had 'punished' Lulu by having a defective heart, then forcing his parents to go through months of appalling anxiety and deprivation.

Now that the worst was over and the baby said to be well and 'normal', Lulu was able to relax and her hostility to the baby began to make itself known via the claustrophobia.

It is of course very difficult for a gentle, conventional, 'good' woman like Lulu to admit to anger towards a four-month-old baby with a congenital heart defect. But anger is the logical inevitable outcome of profound stress, disappointment and exhaustion – anger towards whatever and whoever has caused the misery.

I suggested she should ask her doctor to send her to a psychiatrist to talk about what she'd been through in the last four months.

The last telephone call was from a friend and colleague who'd not long ago started a new job as psychiatrist in the East End of London in a very poor district. She said, 'I understand now why the social services miss out on those children who are eventually battered to death. They just can't cope with the conditions round here. Everyone on the staff here is so exhausted. It's useless thinking of analytical psychotherapy. It's like trying to push a huge stone uphill. It just rolls back all the time. The housing is so appalling, and the poverty and the unemployment and the race hatred – and the drugs, and the violence, and the vandals. There's no way the people who come to the clinic would want to talk about anything except what's going on around them at the moment, and as for doing anything for the children – and I'm supposed to be a child psychiatrist. . . .'

These three conversations illustrate some truths about the benefits and limitations of analytic psychotherapy.

In the first case, Jocelyn could be helped by psychotherapy to understand the causes of her depression and – partly through understanding, partly through the mysterious 'healing' which psychotherapy may bring about – she could 'cope' with her depression when it struck her again. And depression was likely in Jocelyn's case to strike again and again. When she was overtired, overstressed, rejected by a man – or woman – for the ninth time, when she saw or had to deal with a suffering child, especially an abused child, the depressive illness was liable to return.

Psychotherapy might also help Jocelyn in the long run to find and sustain a relationship with another human being. But time was running out for her. She was already in her late forties and far from this achievement. Psychotherapy couldn't remake Jocelyn's psyche, or remake her childhood experiences. Emotionally stunted and immature, Jocelyn was likely to walk, wounded and alone, the rest of her days.

The second person, Lulu, could be and was very greatly helped by psychotherapy. Lulu, strong, intelligent, capable, sufficiently at peace in her environment, was able to understand and accept theories and above all was able to feel, to accept and understand the validity of feeling responses.

Theories are an invaluable aspect of psychotherapy although part of the help people receive is given via their relationship with their therapist. The therapist gives the patient a chance to have a kind of second experience as a child, this time with a parent who often seems to provide what the child in the patient needs and needed: patience, an undemanding nature, uncritical acceptance, responsibility, detachment, caring, being there, being adult without jealousy or competitiveness. (Certain psychotherapists or psychoanalysts prefer to appear to their patient cold and unpleasant, working then with the patient on the basis of what's called a negative transference, in theory allowing the patient to be hostile and aggressive in return.)

It's probably not possible to explain precisely why the patient's relationship with the therapist is so important. There's an element of magic in the help a good therapist gives a patient. The theories are equally important. 'Well, we've got to talk about *something!*', one well-known analyst once said to me – he believing that the relationship between patient and therapist was more important than anything else.

It's true that the patient and therapist must have some material for communication with one another – but I believe that theories are more than conversation fodder. The patient needs a conceptual formula for getting him or her away from the emotional and behavioural patterns of childhood. The theory is like a ladder pushed across the ice to the hole where the patient is struggling. But does it matter which theory is used as a ladder? Possibly not. One set of concepts is probably as useful as another set of concepts. None need necessarily represent reality, provided they 'work'. Newton's theory of gravity was useful – helpful up to the point where it was displaced by Einstein's theory of relativity.

So the most important aspect of a psychoanalytical theory is that it must 'work'. It must make sense to the patient – and particularly 'feeling' sense. Many psychoanalytical theories are more related to the ingenious and often brilliant conceptual notions of an analyst than to reality.

As I keep emphasizing, our only clear link with reality is via feelings, that is, sensations and emotions. When we begin to attribute causes to feelings, we enter the world of concepts and may leave reality behind. We all do, I'm sure, attribute some astounding concepts to the causes of our feelings, to our bodies, to ourselves, to our environment, friends, enemies and neighbours, to every aspect of our being and doing. We symbolize, we codify, we transfer from one to another, we weave fantasies and fairy stories, superstitions, dreams and weird taboos. All this has some validity in its own right but is remote from the basis, the origins of the concepts, that is, the sensory and emotional experiences.

In my view, the nearer the psychoanalytical theory to the feeling experience, the more likely it is to 'work'. To return to Lulu. She could benefit enormously from psychotherapy, changing her old childhood patterns of response, freeing herself of symptoms, living a satisfactory and fulfilled life with her work and family. What psychotherapy might, of course, have failed to achieve, was to help Lulu rid herself of the notion that her baby's damaged heart was not caused by something in Lulu herself – her aggression, a mother's aggression to her child – since the baby fulfilled her original fears.

The third telephone call from my colleague in the East End of London was the most discouraging of all.

Mental and emotional problems are common and severe in people living in conditions of degrading poverty. There's an utter futility in attempting to practise an analytic type of psychotherapy when the patients are living in desperately overcrowded, disintegrating houses and flats, where walls are crumbling with damp, the neighbours scream and quarrel, the people out of work, and flattened with defeated exhaustion.

Two hundred years ago the Declaration of Human Rights was proclaimed in France; a brave ideal. We're as far from solving the fearful social and economic problems of our societies as ever we were. Perhaps, in great cities, in fact, things are worse, for millions of people, than in the past.

The truth is that man does not love his fellow men. In fact, we are largely competitive, jealous and hostile and profoundly selfish by nature. Here are two quotations from distinguished people:

Sir Angus Wilson, the author, when asked for a definition of a civilized society said, 'A group of people who actually rather hate one another but who try to live with one another' (personal communication, 1988). Ralph Bunche, Nobel Prizewinner, United Nations Mediator said, when asked to address a World Conference on brotherhood, 'Let me say a word or two against brotherhood. A lot of people I know I wouldn't want for cousins, let alone brothers. In human relations the concept of tolerance and mutual respect is far more important.' (Brian Urquhard, 'Remembering Ralph Bunche', *The Yale Review*, vol. 76, no. 3, June 1987, p.448.)

While these two views were, of course, meant to amuse and shock, there's some validity to them. It's important to accept that there may be a great deal of hostility in some human relationships. Love is sometimes missing in a parent's feelings for a child and siblings don't always automatically feel positively towards one another. This doesn't mean that a parent might not consciously wish to love a child or a brother a brother or sister. But love doesn't flow on demand.

Our Western societies silently expect that parents should love their children, that siblings should love one another, that children should love their parents. These are misleading and therefore harmful concepts. They're misleading in that they represent family relationships as our society feels they *ought* to be rather than the way they really are.

They are harmful because people, parents and children, feel guilty, angry and anxious if they fail to conform in feelings and behaviour with the idealized version of parent/child relationships. They are harmful because, in trying to be the ideal parents, people do not allow themselves to experience consciously the 'real' feelings. The real feelings (often love, but also aggression, hostility, irritability, anger, boredom) are on the whole not allowed into conscious awareness, although from time to time they flicker through consciousness. There are few parents who'd be able to admit they didn't love their children or that they longed to abandon their children – yet these feeling states are not uncommon.

People don't, as social customs would like us to believe, automatically love a child the moment it's born. Sometimes they look on the arrival of a child with apprehension, sometimes with a mixture of dread and hostility. Their feelings and attitudes depend on their own childhood experience, as I've explained.

Love between parents and child is, of course, immensely desirable – but the notion that all parents love all children (and all their children equally) and that all children love all parents is, like the Declaration of Human Rights, a longed-for vision of a dream future.

Better by far to aim for the achievable. Parents should do their best to respect, tolerate and care for their children, notwithstanding feelings of aggression and hostility. Parental aggression, conscious or unconscious, in its various expressions, is one major reason for damage to children.

The other is parental sexual urges, conscious or unconscious, and their expression physically or emotionally. The social demand is that parents should somehow eliminate the faintest suspicion of sexual desire from their feelings and remain blandly asexual towards their children – another myth. Parents often feel strong sexual passions for their children. Were these feelings allowed in consciousness, perhaps there'd be fewer distortions of sexuality. The emphasis must be on restraint and control of sexual *behaviour*.

A last word on psychotherapy. People 'in' therapy sometimes become distressed, angry and/or depressed as they begin to understand their unhappiness and its causes during childhood. In the course of this process they may conclude that some 'good' deed, or many 'good' actions that they've undertaken, were selfish, rather than altruistic as they'd originally believed. Having little faith in their own value, they'd valued themselves by their 'good' activities. Having suffered as children, they recognized during therapy that they had unconsciously identified with sufferers, people in distress or pain, whom they'd done their best to help. They then concluded that the 'good' deed was largely an act of trying to heal themselves, a self-saving tactic, unconsciously motivated. This is a wrong interpretation. It's true that we're all motivated to act by unconscious stimuli. We may then choose to act – or not to act – by caring for the suffering of others. But alleviating pain is not in any way diminished because the actions spring from a compassion which arose from our own experience of suffering. We couldn't understand the pain of others without an intimate knowledge of pain. All the good deeds of this world must have been undertaken by people who'd suffered themselves, usually in their childhood.

The dimensions of emotional suffering can't be properly grasped second-hand any more than can physical pain. No one could understand pain as the result of a verbal explanation or the sight of a person in pain. Only those who've suffered know.

This understanding of suffering, the identifying with a sufferer, doesn't make a good deed less noble. There are those who choose to act, as I've said – to act to alleviate and help. There are also those who choose to stand back and say, 'I had to get through it on my own – why shouldn't he . . .'?

In this last chapter I've indicated some of the benefits and also the limitations of psychotherapy. Analytic psychotherapy can't make a person who's been very severely damaged in childhood into a whole, healthy, 'new' human being – but it may help that person to have a better life. Analytic psychotherapy can't help people in severe social and economic distress. But analytic psychotherapy can help millions of people to change unconstructive or destructive patterns of feeling and behaviour into more constructive patterns, so that stable and comfortable relationships may be made with others, and children brought up undamaged. Work and leisure activities may also become fulfilling and successful. However, the therapist and the theories offer only the escape ladder. The person in treatment must climb out by his or her own efforts. Some people choose or prefer to stay in their hole in the ice.

Those who stick adamantly to their neurotic patterns are few. Most people struggle valiantly with the help of their therapist to overcome their problems. In my own practice, I was always full of admiration for my patients. The majority of them persevered with courage and determination to co-operate with our investigation of the past and our attempts to understand the present in relation to the past. Journeys into the past are often difficult, the going rough and tough. Shedding illusions, facing reality can be bleak and depressing. The truth is often shocking or, at best, disappointing.

I felt great respect for my brave patients and great affection for them as we worked together to overcome and change destructive patterns of feeling and behaviour. It's true, I believe, to say that for most of them, at the end of the journey, the quality of their lives had improved. It's usually possible, with the help of psychotherapy, to survive with a flourish, no matter how hard a childhood has been and even though some emotional disability (the equivalent of a physical scar) remains. It's easier by far to overcome an emotional disability if its causes are understood.

Appendices

ONE

How to Obtain Psychotherapy

In Britain, those who feel they may need or might benefit from a course of psychotherapy must first pay a visit to their general practitioner. Psychotherapeutic treatment is often available in the psychiatric outpatient department of most big general hospitals. It's also available at certain special clinics. It's not possible, within the National Health Service, for a person to go directly to a psychiatrist or psychotherapist. There must be a referral by the doctor.

If your doctor says he doesn't think it's necessary, you may nevertheless insist on his referring you, if you yourself believe you really need help. It's not absolutely essential to tell your doctor your reasons for wanting treatment. A sensible and sensitive doctor will arrange referral without asking a great number of questions.

As with all referrals to specialists under the National Health system, your doctor must send you to a hospital or clinic in the area where you live – your 'catchment area' as it's called. Some general practitioners – and other doctors – are opposed to psychiatry and psychotherapy. If your doctor adamantly refuses to refer you for treatment in spite of your serious and considered request for treatment, it might be better to change to another general practitioner.

Unless you have the means to pay fees for psychotherapy as a private patient, you'll have no choice regarding the therapist nor the kind of therapy arranged for you under the National Health system. But if you have some modest means and are prepared to pay for therapy, your doctor may refer you, in London, to:

The Group Analytic Practice
88 Montagu Mansions
London W1
Tel: (071) 935 3103, 935 3085

Here psychotherapy is practised in group situations, often as effective and helpful as one-to-one therapy. Psychiatrists at the centre will talk to you initially and decide whether you are suitable for a group, or whether individual treatment would be better for you. Individual treatment may be arranged there before or simultaneously with group therapy.

British Association of Psychotherapists
121 Hendon Lane
London N3
Tel: (081) 346 1747

Portman Clinic
8 Fitzjohns Avenue
London NW3
Tel: (071) 794 8262

These organizations treat people from any area out of London. The person in touch with local psychotherapeutic centres is your general practitioner who must, in any case, initially refer you for treatment.

For those who are more privileged financially, psychotherapy as a private patient is available almost anywhere in the United Kingdom. Once again, it's up to your general practitioner to arrange this and refer you to a suitable person.

A 'suitable' person is a skilled psychiatrist who practises psychotherapy, or a lay psychotherapist. It's not necessary to like or feel empathy with your therapist. If after several months of treatment you feel you've made no progress at all, it's suitable and appropriate to go back to your doctor and ask him to refer you to another person.

Remember, however, that progress will be made without very visible results. It takes a long time for deeply established childhood patterns of feeling and behaviour to undergo a change.

Psychoanalysis involves, as I explained in Chapter I, a different technique. Psychoanalysis is available mainly to fee-paying patients; and it involves a lengthy commitment. Each school of psychoanalysis has its own institute (Freudian, Jungian and so on) where advice may be obtained regarding psychoanalysts. (These institutes do take on very few non fee paying patients.)

If you live out of the London area, your general practitioner will usually know where to send you for psychotherapeutic help.

TWO

Useful Addresses

Alcoholics Anonymous
PO Box 1
Stonebow House
York YO1 2NJ
Tel: (0904) 644026

London Region Telephone Service
Tel: (071) 352 3001

Mutual, non-judgemental support for those with alcohol problems. Many local groups – contact head office for details.

Al-Anon
61 Great Dover Street
London SE1
Tel: (071) 403 0888
Support for families and partners of those with alcohol problems.

British Association For Counselling
37A Sheep Street
Rugby
Warwickshire CV21 3BX
Tel: (0788) 78328

Publishes directories of counsellors, as well as helping with psychosexual problems. Please send SAE.

Capital Radio Helpline
Euston Tower
London NW1 3DR
Tel: (071) 388 7575

A confidential off-air advice and information service for people
in London. Experienced counsellors will try to advise on any
sort of problem, or put you in touch with a relevant organization who could help.

Family Welfare Association
501–505 Kingsland Road
London E8 4AU
Tel: (071) 254 6251

Professional counselling service for families in distress. Ten
local branches in the U.K.

Incest Crisis Line
PO Box 32
Northolt
Middlesex UB5 4JG
Tel: (081) 422 5100 or 890 4732

Marriage Guidance Council (Relate)
Herbert Gray College
Little Church Street
Rugby
Warwickshire CV21 3AP
Tel: (0788) 73241

Relate has about 160 local centres for marriage guidance. Look
in your local telephone book for details.

Mind (National Association for Mental Health)
22 Harley Street
London W1N 2ED
Tel: (071) 637 0741

Campaigning group on a range of issues to do with mental
health. Publishes booklets and leaflets on a variety of issues
concerned with psychiatric illness. Has a legal department
which will help with any mental health problem which
requires this sort of advice, e.g. discharge from a psychiatric
hospital. Two hundred local groups – see telephone book.

Narcotics Anonymous
Tel: (071) 351 6794 or 351 6066

National Society for the Prevention of Cruelty to Children
(NSPCC)
67 Saffron Hill
London EC1N 8RS
Tel: (071) 242 1626

Child Protection Line (24 hours): (071) 404 4447

Runs about sixty local child protection groups. If you or your
family need help, they have child protection officers who can
act on your behalf – phone the Child Protection Line.

Parents Anonymous
6 Manor Gardens
London N7
Tel: (071) 263 8918
Provides support for distressed parents.

Samaritans
17 Uxbridge Road
Slough
Berkshire SL1 1SN
Tel: (0753) 32713/4

About 180 local branches (see telephone book) give a confidential service over the phone for anyone in despair.

Tranx UK (National Tranquillizer Advisory Council)
25A Mansons Avenue
Wealdstone
Harrow
Middlesex HA3 5AH
Tel: (081) 427 2065

Advice and support for people using minor tranquillizers on
a long-term basis – and help to get off them.

Index

Emotional disturbances, and illness,
208
Emotional shock, and illness, 209
Emotional stress, and crime, 187
Emotional suffering, as symptom, 5
Emotions, human intensification, 30–1
cauterization, *see* Stoicism
see also Feelings
Environment and personality, 46
Envy, *see* Jealousy
Esprit de l'escalier, 75
Evolution, Darwinian, 10, 22, 27, 29,
59, 73
Exorcism of aggression, 63
Extended families, 128
Extroverts, 47–8

Family life, 'normal', 128
Family love, excessive, 100
Father, lost and found, by orphan,
42–3
Father/children, jealousy, 117–18
Father/daughter relationships, 17–18,
117
case studies, 42–3, 77–9, 205–6
sexual aspects, case studies, 85,
91–2
Father/son relationships, case studies,
6–7, 9, 119–20, 184–5, 205–7
Father figure, 6, 7
Fatness, *see* Obesity
Fear, of authority figures, 6, 7
Fears, *see* Phobias
Feelings, ability to experience, 28–31
aggressive, 61–2
in animals, 30
truth of, 10
variety and importance, 222–3
Feelings, *see also* Emotions;
Repression
Fetishes, sexual, 86–7
Foetus, and pregnancy, 143
Freud, Sigmund, 32, 85
Freudian school of psychotherapy, 12
Frigidity, 94–5

Gentleness, quality despised, 76
Good and evil, *see* Morality
Group therapy, 15, 42–3
facilities, 230
Guidance, addresses for, 232–4

Guilt, 53–7
case histories, 55–7
cause of impotence, 95
desire to give, 202
over parent's death, 129
re siblings, case study, 20–2
susceptibility to, 48

Happiness, 28–9
Hay fever, 210
Heights, fear of, 82
Hereditary factors in nervous illness,
209
Homosexuality, 83, 92
father/son case study, 184–5
result of seductive mother, 91, 97–8
Hope (false), as child's reaction, 172–7
case studies, 172–4, 174–6
Hostility, mother to child, over
pregnancy, 146
case study, 218–19
Husband/wife relationships, 18–20,
21–2, 66–7, 78–9, 80–2, 108–10,
167–8, 174–5, 195–6, 203–4,
204–5

Identification, with another person,
39–40
Identity, personal, 36–45
Ill-treatment of children, 3
Illness, anger with, 109–10
attitudes towards, 54
as expression of personality, 48
fear of, 73
manifestation of anger, case study,
108–10
psychosomatic, 208–12
requiring psychiatric help, 5
Image of self, 36–45
Impotence, sexual, 94–5
case studies, 78–9, 86–7, 90, 162
Incest, 84–5, 89–93
organizations to help victims, 232–4
Indulgence towards children, 65
Infanticide, 107–8
Inferiority, sense of, as spur to
success, 37
Inherited abilities, 58–123
Inhibitions, 12
Instincts, in animals, 27
and man, 28